Additional Praise for
The World in the Trinity

"Our Trinitarian God is in the world, and the world is in God. Just how do we explain this so that God doesn't get stuck in the world, like a fly gets stuck in flypaper? Joe Bracken has been trying to explain this for decades. This is his most thoughtful and illuminating explanation yet."

Ted Peters
Pacific Lutheran Theological Seminary and the Graduate Theological Union

"In this bold volume, Joseph Bracken seeks to do in our day what St. Thomas did in his: to interpret classical Christian doctrine using the best of contemporary scientific and philosophical resources. The escalating warfare between naturalists and supernaturalists will end, he suggests, only if science and theology both embrace a shared metaphysic built on integrated systems or processes of activity. In chapter after chapter, Bracken effectively demonstrates the fruitfulness of these new concepts for overcoming traditional challenges to the theology of the Incarnation, the Trinity, the church, miracles, resurrection, and life after death. A cutting-edge contribution to today's theology-science dialogue…"

Philip Clayton
Claremont School of Theology

The World in the Trinity

The World in the Trinity

Open-Ended Systems in Science and Religion

Joseph A. Bracken, S.J.

Fortress Press
Minneapolis

THE WORLD IN THE TRINITY

Open-Ended Systems in Science and Religion

Cover image: MarcelC/153685168/iStock/Thinkstock

Cover design: Alisha Lofgren

Library of Congress Cataloging-in-Publication Data

Print ISBN: 978-1-4514-8205-8

eBook ISBN: 978-1-4514-8755-8

This book was produced using PressBooks.com, and PDF rendering was done by PrinceXML.

Contents

Acknowledgments

As a self-declared systems thinker with its strong emphasis on the dynamic interconnection of component parts or members to produce a new objective reality, I certainly should acknowledge with gratitude the significant participation of key people besides myself in the production of this book. Michael Gibson, Acquisitions Editor for Fortress Press, showed keen interest in my hypothesis at an early stage in the composition of the book and offered me a contract to publish it upon completion. I am very grateful to him for his support and encouragement at a key stage of the process. Other members of the Fortress Press management to whom I owe much would be in the first place Development Editor Lisa Gruenisen who kept me moving to stay on schedule in the pre-publication process, and Amy Sleper who secured some very flattering endorsements for my book from colleagues in systematic theology. Two brother Jesuits should be singled out for their involvement in bringing this book to completion. My Provincial Superior, Rev. Walter C. Deye, S.J., moved with dispatch in granting official approval of the Society of Jesus for publication of my book. But in the actual composition of the book I owe very much to William R. Stoeger, S.J., astrophysicist at the Vatican Observatory and longtime participant in the ongoing international religion and science discussion. Bill was trying to recover from a recurrence of prostate cancer when he agreed to read and comment at length on the natural science material in Part One of the book. He died earlier this year (March 24, 2014). To him this book is fondly dedicated. In the highly competitive world of academic scholarship, Bill was a genuine wisdom-figure for all of us.

Introduction

In the years since Ian Barbour's first set of Gifford Lectures titled *Religion in an Age of Science*,[1] the contemporary literature on the topic of religion and science has expanded exponentially. While this extended conversation between theologians and scientists has opened up many new avenues for fruitful exchange of views on controversial issues, other "doors," so to speak, remain closed. For example, scientific materialists consciously or unconsciously seem to be proposing the equivalent of a secular religion, that is, a belief-system opposed to the belief-systems of the various theistic religions; but their own secular belief-system can no more be proven to be true than the belief-systems of their theistic opponents. At the same time, many proponents of theistic religions confidently assert that the doctrines or truth-claims of their religion testifying to the presence of the supernatural in the form of miracles or other alleged types of divine intervention into the normal workings of nature are justified simply because their scriptures make clear that this is what actually happened. Wentzel van Huyssteen offers an interesting middle-ground position between these rival belief systems in the form of a new kind of interdisciplinary rational reflection, namely,

1. Ian G. Barbour, *Religion in an Age of Science: The Gifford Lectures 1989-1991,* vol. 1 (San Francisco: HarperSanFrancisco, 1990).

1

what he calls "transversal rationality."[2] This new type of rationality is not purely cognitive but likewise a performative praxis: "the practice of responsible judgment, that is at the heart of a postfoundationalist notion of rationality, and that enables us to reach fragile and provisional forms of coherence in our interpersonal and interdisciplinary conversations."[3]

While I am very sympathetic to this notion of transversal rationality as an effective strategy for continued dialogue among proponents of different academic disciplines on matters of religion and science, I believe that, taken by itself, it is not enough to adjudicate between rival truth-claims on sensitive issues in this context. What is needed in my judgment is a new socially oriented worldview that emphasizes the ontological priority of relationships to the entities, both individual and corporate, that are thus dynamically interrelated. That is, all appearances to the contrary notwithstanding, reality is not constituted by individual things existing in their own right but also involved in contingent relationships to one another. Rather, reality consists in an ever-expanding network of processes or systems in which the patterns of existence and activity that exist between and among their component parts are more important than the parts themselves. The individual component parts are replaceable or in some other way time-bound, but the system or process as a whole remains intact because it sustains a persistent pattern of existence and activity between and among those same parts. The institutional process constituting civil society, for example, is constantly adding or losing members; but the process itself as a corporate reality undergoes significant structural change much more slowly. One can call this new worldview a metaphysics of becoming

---

2. J. Wentzel van Huyssteen, *Alone in the World? Human Uniqueness in Science and Theology* (Grand Rapids: Eerdmans, 2006), 23.
3. Ibid.

(rather than of being) or an event ontology, since the enduring entities of commonsense experience are in fact the byproduct of a sustained pattern of interrelated transient events.

Systems Rather than Things

More will be said in the early chapters of this book about our human tendency to confuse ongoing processes with enduring things. Commonsense experience long ago led human beings to recognize and deal with things rather than with complicated processes in the day-to-day struggle for survival in a highly competitive world. But for now I simply propose that ongoing processes or systems are productive of the things of ordinary experience, not vice versa. That is, we human beings and all other creatures of this world do not first exist and then act according to our predetermined nature or essence, as in classical metaphysics (*agere sequitur esse*). Instead, from moment to moment we find ourselves already involved in various kinds of activities and only over time reflexively understand what that means in terms of our ongoing self-identity, what makes us different from others (*esse sequitur agere*).

Yet, if this is in fact the case, then the professional language of science, on the one hand, and equally professional language of the humanities (above all, philosophy and theology) should reflect the reality of living in a world of intricately interrelated processes or systems rather than in a world populated by individual entities that first exist in their own right and then take on relationships that add to or somehow diminish what they are in terms of their nature or essence. For only then will we consciously take into account similarities and differences among us that can cause unneeded friction and even overt conflict among us as we struggle to assert who we are and what role we play in the world around us.

Perhaps the best example of what I have in mind here is the longstanding debate among academics about the existence of God and the reality of a supernatural order of events over and above the natural order to be found in this world. People of a more empirical or even materialistic mindset are very skeptical about the truth-claims of the major world religions about God/Ultimate Reality as both transcending this world and yet immanent within it in ways that cannot be empirically verified. Theists, on the contrary, find it all but impossible to deny the reality of God and the workings of the supernatural order in their lives simply as a matter of personal experience. As they see it, one does not logically argue to belief in the existence of God; one experiences the workings of God and Divine Providence in one's life in ways that allow for but go beyond purely rational argument. But, if one changed the language of discourse between materialistic empiricists and religiously oriented idealists, could the often heated exchange of views between them be significantly altered for the better?

In other words, if both sides could agree to think in terms of integrated processes rather than individual things as constitutive of reality, would it be possible for hardcore empiricists and religiously oriented trans-empiricists to assert that their respective truth-claims are valid within certain limits but in need of further qualification from proponents of the other point of view? If, namely, the natural order and the alleged supernatural order are in fact dynamically interconnected processes or systems that together constitute a richer reality than what either the natural order or the supernatural order, taken alone, can provide, then the naturalist can with complete justification claim that there has to be a natural explanation for everything that happens in this world and the supernaturally oriented person can with equal justification claim that the full intelligibility of any event happening in the natural order is only satisfied by an appeal to the invisible workings of Divine Providence or some other supernatural nonempirical agency.

In principle, of course, this subtle coordination of natural and supernatural agencies so as to produce a single empirical effect in the natural order could possibly be achieved by reference to natural and supernatural entities (e.g., God) in their causal relations to one another. But thinking in this way immediately raises thorny questions about how this can take place without conflict of interest, that is, the dominance of the supernatural order of things over the natural order of things or vice versa. If, however, one thinks of agency in terms of interdependent processes that require one another to achieve some common goal or value in the natural order, then the tension between proponents of a naturalistic and a supernatural approach to physical reality might well dissipate. For, both sides should in principle admit that coordination of separate processes so as to produce something by way of a higher-order common effect is in fact everywhere at work in the natural order.

An atom, for example, if seen as a micro-process (i.e., a temporally ordered sequence of atomic "events" with empirically identifiable characteristics), still retains its ontological integrity as an atom when it becomes part of a molecule as a still larger process of nature. Likewise a molecule retains its ontological identity as a molecule even after it becomes part of the still more comprehensive processive reality of a cell. Finally, a cell retains its own identity as a cell when it becomes part of the process constituting a multicellular organism. As a result of this dynamic interrelationship between the parts and the whole at work in nature on a universal scale, the present world has come into being in all its wonderful order and complexity. We human beings, accordingly, might have something important to learn from observation of the workings of the nonhuman natural order so as better to deal with one another in the solution of controversial issues peculiar to ourselves as human beings. Nature seems to tell us that what counts in the end is the success or failure of the overall process, not how much this or that individual entity contributed to the success or failure of that process.

Overview of the Chapters

After this brief introduction to my governing hypothesis, I will in the chapters that follow try to establish its rational plausibility in the following manner. In chapter 1, I reflect on how the language that we customarily use to describe our experience unconsciously shapes the way in which we perceive reality. Our Western emphasis on nouns rather than verbs in our use of language preconditions us to see reality in terms of things in themselves rather than as the here-and-now byproduct or result of ongoing processes. In chapter 2, I use the metaphysics of process-oriented thinkers like Alfred North Whitehead and Pierre Teilhard de Chardin to argue that there is invariably a spirit-dimension, an "inside," to every physical reality as counterpart to its "outside" or material embodiment here and now. In Whitehead's metaphysical scheme, this spirit-dimension is envisioned as the workings of an actual entity, an immaterial self-constituting subject of experience in dynamic interrelation with its environment. Yet every actual entity has a material counterpart in its "superject," the empirical result of its self-constituting "decision."[4] Then in the next two chapters I analyze various theories both pro and con on the value and significance of the relatively new notion of panentheism in philosophical and theological circles. For, if panentheism is taken seriously, it is, so to speak, a test-case for my hypothesis that

---

4. Alfred North Whitehead, *Process and Reality: An Essay in Cosmology*, corrected edition, ed. David Ray Griffin and Donald W. Sherburne (New York: Free Press, 1978).

interrelated processes, not individual entities in various forms of contingent relationship, make up the world in which we live.

That is, if God is "pure Spirit," a strictly immaterial individual entity, there is no way that the things of this world as material entities can be literally said "to live, move and have their being" (Acts 17:28) in God. Even human beings as simultaneously both material and spiritual entities in their ongoing pattern of existence and activity cannot literally share in the divine life apart from a special divine dispensation. But within a process- or systems-oriented approach to reality, it is quite easy to picture the communitarian life of the three divine persons of the Christian doctrine of the Trinity as being the Alpha and Omega of the current cosmic process. That is, the ongoing process of the divine life is the transcendent reality from which the time-bound cosmic process originated and to which it will return at the end of its existence. For only in this way, as I explain in the third chapter of this book, does the term panentheism upon closer inspection not reduce to a new name for either classical dualism (God and the world in opposition to one another) or for classical pantheism (God absorbed into the empirical reality of the world or the world absorbed from moment to moment into the transcendent reality of God).

Then in the second part of the book, chapters 5 to 9, I apply this process- or systems-oriented model of the God-world relationship to a rethinking of some of the basic truth-claims of the Christian tradition. In chapter 5, for example, I inquire whether in substituting the word "process" or "system" for the word "nature" in explaining the Christian doctrine of the Incarnation, one could more readily understand how the divine and the human natures of Jesus as the Incarnate Word of God are "unconfused, unchangeable, undivided and inseparable."[5] For, "natures," when understood as unchanging principles of existence and activity or essences for different things, makes understanding how divinity and humanity are simultaneously constitutive of the personhood of Jesus much more difficult. But, if instead there are two dynamically interrelated processes at work in Jesus so as to produce all the events in his life-history, then the doctrine of the Incarnation could be more rationally plausible to all those who on scientific grounds believe that the natural world is constituted by hierarchically ordered processes that work together to produce a common effect from moment to moment. Similarly, in applying this process- or systems-oriented paradigm to the interpretation of the Christian doctrine of the Trinity (one God in three persons) in chapter 6, there seems to be no logical contradiction in claiming that the divine persons are each a personally ordered subprocess or subsystem within the all-encompassing corporate process of their life in community. The process proper to the divine community, in other words, cannot exist apart from the ongoing interplay of the three subprocesses proper to the divine persons, and the divine persons cannot be regarded as one God, rather than three gods, except insofar as they together constitute the corporate reality of God as a never-ending communitarian process or system. If, on the other hand, stress is instead laid on the divine persons as separate individual entities, then one is invariably tempted to think of the divine community as a tightly knit aggregate of individual entities rather than as a corporate reality in its own right. Aquinas well understood this conceptual problem and solved it with his notion of the divine persons as "subsistent relations," three entities that are themselves only in terms of their ongoing relations to one another.[6] But the expression "ongoing relations" seems to imply a

5. *The Teaching of the Catholic Church*, ed. Josef Neuner, Heinrich Roos, and KarlRahner, trans. Geoffrey Stevens (Staten Island, NY: Society of Saint Paul, 1967).
6. Thomas Aquinas, *Summa Theologiae* (Madrid: Biblioteca de Autores Cristianos, 1951).

process-oriented understanding of the Trinity without conscious use of process terminology.

Chapter 7 provides a process- or systems-oriented approach to the understanding of the Church as a historical process as well as a divinely intended trans-historical or atemporal reality with goals and values that transcend the boundaries and inevitable limitations of different cultures and civilizations. My contention in this chapter is that the Church (in this book, primarily the Roman Catholic Church) is both an institutional entity and an institutional process at the same time. Yet, given the proposed ontological priority of action over being (*esse sequitur agere*) and with close attention to historical changes in Church life and government over the centuries, I contend that the Church was originally more a charismatic movement or new way of life for the disciples of Jesus after his death, resurrection, and ascension and only over time developed the institutional structures needed to sustain the enduring meaning and value of the movement. Divine Providence, to be sure, was likewise invisibly active in the pragmatic decisions of church leaders over the centuries to pursue one course of action rather than another in dealing with an often hostile environment. So in this chapter as in all the others, I emphasize the interplay between the natural order and the supernatural order of things so as to produce a unified and empirically verifiable reality. The Church is what it is today as a result of its historical evolution and the work of Divine Providence. It will inevitably keep changing, albeit in incremental ways more than in a "great leap forward," because this is the way that evolution for the most part works elsewhere in the natural order.

Chapters 8 and 9 are closely linked in terms of their approach to the same theme. That is, in chapter 8 I explore the role of miracles within the natural order of things, above all, with reference to the recurrent problem of natural and moral evil within a panentheistic understanding of the God-world relationship. On the one hand, miracles, supernatural intervention into the normal processes of nature for a higher purpose, should not be necessary if the system proper to the world is a subsystem within the process or system of the divine communitarian life. But, given that natural and moral evils occur on a regular basis in this world so that a miraculous intervention by God into the workings of nature is often needed to set things right again, why do divine miracles show little or no predictability? Does God favor some human beings and neglect the needs of others? Then in chapter 9, I offer a rationally plausible explanation of the greatest miracle of all, the resurrection of Jesus after his passion and death and the promise of resurrection of the body for all human beings and of a New Creation for the cosmic process as a whole. The key philosophical issue at stake here is the nature of the human body and indeed of all material entities if they are to be assimilated into the divine communitarian life after existence in this world. How is one to understand what St. Paul calls a "spiritual body" (1 Cor. 15:44)? Likewise, a new understanding of "the four last things" (death, judgment, heaven, and hell) will be set forth to show the basic consistency of this more rationalistic approach to traditional Christian belief in the resurrection of Jesus and continuing life after death for all finite entities, above all, human beings.

Finally, in a brief Conclusion, I compare my systems-oriented understanding of the God-world relationship with the efforts of the late Gordon Kaufman to work out an acceptable worldview that can be employed by both Christian theologians and natural scientists to achieve common ground in dealing with controversial issues that up to the present have set them at odds with one another. Christian theologians will thereby be challenged to take a "leap of faith" to use the systems- and process-oriented language of contemporary science to rethink and interpret anew the key articles of Christian belief that have been passed down over the centuries to new generations of Christians. Yet natural scientists will likewise be challenged to give up a largely instrumentalist approach to knowledge of the natural order ("saving the phenomena") and begin asking themselves about the underlying laws of nature that produce the phenomena, the appearances of things to human observers. The result, of course, will be a theory that cannot be empirically verified in every respect but still makes overall good sense both for deeper understanding of the laws of nature and for the work of Christian philosophers and theologians in dealing with the proper interpretation of Sacred Scripture and the doctrinal teaching of the Church.

PART I

1

Language and Reality

Does language simply reflect the world in which we live, or instead shape it so that we see things differently as a result of using one language to express ourselves rather than another? On the basis both of personal experience and of the conclusions reached by some major European philosophers, I would say "yes" to the second alternative. With respect to personal experience, for example, in the 1960s after being ordained a priest at a Jesuit seminary here in the United States, I received permission from my religious superiors to do a final year of spiritual reflection and pastoral training in Austria and then to study for a doctorate in philosophy at the University of Freiburg in southwest Germany. Both in Austria and above all in Germany, I confronted not just a problem of translating English into German but a new and different way of looking at reality. At least in a formal academic context, use of the German language is very orderly and precise with the verb normally at the end of a sentence rather than closely connected to the noun or grammatical subject of the sentence at or near its beginning. For a foreigner like myself, there was a regular tendency to forget what verb I originally planned to use at the end of the sentence that I was currently speaking. In addition, I quickly realized that the German language readily lends itself to logical abstractions; verbs are easily converted into nouns, by adding a customary prefix or suffix to the verb. It was no wonder to me that academically oriented Germans became world renowned as theoreticians: in the humanities as philosophers and theologians and in the natural sciences as mathematicians and natural scientists.

At the same time, German preoccupation with orderly and precise language seems to have inspired a number of German philosophers and theologians in the twentieth century to study carefully the influence of language on human thinking and behavior. Martin Heidegger, the author of the groundbreaking book in phenomenology and existentialism *Being and Time*, referred to language as "the house of Being."[1] By that he presumably meant that Being or the world in which we live presents itself to us in and through language. Hence, the reality of the world in our experience is radically shaped by the language we use to describe it. Similarly, Hans-Georg Gadamer, Heidegger's student and junior colleague in philosophical studies, first at Freiburg and later at Marburg University in Germany, saw the connection between language and reality in much the same way. In his book *Truth and Method*, for example, he says: "[M]an's being-in-the-world is primordially linguistic."[2] That is, without language as a way to communicate personal thoughts and feelings, a human being is totally isolated from others and even from him- or herself. Finally, the Austrian philosopher Ludwig Wittgenstein in his book *Philosophical Investigations*, originally

1. Martin Heidegger, "Letter on Humanism," in *Pathmarks*, ed. William McNeill, trans. Frank A. Capuzzi (New York: Cambridge University Press, 1998), 254, 272.
2. Hans-Georg Gadamer, *Truth and Method*, 2nd edition, trans. Joel Weinsheimer and Donald G. Marshall (New York: Crossroad, 1992), 443.

published in 1953 after his death, refers to language as a "game," that is, as an activity or form of life.[3] In other words, language has many more uses in human life than simply direct communication of information.

Naturally, still other twentieth-century philosophers who are not Germans, such as Paul Ricoeur in France and Alfred North Whitehead in Great Britain, both of whom lived and worked in the United States later in life, have analyzed carefully both the underlying structure of language and the way it influences human thinking and behavior. So the so-called "linguistic turn" in twentieth-century philosophy has had an enduring influence on our Western way of life. This is not to claim, of course, that we are completely determined in our understanding of reality by the language that we use. Nor is it to claim that outside of our own language context we find it virtually impossible to communicate with people using another language. I myself, for example, learned over time to think, talk, and write reasonably well in German so that to this day certain German words and phrases come more readily to mind than their English equivalents. Furthermore, much of basic interpersonal communication is grounded in feeling even more than in concepts and words. These feelings, to be sure, are themselves conditioned by our cultural upbringing, which in turn is partly shaped by the language that we habitually speak. But certain primitive feelings, for example, love, hate, joy, and sorrow, seem to transcend the limitations of language since they are personally felt and mutually shared through the body with its gestures and facial expressions rather than through the mind with explicitly verbal communication. Nonverbal symbolism, in other words, with its strong appeal to the memory and imagination of a human being, is just as powerful as the

3. Ludwig Wittgenstein, *Philosophical Investigations*, trans. G. E. M. Anscombe (New York: Macmillan, 1968), 23.

spoken word in expressing how we think and feel about life going on around us and how we share it with others.[4]

But, to return to the question that I posed in the Introduction and again at the beginning of this chapter, does language not just reflect but actually shape the way that we experience reality? In particular, does an unconscious focus on nouns shape one way of looking at the world and an implicit focus on verbs reveal still another way? Here too I say "yes." A focus on nouns subtly induces one to look for ongoing permanence within the flow of experience; a focus on verbs leads one to see ongoing change as more persistent than permanence within human experience of reality. Clearly, both change and permanence characterize our human experience of ourselves, others, and the world. But in the end one finds what one is already unconsciously looking for and instinctively comes to the conclusion that this is the way things are. To make this point more obvious, I now briefly review the history of Western philosophy.

From Plato to Kant

Prior to the time of Aristotle and Plato there were already various schools of thought among the ancient Greeks on the nature of physical reality, different philosophical cosmologies. Two of the more prominent schools of thought were represented by Heraclitus and Parmenides, who held opposite views about the nature of reality. Heraclitus is quoted by Plato in the dialogue *Cratylus*[5] to the effect that no one ever steps into the same river twice. So for Heraclitus the only thing that is permanent is ongoing change. Parmenides, on

---

4. Alfred North Whitehead, *Symbolism: Its Meaning and Effect* (New York: Fordham University Press, 1985), 60–88.
5. Plato, "Cratylus," in *The Collected Dialogues*, ed. Edith Hamilton and Huntington Cairns (Princeton: Princeton University Press, 1961), 402A.

the contrary, believed that all change in this world is illusory. Being really exists; nonbeing does not exist except in thought. Hence, being is timeless, permanent, and unchanging. Put otherwise, Heraclitus believed in the unity of opposites, change and permanence being two dimensions of one and the same reality. Parmenides believed that reality is one-dimensional. Permanence is real; change is illusory. Plato favored the view of Parmenides over that of Heraclitus but still wanted to give due credit to Heraclitus' intuition that change is a constant feature of human experience of the world. So, in his celebrated analogy of the cave in *The Republic*, he distinguished between Being and Becoming, with Being characterizing reality and Becoming linked to appearance. Using their minds properly, human beings can attain certain knowledge of the unchanging intelligible Forms of things. In sense experience, on the contrary, human beings are only dealing with the constantly changing appearances or contingent manifestations of these unchanging Forms.[6]

Plato's disciple, Aristotle, was more of a naturalist, a close student of the physical appearance and activity of things, than Plato who was an idealist, interested in the unchanging Forms of things. So Aristotle gave a new meaning to Plato's doctrine of unchanging Forms. They do not primarily exist as intelligible structures apart from the things in which they are manifested, but exist in things as their unchanging substantial form or essence.[7] As such, they have contingent properties that vary from individual to individual and even over time within one and the same individual entity at different stages of its development (e.g., youth as opposed to old age within human beings and other animal species). But what gives things their "suchness" or universal intelligibility is their substantial form, which can be grasped by the

6. Plato, *The Republic*, trans. Francis MacDonald Cornford (New York: Oxford University Press, 1962), 509D–511B, 514A–521B.
7. Aristotle, *Metaphysics*, trans. Hippocratus G. Apostle (Grinnel, IA: Peripatetic, 1979), 1038B–1041B.

human mind as a reality underlying all the contingent properties of the thing. In turn, this insight led to Aristotle's exposition of formal logic, the relationship of unchanging grammatical subjects to their ever-changing verbs or predicates within sentences. This prioritizing of unchanging subjects of sentences over the ever-changing verbs that express their contingent existence and activity has had enormous influence on Western culture. For our purposes in this chapter, it leads us to assume without question that our conventional way of speaking reflects the way that things are. Only with the transcendental philosophy of Immanuel Kant in the late eighteenth century and, above all, with the controversial issues associated with subatomic physics (e.g., the wave/particle complementarity as the underlying character of reality at the quantum level) have we Westerners seriously begun to question this basic assumption that language closely reflects reality and reality is clearly reflected in the way that we conventionally use language.

To shift from Aristotle to Immanuel Kant, of course, leaves out much detail about the intermediate history of Western philosophy. But it is justified by the narrow focus of our search: namely, the proper relationship between the structure of language and the structure of reality. Thomas Aquinas and other medieval thinkers, for example, basically accepted the metaphysics of Aristotle as the basis for their own philosophical/theological reflections about the God-world relationship. The substantial forms or essences of things and their order to one another and to God were created by God as their source and final end. In the late Middle Ages, to be sure, William of Ockham challenged the Aristotelian/Thomistic presupposition that universal ideas in the mind correspond to the essences of things outside the mind. From his perspective, universals are simply mental constructs for cataloguing and ordering to one another empirical data. This emphasis on particular things rather than their universal essences helped to establish the growth of early modern natural science. But early natural scientists like Galileo and Newton not only studied individual things in terms of their physical appearances; they used mathematics to formulate the laws of nature governing those things. Thus a new form of universal statements arose, grounded in mathematically formulated relations between empirical things rather than in *a priori* relations between universal ideas. Yet, even with this new methodology for studying the workings of nature, not only natural scientists but everyone else as well believed that the human mind is still in regular contact with reality itself.[8]

William of Ockham's challenge to the classical assumption that universals in the mind directly correspond to the essences of things in nature, however, did not get lost. The suspicion was growing that maybe all we know are our own subjective ideas about things. For example, René Descartes, a brilliant French mathematician, and John Locke, a celebrated English physician, questioned whether we know things in themselves or only our clear and distinct ideas about them.[9] This still assumes, of course, that there is a direct correspondence between these clear and distinct ideas in the mind and the physical things of this world. For Descartes, rational reflection would yield the needed clear and distinct idea corresponding to the essence of a physical reality. For Locke, being more empirically oriented, it was continued observation of the thing in question that would distinguish between its nominal and its real essence. But the Scottish philosopher David Hume questioned the assumptions of both Descartes and Locke. For he doubted whether or not there is any correspondence at all between ideas in the mind and the underlying essence of things

---

8. Joseph A. Bracken, *Subjectivity, Objectivity, and Intersubjectivity: A New Paradigm for Religion and Science* (West Conshohocken, PA: Templeton Foundation, 2009), 24–28.
9. Ibid., 28–37.

in nature. Hume claimed that all human knowledge is based on the succession of sense impressions in human consciousness which yield at best probabilities for their recurrence in nature. Likewise, given that the time-honored law of cause-and-effect is then no more than a fallible generalization from the succession of sense impressions in human consciousness, one cannot even be certain that there is an enduring self as source of human consciousness. Perhaps human consciousness is nothing more than a stage play without a script and without anyone in the audience to watch it.[10]

Immanuel Kant came to the rescue of the laws of nature and the legitimacy of natural science with his so-called Second Copernican Revolution. That is, just as Copernicus displaced the commonsense experience of the sun revolving around the earth (rising in the East and setting in the West) with his counterintuitive proposal that the earth rather revolves around the sun, so Kant proposed that the laws of nature come from the internal workings of human consciousness rather than from the external workings of nature. In his preface to the second edition of the *Critique of Pure Reason* he asserts: "Hitherto it has been assumed that all our knowledge must conform to objects. But all attempts to extend our knowledge of objects by establishing something in regard to them *a priori*, by reason of concepts, have, on this assumption, ended in failure. We must therefore make trial whether we may not have more success in the task of metaphysics, if we suppose that objects must conform to our knowledge."[11]

As he explains, "reason has insight only into that which it produces after a plan of its own"; hence, in dealing with nature, reason "must itself show the way with principles of judgment based upon fixed laws [of the mind], constraining nature to give answers to questions

---

10. Ibid., 42–46.
11. Immanuel Kant, *Immanuel Kant's Critique of Pure Reason*, trans. Norman Kemp Smith (New York: St. Martin's Press, 1956), B:xvi. N. B.: "B" refers to the second edition of the *Critique*.

of reason's own determining."[12] Kant's presupposition in this hypothesis, of course, was that the laws of the human mind are *a priori* (already given) and universal, the way in which all human minds necessarily work in dealing with physical reality. Basically, Kant's proposal here simply reflected what was already being taken for granted by many natural scientists of his day in their dealing with physical reality. Likewise, it remains the standard procedure for natural scientists to this day. That is, a scientist first observes what is going on in nature at some time and place, conceives a hypothesis as to the natural laws that must be operative there, and finally tries to verify that hypothesis through a series of experiments on the empirical data. If the hypothesis reasonably matches what is going on in nature, then the scientist can claim that she has provisionally discovered a law of nature. It is a provisional truth rather than an absolutely certain law of nature because the scientist herself or someone else could at a later date come up with an even more satisfactory hypothesis to match the same empirical data and thus replace the current understanding of the law of nature.

Kant's thinking here, to be sure, sets up a tension between *phenomena*, the physical appearances of things, and the *noumena*, things in themselves apart from human experience. Even more mysterious are the workings of what Kant called the transcendental self,[13] the hidden source for all the mental categories that order the phenomena or physical appearances of things. Also presupposed, of course, are the Postulates of Practical Reason, the prerequisites of human morality: the nonempirical self, God, and the world as a totality or comprehensive whole.[14] So it is not surprising that the next generation of German philosophers (e.g., Fichte, Schelling, and

12. Ibid., xiii.
13. Ibid., 132.
14. Immanuel Kant, *Critique of Practical Reason and Other Writings in Moral Philosophy*, trans. Lewis White Beck (Chicago: University of Chicago Press, 1949), 234–35.

Hegel, the so-called German Idealists) tried to synthesize the phenomena and the noumena into a unified system in which God as transcendent Spirit is ultimately responsible for the existence of both. For our purposes in this chapter, what is most important here is that the things of this world are now being explained in terms of interrelated processes. Things are still things (substances); but the focus is now on an overall process of becoming, guided by the Divine Spirit. It was only at the beginning of the twentieth century, however, that reality became more and more defined in terms of Becoming (process or system) rather than Being (substance and accident as in classical metaphysics). Two prominent process-oriented philosophers of the first half of the twentieth century were Henri Bergson and Alfred North Whitehead. Here I provide only a brief summary of their rival philosophical positions.

Two Contrasting Views on Movement

Both Bergson and Whitehead were convinced that the mechanistic worldview of early modern science (such as that espoused by Galileo, Newton, Robert Boyle, etc.) was well adapted to the mathematical analysis of the things of this world but that it only worked so well because scientists could thereby abstract from the full reality of those things. For, things in their full reality cannot be reduced to a set of equations governing their moving parts like the blueprint for automobiles to be produced on an assembly line. An individual thing, and in its own way all of nature, is built like an organism, a whole or totality that is somehow more than simply the sum of its parts as is the case in the functioning of a properly assembled machine. But if individual things and nature as a whole are in this way alive, not dead, then a new worldview, a new sense of how things operate in conjunction with one another, is needed. But what should be that new worldview based on principles of Becoming rather than of Being? Here is where Bergson and Whitehead dramatically differ.

In his book *The Creative Mind*, for example, Bergson describes the experience of movement in human consciousness as follows: "We shall think of all change, all movement, as being absolutely indivisible," something that cannot be divided into a series of points or spatial locations without ceasing thereby to be movement.[15] For, in this way movement as an intuitively experienced physical reality is lost. Movement is thereby reduced to "a position, then another position, and so on indefinitely. We say, it is true, that there must be something else, and that from one position to another there is the *passage* by which the interval is cleared. But as soon as we fix our attention on this passage, we immediately make of it a series of positions, even though we still admit that between two successive positions one must indeed assume a passage."[16] Given that presupposition, Bergson then stakes out his own metaphysical position: "There are changes, but there are underneath the change no things which change. There are movements, but there is no inert and invariable object which moves."[17] Much akin to the worldview of Heraclitus, therefore, everything flows; nothing endures.

Yet, from Whitehead's perspective, this is only half-true. Becoming is indeed ontologically prior to Being, but there are nevertheless beings, things that are the outcome here and now of an antecedent process of becoming. For this reason he stipulated that "the final real things of which the world is made up" are actual entities, momentary self-constituting subjects of experience that in rapid succession have as their conjoint effect the sense of a continuously existing organic reality or self. Moreover, since these

15. Henri Bergson, *The Creative Mind [Pensée et le mouvant]*, trans. Mabelle L. Andison (New York: Greenwood, 1968), 167–68.
16. Ibid., 171.
17. Ibid., 173.

actual entities or "actual occasions" of experience are self-constituting, the result of an internal process that in each case somehow takes account of the past but anticipates the future, Whitehead can still agree with Bergson that agents, entities that act, are the result rather than the source of action or movement. This is, to be sure, contrary to commonsense experience, which stipulates that things first exist and then perform certain actions. For example, in the picture books that teach young children how to read, the first picture is labeled "See Dick" and then second is titled "See Dick run." Likewise, as already noted, Aristotelian formal logic has heavily influenced the sentence structure of the various Western languages. Subjects of sentences are primary; verbs and other qualifiers are secondary. Subjects endure over time; predicates change over time. But Whitehead himself may have erred in the opposite direction. That is, he may have overemphasized the sheer multiplicity of actual entities and failed to make clear that in rapid succession they not only give the impression of movement to an outsider but in a carefully qualified sense (see below, chapter 2) constitute movement as a physical reality even for themselves as a "society" or closely knit aggregate of actual entities that share "a common element of form" or defining characteristic.[18]

From his own words, to be sure, it is clear that Whitehead did not want to reduce these "societies" to the sum of their component parts (their actual entities):

> The point of a "society," as the term is here used, is that it is self-sustaining; in other words, that it is its own reason. Thus a society is more than a set of entities to which the same class-name applies. . . . To constitute a society, the class-name has got to apply to each member by reason of genetic derivation from other members of that same society. The members of the society are alike because, by reason of their

18. Alfred North Whitehead, *Process and Reality: An Essay in Cosmology*, corrected edition, ed. David Ray Griffin and Donald W. Sherburne (New York: Free Press, 1978), 34.

common character, they impose on other members of the society the conditions which lead to that likeness.[19]

The details of how actual entities, self-constituting subjects of experience, have internal rather than purely external relations to one another and thereby transmit from one set of actual entities to another this common element of form or common characteristic will be part of the subject matter of chapter 2. For now, it is only important to note how through the influence of Bergson and Whitehead and many other contemporary philosophers, the mindset of even the average person here in the West is that reality is not permanent or fixed but dynamic, always on the move. Change is not always welcome, but everyone senses that change is "the name of the game" for contemporary life in this world. In the remaining pages of this chapter, I indicate briefly how the naturalist Charles Darwin with his theory of natural selection in the workings of nature and how early twentieth-century theoretical physicists with their research on subatomic reality likewise have contributed to this new commonsense understanding of physical reality as constantly evolving and thus as significantly different from the classical worldview with its own emphasis on Being or permanence rather than on Becoming or change.

Darwin on Evolution

In his early years, Darwin first studied medicine at the urging of his father, himself a physician. Since the young Darwin disliked the practice of surgery, his father then arranged for him to study for the Anglican priesthood at Cambridge University. Here Darwin like every other seminarian was required to read William Paley's

---

19. Ibid., 89.

celebrated *Natural Theology*, which established on philosophical grounds the need for a Creator God as ultimate cause of the marvelous order and design of the universe. Paley is perhaps best known for his watchmaker analogy. If one finds a stray stone on the heath, a stretch of relatively uncultivated land, one presumes that it is there by chance, simply the result of a coincidence of natural forces. But, if one finds a watch on the heath, one sees an order and design that could only have come from a watchmaker. In similar fashion, the order and design of the universe could only have come about through the work of a divine watchmaker. Given that there was already in academic circles a strong belief in the gradual evolution of the world of nature, Paley's watchmaker argument still upheld the need for a Creator God to oversee this gradual change in the history of the universe. In those years as a seminarian Darwin was quite convinced that Paley's teleological argument for the existence of God was correct. At the same time he was also much impressed by Charles Lyell's *Principles of Geology* with its presupposition of the overall uniformity of the changes in nature. The laws of nature that exist today are the same laws that have been responsible for the gradual formation of the earth's crust over the centuries.

The seismic shift in Darwin's thinking about the workings of nature came about as a result of a five-year journey on the HMS *Beagle* as a companion to its captain, Robert Fitzroy, in exploring the coast of South America and making a lengthy stop at the Galápagos Islands in the Pacific Ocean west of Ecuador. Here he saw firsthand the divergence of "daughter" species from one another and the parent-species, seemingly as a result of exposure to different natural environments on the various islands. So, after returning to England and getting considerable publicity in scientific circles as a result of his research on the diversity of plant and animal species, he began work privately on a theory that would account for these changes in nature by divinely ordained natural laws. What he eventually came up with was his theory of natural selection, namely, that nature itself operating in virtue of its own God-given laws would "select" the organisms best adapted to their environment for survival and reproduction. This seemed to Darwin at the time to be much more in line with the subtle workings of Divine Providence than an explanation of change as a result of direct divine intervention into the way that nature functioned. Natural selection is clearly God's preferred way to produce the species changes that he had observed while visiting foreign shores.[20]

Another major factor in his thinking during this creative period of his life was the work of Thomas Malthus in his book *An Essay on the Principle of Population*, first published in 1798. Therein Malthus, an Anglican clergyman, argued that human population tends to rise much faster than any increase in the production of food available to feed the population. As a result, Divine Providence allows for positive and negative checks on the excessive growth of the human population. Positive checks include hunger, disease, and war; negative checks include birth control, abortion, prostitution, postponement of marriage, and celibacy.[21] After reading and thinking about Malthus's book, Darwin concluded that not God, but nature itself operating in virtue of its own laws "selects" for survival and reproduction those organisms that are best adapted to deal with these positive and negative checks on population growth. God in turn uses this law of natural selection, this "struggle for existence," to bring about the highest good of the cosmic process, the creation of human beings and other higher-order animal species. But, as time went on, Darwin saw more clearly the pain and suffering that

20. James Moore, "Charles Darwin," in *Science and Religion: A Historical Introduction*, ed. Gary Ferngren (Baltimore: Johns Hopkins University Press, 2002), 208–11.
21. T. R. Malthus, *An Essay on the Principle of Population*, ed. Geoffrey Gilbert (New York: Oxford University Press, 1993), 28–45.

inevitably accompanied the demise of defective individuals and of entire species as a result of this law of natural selection. Likewise, he felt the pain of personal loss in the death of his father in 1848 and, above all, of his beloved daughter Annie at the age of ten, three years later. As a result, by the time that he wrote *The Descent of Man* in 1871, he had become an agnostic, one who doubted the existence of a benevolent and caring God, given the impersonal cruelty in the functioning of the law of natural selection, but never an atheist even though many atheists of his day sought to enlist him in their ranks. His wife Emma was a devout Anglican churchgoer who prayed for her husband's conversion, fearing that in the next life she might never see him again. But he died, surrounded by his wife and daughters and whispering to them "I am not in the least afraid to die." He was buried with much ceremony in Westminster Abbey in London.[22]

Darwin's theory of evolution through a process of natural selection for both individuals and entire species appeared, of course, in the midst of considerable controversy both in England and elsewhere over how to understand the term "natural history." On the one hand, religiously minded scientists and Anglican theologians endorsed what was called Physicotheology, in which advances in knowledge of the complex adaptation of plants and animals to their environments were seen as further proof of the existence of God and of the wisdom of God at work in the world. But, on the other hand, a secular, nonreligious understanding of changes in physical reality increasingly prevailed in scientific circles, where references to God as source of these changes became less and less common even among those scientists who still believed in the existence of God and the activity of God in creation. The publication of Darwin's *Origin of Species* did not settle that controversy but only intensified it. For

22. Moore, "Charles Darwin," 211–17.

Darwin proposed new lines of evidence to show how evolutionary theory could explain physical changes in nature in and through a new and potentially more materialistic mechanism of evolution.[23] That is, changes in nature were not the result of a divine plan of creation but simply of chance happenings that over time favored some members of the species in question but not others, or favored one species over another in successfully adjusting to presumably irreversible changes in the natural environment. Yet, as already noted, Darwin insisted on remaining agnostic on this point even though he experienced considerable pressure from atheists in England to endorse their militantly anti-religious movement.[24] His agnosticism seems to have arisen only over time as he thought through the inevitable consequences of his own theory of natural selection. The strictly impersonal and seemingly heartless notion of advance in nature through grim competition among individuals and entire species for survival and reproduction and the gradual extinction of some of those individuals and species who were less equipped to adapt to changes in the environment seemed to be incompatible in his mind with belief in the omnipotent, omniscient, and loving God of biblical revelation.

That controversy, whether evolutionary theory is necessarily secular and materialistic, effectively denying the existence of a Creator God actively at work in nature, or whether it can be reconciled with traditional belief in the existence of God as revealed in the Bible and the sacred scriptures of other world religions is, of course, still unsettled. In my judgment, it will not be settled simply through new advances in natural science or through a new interpretation of the Scriptures by the mystics and theologians in each world religion, but only through a new worldview, a new

23. Peter J. Bowler, "Evolution," in *Science and Religion: A Historical Introduction*, ed. Gary B. Ferngren (Baltimore: Johns Hopkins University Press, 2002), 222.
24. Moore, "Darwin," 216.

evolutionary metaphysics, that can make sense of the truth-claims both of science and of the various world religions and show their complementarity, their deeper reality of being different but still interrelated dimensions of one and the same physical reality. To sketch how this might be possible, of course, is the aim of this book as a whole. But, before plunging into a defense of such a claim, I conclude this chapter with an advance look at the way new knowledge of subatomic physics, physical reality at its foundational level, is also implicitly appealing for a new worldview in which contingency or chance can play a key role in the evolutionary process and yet not throw into question all the traditional laws of nature that seem to presuppose a directionality, if not a predetermined goal, for that same process.

Whitehead and Quantum Physics

There have been many books written about the "weirdness" of quantum physics, the study of subatomic reality. "Grasping quantum reality requires changing from a reality that can be seen and felt to an instrumentally detected reality that can be perceived only intellectually. The world described by the quantum theory does not appeal to our immediate intuition as did the old classical physics. Quantum reality is rational but not visualizable."[25] The weirdness of quantum theory is that it makes rational sense but can't be directly visualized. It can only be visualized in terms of what appears to be entities with different properties or modes of operation, namely, waves and particles.[26] Common sense tells us that we live in a world

---

25. Heinz R. Pagels, *The Quantum Code: Quantum Physics as the Language of Nature* (New York: Bantam, 1982), xiii; 47.

26. Cf. Daniel Athearn, *Fruits of Time: Nature and the Unfolding of Difference* (Universal Publishers [upublish.com], 2003), 1–48, esp. 12–13. Athearn challenges the conventional understanding of particles and waves in theoretical physics, claiming that these terms are derivative from

where things remain stable for extended periods of time; they do not dramatically change character from moment to moment. Thus we have no reason to doubt the testimony of our senses until we are confronted with theories both from natural science and various process-oriented metaphysical systems that, as noted in the beginning of this chapter, presuppose that there are in the end no things, but only processes that from moment to moment look like things. In other words, things are the momentary byproducts or results of complex processes or systems within us and all around us that we have to "freeze" or hold in place in order to understand and control for our own purposes. Yet the sense of weirdness still remains because it contradicts commonsense experience. We may grasp the objective rationality of a process- or systems-oriented approach to reality, but, as Pagels says, we cannot directly visualize it; and so we tend to treat it with suspicion, even total skepticism, at the beginning.

The wave-particle complementarity, noted above, is a classic example of this affront to commonsense experience. Different experiments in the field of quantum physics give testimony to the belief that the same reality (e.g., light) is somehow both particle and wave but not both at once. Yet the notions of wave and particle are completely different from one another. Waves radiate out from a central source (like light from the sun) and bend around the objects they encounter. Particles are very small bits of matter that like every other material object should be located at a definite position in space and time at any given moment. But, if and when they move or change location, they strike any object that they encounter in a clearly defined place like a bullet striking a target. The so-called double-slit experiment, however, is more ambiguous in terms of its results. For example, an electron shot from an electron gun can travel

mathematical formulas used to analyze and control the workings of physical reality rather than from a consistent metaphysics or philosophy of nature.

through a plate with two slits in it so as to allow the electron to pass through it and strike a screen behind it. The electron will exhibit particle-like behavior if only one slit is open and wave-like behavior if both slits are open. Hence, one has to conclude that an electron is somehow both particle and wave but not both at the same time.[27] The German physicist Max Born in 1926 proposed a solution to the wave-particle complementarity, namely, that waves are not "matter-waves" as the Austrian Erwin Schrödinger proposed but probability-waves, expressing the probability that a given particle will be found at one place on the mathematical trajectory of the particle at any given moment.[28]

But is this solution to the wave-particle duality resolved at too high a price, namely, the loss of objectivity about the way the world works? That is, if what we observe depends crucially upon the type of experiment performed, then are we human beings with our choice of measuring apparatus separate from what is being observed as in early modern science and classical metaphysics? Or are we an integral part of the measurement process? Do we affect the outcome of the experiment simply by the way we conduct the experiment? The laws proper to quantum mechanical interactions, after all, are fully determinate in virtue of the linear Schrödinger equation. Indeterminacy in the results comes from the macroscopic observation of the results with a given measuring apparatus. To date, this controversy about whether the wave-particle complementarity is grounded in ontology, the nature of reality, or in epistemology, the inevitable limits of human observation and experiment, remains unresolved. What seems to be needed to resolve this impasse would be a new understanding of physical reality in which one and the

---

27. Pagels, *The Quantum Code*, 113–24.
28. Andrew Whitaker, *Einstein, Bohr and the Quantum Dilemma: From Quantum Theory to Quantum Information*, 2nd ed. (New York: Cambridge University Press, 2006), 145–46.

same reality can be in quick succession first wave and then particle as integral components of an evolving physical process or system. Whitehead's metaphysical scheme might be useful here. For a Whiteheadian actual entity as a momentary self-constituting subject of experience is first potentiality and then actuality in rapid succession. As potentiality/subject of experience it receives energy-waves with a given pattern or mode of operation from predecessor actual entities in its environment; as actuality it chooses which one of those information-carrying energy waves to actualize so as itself to exist as a determinate subatomic particle in a specific location. Then this fully self-constituted actual entity "superjects"[29] its information-laden energy wave into the encompassing society or field of activity that it shares with other contemporary actual entities. In this way multiple information-laden energy waves are now available for the next generation of actual entities to choose as the pattern or mode of operation for their own process of self-constitution.

What is intriguing about this Whiteheadian solution to the wave/particle issue in subatomic physics is that it stands midway between two classical positions among theoretical physicists on that same topic. Albert Einstein and David Bohm insist that subatomic particles have a definite position and momentum at every moment, quite apart from human observation of the wave-like or particle-like behavior of the electron (or some other subatomic particle) using the two-slit experiment described above.[30] Others, like Niels Bohr, in line with his principle of complementarity insist that the electron is both wave and particle, but not at the same time. So for Bohr much depends upon the choice of experiment by the human observer whether the electron is detected as a particle or as a wave.[31] But if an electron is

29. Whitehead, *Process and Reality*, 26, 28.
30. Whitaker, *Einstein, Bohr and the Quantum Dilemma*, 225–54.
31. Ibid., 205–10.

hypothetically seen as a Whiteheadian actual entity, then the electron would be initially a self-determining subject of experience within an already-structured field of activity; that is, the electron would be something internally as well as externally or environmentally determined. Then as a superject or fully self-constituted actuality, the electron would have a definite location in the space-time continuum. Finally, before ceasing to exist as this or that determinate physical actuality, the electron would transmit to future electrons/electromagnetic actual entities in the same society or shared field of activity its pattern of existence and activity in the form of an information-laden energy-wave.[32] Thus in terms of this hypothetical conjunction of electron and actual entity, it is not necessary for human observers with their scientific experiments to "collapse" the wave function so as to fix the physical location of a subatomic particle at that moment. The particle, when understood as a fully self-constituted actual entity with a definite pattern of existence and activity within the space-time continuum has already "collapsed" the wave function as part of its own process of self-constitution. Yet, insofar as the electron/actual entity then transmits the pattern of its momentary existence and activity to future electrons/actual entities in the same society or field of activity before ceasing to exist, it still retains the reality of an information-laden energy-wave. Thus the electron is both particle and energy-wave in rapid succession, not simultaneously, as Bohr stipulated. In this way, an electron being both particle and wave in quick succession simply represents two interrelated functions or modes of operation within one and the same open-ended system or process at the subatomic level of existence and activity within nature. What is totally confusing if viewed in terms of interaction between quite different individual entities becomes

32. Alfred North Whitehead, *Science and the Modern World* (New York: Free Press, 1967), 133–37.

readily intelligible if interpreted as dynamically interrelated functions or modes of operation within a complex physical system.

All this, of course, is abstract speculation on my part about a controversial topic in contemporary quantum physics, which is obviously much more complicated than what I have laid out thus far. But for our purposes in this book, it seems safe to say that likewise from the perspective of natural science physical reality is not what we conventionally take it to be. We do not live in a world of things, relatively fixed and unchanging material objects, but in a world of interrelated processes or systems in which the things that we perceive are the momentary byproduct or result of these processes both within us and around us that we cannot directly perceive but can only infer on the basis of rational reflection upon empirical data.

2

The "Inside" and the "Outside" of Everything

At the end of the last chapter, I indicated the problem posed by the wave-particle complementarity (or, in the view of some, duality) for theoretical physicists working in quantum mechanics. A scientist can no longer stand apart from and objectively analyze the empirical data as was generally assumed to be the case in early modern natural science. The scientist, with his choice of experiment and equipment for accurate measurement of the data, is an integral part of the experiment and the results thereby achieved. She also has to take into account her own finite powers of perception and understanding. As a result, some notable physicists such as Niels Bohr and, above all, Werner Heisenberg with his Uncertainty Principle, contend that physical reality as a whole might well be open-ended and indeterminate in its workings so that the wave-particle complementarity would reflect the way nature itself works as well as the way that the human mind works with the instruments at its disposal.[1] Bohr and Heisenberg, however, did not provide a philosophical explanation for this alleged wave-particle complementarity in nature. Yet, as already noted in the last chapter, Alfred North Whitehead with his notion of an actual entity, a momentary self-constituting subject of experience with an objective material counterpart, might point the way to such a dual-dimensional explanation of physical reality.

That is, if every actual entity is not only an immaterial subject of experience but also a "superject" or material self-expression of that actual entity in virtue of its self-constituting "decision,"[2] then an ongoing series of these superjects with the same pattern of existence and activity will be detected empirically as an "enduring object" or material reality.[3] In this way, reality is not made up exclusively of one kind of stuff (monism of either spirit or matter) nor of two totally different kinds of stuff (dualism: spirit and matter in opposition to one another), but of a two-dimensional "stuff" (matter and spirit in combination, albeit in different proportions in each instance). Inanimate "things," for example, exhibit a preponderance of matter over spirit in their quasi-mechanical workings. Organisms or living "things," especially those that are highly complex in their mode of operation like human beings or other higher-order animal species, exhibit a clear preponderance of spirit over matter in their mode of operation.

---

1. Ian G. Barbour, *Religion and Science: Historical and Contemporary Issues* (San Francisco: HarperSanFrancisco, 1997), 167–73.
2. Alfred North Whitehead, *Process and Reality: An Essay in Cosmology*, corrected edition, ed. Davis Ray Griffin and Donald W. Sherburne (New York: Free Press, 1978), 26–28. Hereafter: *PR*.
3. Ibid., 35.

Teilhard and Whitehead

In his widely read book *The Phenomenon of Man*, the Jesuit scientist turned philosopher-theologian Pierre Teilhard de Chardin made much the same claim: "[I]n every region of space and time—in the same way, for instance, that it is granular: *co-extensive with their Without, there is a Within of things.*"[4] The Without of things is their material reality; the Within of things is their psychic energy. According to Teilhard, "all energy is psychic [but] divided into two distinct components: a *tangential energy* which links the element [e.g., subatomic particle] with all others of the same order (that is to say, of the same complexity and the same centricity) as itself in the universe; and a *radial energy* which draws it towards ever greater complexity and centricity—in other words forwards."[5] Implicit in this statement is Teilhard's belief that the motive force for cosmic evolution is what he calls the "Law of complexity and consciousness."[6] At the beginning of cosmic evolution there existed only a multiplicity of elements [subatomic particles], but with the passage of time the multiple elements have become more and more unified with a consequent growth in internal consciousness. Progress in cosmic evolution is thus marked by ever-greater complexity (tangential energy) and centricity (radial energy).

At the end of cosmic evolution, the collective consciousness of the universe (the *noosphere*)will be released from its "material matrix," its connection to matter, and be absorbed into the Omega Point, God as the "Hyper-Personal."[7] Cosmic evolution is thus ultimately "personalizing";[8] all the centers of consciousness both human and

4. Pierre Teilhard de Chardin, *The Phenomenon of Man*, trans. Bernard Wall (New York: HarperTorchbooks, 1965), 56.
5. Ibid., 64–65.
6. Ibid., 61.
7. Ibid., 260.
8. Ibid., 260–62.

nonhuman, while retaining their individual identity, are nevertheless united with a transcendent Center, God as the Hyper-Personal. What remains afterwards as matter apart from spirit will become increasingly disordered and chaotic as a result of the workings of the principle of entropy. Only that which has been "personalized," above all, human beings but nonhuman creation as well, will be drawn into ever-greater spiritual union with God as Omega Point: "To make room for thought in the world, I have needed to 'interiorize' matter: to imagine an energetics of the mind; to conceive a noogenesis rising upstream against the flow of entropy; to provide evolution with a direction, a line of advance and critical points; and finally to make all things double back upon *someone*."[9]

There is clear affinity here between the thought of Teilhard de Chardin and the metaphysical scheme of Whitehead. Above all, the dual-dimensional reality of everything in the cosmos as simultaneously both spirit and matter is common to both authors. But whereas Teilhard ultimately absorbs matter into spirit, Whitehead keeps them interrelated but still distinct from one another forever. There is, to be sure, also a certain primacy to spirit in Whitehead's scheme since logically an actual entity must be first an immaterial self-constituting subject of experience and only as a result of its internal process of decision-making a superject, i.e., a momentary material reality. But he still insists in *Process and Reality* that an actual entity is simultaneously both subject and superject.[10] It is strictly nondual or dual-dimensional in its physical reality. But how is this achieved? To deal with this and other questions about the relationship between spirit and matter, I here summarize my revised understanding of Whitehead's metaphysical category of society as more than simply a tightly organized set of component parts (actual

9. Ibid., 290.
10. Whitehead, *PR*, 28.

entities). Each superject or external self-manifestation of an actual entity is indeed a material reality, but it is not a "thing" in the normal sense. It is instead a momentary pattern of self-constitution for an actual entity that is immediately integrated into an energy-field progressively structured by the patterns proper to each new set of constituent actual entities. So the materiality of a Whiteheadian society (or system in my scheme) is real enough in terms of its tangible material effects but as the cause of those effects it is intangible. That is, one sees the material effects of a system, but the system itself is hidden from view. It looks like an enduring thing but actually exists as an ongoing system of ever-new dynamically interrelated parts or members.

A Field-Oriented Approach to Reality

In chapter 1, I emphasized that the commonsense experience of a world of things is illusory. What appears to be stable and unchanging is actually in ongoing process, never quite the same from one moment to the next, all appearances to the contrary notwithstanding. So to think of physical things as energy-fields progressively structured by the succession of events taking place within the field in question is not as outrageous as it might initially seem.[11] Furthermore, description of physical reality in terms of interacting energy fields that can be integrated with one another to produce further even more complex energy fields was validated in the late nineteenth century with James Clerk Maxwell's formulation of equations governing electromagnetism. He and his successors thereby proved that the ongoing integration of an electrically charged field and a magnetic field produces the electricity needed to power electric motors.

11. Cf., e.g., Daniel Athearn, *Fruits of Time: Nature and the Unfolding of Difference* (Universal Publishers [uPublish.com], 2003), 25–34, 47–48.

Furthermore, the electromagnetic field which results from this integration of two different fields of activity permeates all of nature and is recognized as one of the four fundamental forces of nature, the others being gravitation, the weak force, and the strong force. From my neo-Whiteheadian perspective, one can also claim that individual persons and things (both animate and inanimate) are in fact more specialized subfields of activity within the electromagnetic field. But neither the electromagnetic field nor any of the other fundamental forces of nature is empirically visible in itself; only its physical effects are visible in the form of the activity and behavior of the persons and things to be found in commonsense experience.

I propose this modest revision in Whitehead's scheme because in my judgment his explanation of the nature of societies in his own philosophy is incomplete. For example, he describes a society in *Process and Reality* as follows:

> The point of a "society," as the term is here used, is that it is self-sustaining; in other words, that it is its own reason. Thus a society is more than a set of entities to which the same class-name applies: that is to say, it involves more than a merely mathematical conception of "order." To constitute a society, the class-name has got to apply to each member by reason of genetic derivation from other members of that same society. The members of the society are alike because, by reason of their common character, they impose on other members of the society the conditions which lead to that likeness.[12]

An aggregate, of course, is a group of (actual) entities that find themselves linked together in the same place and at the same time more or less by accident. The entities constitutive of a society, on the contrary, all share a defining characteristic or common element of form from moment to moment in virtue of their dynamic interrelation at each moment.[13] They have as a result internal rather

---

12. Whitehead, *PR*, 89.

than purely external relations to one another.[14] That is, what each actual entity is becoming in terms of its specific form of existence and activity is shared with all the other actual entities in the society in terms of their internally related but still individual processes of self-constitution.

At this point, Whitehead's analysis of a society ends. But what he leaves unspecified is whether the defining characteristic or common element of form for the society as a whole is simply a logical abstraction from the individual patterns of self-constitution proper to its constituent actual entities at that moment or whether this common element of form for the society as a whole has an affinity with but is not identical with any of those individual patterns of existence and activity among the constituent actual entities. If the common element of form for the society as a whole is simply a logical abstraction from the diversity of patterns to be found among the constituent actual entities,[15] then the society is still an aggregate. It is nothing more than the sum of its constituent parts. But, if the common element of form for the society as a whole is related to but still different from the patterns of self-constitution for its constituent actual entities, then the society is an objective reality in its own right. It is more than the sum of its parts; it represents a higher-order level of existence and activity than that proper to its constituent parts or members. It is emergent out of the dynamic interrelationship of its constituent actual entities at any given moment but in itself it is something new and different.

But, even if we grant the legitimacy of this revision of Whitehead's notion of society, would it not be simpler to call a Whiteheadian society a substance as the term is conventionally understood in classical metaphysics? After all, for Aristotle and Thomas Aquinas a

13. Ibid., 34.
14. Ibid., 41, 50.
15. Ibid., 22–23.

substance is what exists in its own right and thus is other than and more than its accidental/contingent characteristics here and now.[16] But logically a Whiteheadian should not make that claim. For substances in the philosophy of Aristotle and Aquinas do not change in their substantial form or basic intelligibility. They come to be and eventually cease to be with the same substantial form or essence from beginning to end, even though their accidental characteristics (size, shape, weight, etc.) over time may vary considerably. But Whiteheadian societies in their common element of form or distinguishing characteristic evolve, that is, gradually change character over time as the dynamic relationships between their constituent actual entities are in some measure different from moment to moment.[17] Societies, to be sure, do not change with the rapidity of the changes between the constituent actual entities. Otherwise, a Whiteheadian society would be nothing more than a pure aggregate, a passing combination of characteristics that will be different in the next moment. Yet a Whiteheadian society in principle can undergo the equivalent of a species change as result of the continued interaction of its constituent actual entities both with one another and with the external environment from moment to moment.

Moreover, Whitehead himself wanted to get away from the customary subject-predicate relation in Western language usage wherein predicates change with the passage of time but not the subject of the sentence (cf. chapter 1). For Whitehead the only unchanging reality is what he calls creativity, the dynamic principle of novelty in the creative process which functions differently in the self-constitution of each actual entity but in itself never changes in

16. Aristotle, *Metaphysics*, trans. Hippocratus G. Apostle (Grinnel, IA: Peripatetic, 1979), 1025, 1038b: 20–32; Thomas Aquinas, *Summa Theologiae* (Madrid: Biblioteca de Autores Cristianos, 1951), I., q. 66 resp. and *ad* 3.
17. Whitehead, *PR*, 89–91.

its basic function and intelligibility within his metaphysical system.[18] For both of the above-mentioned reasons, Whitehead could not call a society a substance in the classical sense without contradicting himself. As a result, he appears to have dodged the issue by detailing instead the various grades of actual entities: some living and some nonliving, some endowed with consciousness but with the great majority lacking consciousness in their process of self-constitution.[19] In a later work after *Process and Reality*, namely, *Adventures of Ideas*, he conceded the affinity of the concept of a society to the classical notion of substance, in that both imply an enduring reality.[20] But Whitehead never developed how they were different from one another. This is why I prefer to call Whiteheadian societies systems; systems better convey the impression of something objectively real and yet are a different kind of reality than an Aristotelian substance or material thing.

Furthermore, the notion of a Whiteheadian society as an ongoing structured field of activity for its constituent actual entities from moment to moment can in some measure be found in Whitehead's metaphysical scheme, provided one allows for a modest extension and refinement of what Whitehead himself says. In his masterwork *Process and Reality*, for example, there are at least two passages that in my judgment allow for an implicit field-oriented approach to Whiteheadian societies. Both are to be found in the chapter on "The Order of Nature," where Whitehead analyzes the underlying structure of physical reality. The first reads as follows:

> Thus a society is, for each of its members [constituent actual entities], an environment with some element of order in it, persisting by reason of the genetic relations between its own members. . . . But there

18. Ibid., 7.
19. Ibid., 177–78.
20. Alfred North Whitehead, *Adventures of Ideas* (New York: Free Press, 1967), 204.

is no society in isolation. Every society must be considered with its background of a wider environment of actual entities, which also contribute their objectifications to which the members of the society must conform. . . . But this means that the environment, together with the society in question, must form a larger society in respect to some more general characters than those defining the society from which we started. Thus we arrive at the principle that every society requires a social background, of which it is itself a part.[21]

In simpler language, Whitehead claims here that societies are hierarchically ordered with the least complex societies in terms of their defining characteristic at the bottom and the most complex at the top.

Can such hierarchically ordered environments with varying degrees of order in them be regarded as structured fields of activity for constituent actual entities? In favor of this interpretation of environments as structured fields of activity is the fact that unlike material things in the conventional sense, fields have flexible boundaries. Fields, in other words, can readily fit into one another, with the structure of one field serving as the infra-structure and the structure of the other field serving as the super-structure for their combined existence and activity. An atom within a molecule, for example, remains an atom in its basic structure and activity, but that structure and activity of the atom is now integrated into the more complex structure and activity of the molecule. The atom is not as "free" and unconstrained in its "atomic" existence and activity as it would be apart from inclusion in the molecule.[22] Similarly, the structure and activity of the molecule is conditioned by its constituent parts, namely, atoms, each with its own internal structure and mode of operation. Atoms and molecules thus condition one another's existence and activity in a way that would be impossible for two

21. Whitehead, *PR*, 90.
22. Ibid., 106.

things separated in space and time that can have only external rather than internal relations with one another. That is, in virtue of their external relation to one another, two entities do not play a major role in one another's self-constitution. They just happen to be together in some way at the same time and in the same place. Entities with internal relations to one another, on the contrary, heavily influence their mutual self-constitution even as they thereby co-constitute a structured field of activity for their dynamic interrelation. Evan Thompson refers to this as "dynamic co-emergence" in discussing emergence and downward causation in nonlinear dynamic systems.[23] Parts and whole mutually "constrain" one another in such a system.

The second passage from *Process and Reality* that seems to hint at a field-oriented interpretation of Whiteheadian societies is the following: "The causal laws which dominate a social environment are the product of the defining characteristic of that society. But the society is only efficient through its individual members [constituent actual entities]. Thus in a society, the members can only exist by reason of the laws which dominate the society, and the laws only come into being by reason of the analogous characters of the members of the society."[24] Here too we have the picture of a field with its governing structure conditioning the activity of the (actual) entities within the field and the entities in turn through their ongoing dynamic interrelation gradually reshaping the governing structure of their conjoint field of activity or environment. The entities in question are, to be sure, Whiteheadian actual entities, interrelated self-constituting subjects of experience that are themselves mini-processes or subfields of activity within the higher-order field of activity that counts as their environment. Thus physical reality is

---

23. Evan Thompson, *Mind in Life: Biology, Phenomenology, and the Sciences of Mind* (Cambridge, MA: Harvard University Press, 2007), 411.
24. Whitehead, *PR*, 90–91.

ultimately made up of dynamically interrelated and hierarchically ordered fields of activity for the events (actual entities as momentary self-constituting subjects of experience) taking place within them. But, if all this is true, then the commonsense world of persons and things that exist apart from one another in space and being and are relatively unchanged by the passage of time is completely overturned. All that really exist are fields of activity whose constituents are dynamically interrelated processes or systems, each of which consists of a series of events with a serial pattern of existence and activity, what Whitehead calls a distinguishing characteristic or common element of form.[25]

Field-Theory in Theoretical Physics

Admittedly, theoretical physicists do not often use field-language to describe their scientific research to one another and, even more importantly, to the general public. On those occasions, they still conventionally use the language of "things" to describe what they have observed and analyzed. Yet, when asked for further information on what they have said in a general way, they freely admit that the things they are talking about are very elusive. Waves (e.g., water waves, sound waves, light waves) are constantly on the move, now in one place, now somewhere else. Likewise, subatomic particles are not tiny inert bits of matter but localized concentrations of energy that exist for a moment and then are gone. As the British physicist Paul Davies comments in his book *The Cosmic Blueprint*, "Today, the truly fundamental material entities are no longer considered to be particles, but *fields*. Particles are regarded as disturbances in the fields, and so have been reduced to a derivative status."[26] Yet, having said

25. Ibid., 34.

that, he then implicitly reverts to the language of things in describing the relation between DNA molecules and the field in which they are located: "If the fields tell the DNA molecules where they are located in the pattern, and the DNA molecules tell the fields what pattern to adopt, nothing is explained because the argument is circular."[27]

That theoretical problem, however, could conceivably have been avoided if he had remembered to think of DNA molecules not as mini-things but as mini-fields of activity with their own structure within the more comprehensive field of activity proper to a cell with its governing structure. The structure of the DNA molecule as a mini-field of activity influences the structure of the cell as a more comprehensive field of activity, and the latter in turn with its more slowly evolving governing structure influences the structure of its constituent DNA molecules. Each DNA molecule, of course, is itself a comprehensive field of activity for the tiny fields of activity represented by its constituent atoms. In brief, then, the language of molecules as mini-things confuses the issue of the dynamic interplay between wholes and parts, larger and smaller fields of activity, in molecular biology. Only dynamically interrelated and hierarchically ordered processes can make clear how parts can explain the whole, even as the whole explains the mode of operation of the parts at the same time. As I see it, this is what Whitehead was trying to make clear in the second citation from *Process and Reality*, quoted above, on the mode of operation of actual entities and societies in his metaphysical scheme.

Davies further objects that if all the DNA molecules possess the same global plan for the organism [the overall structured field of

---

26. Paul Davies, *The Cosmic Blueprint: New Discoveries in Nature's Creative Ability to Order the Universe* (Philadelphia: Templeton Foundation Press, 2004), 12. Cf. also Athearn, *Fruits of Time*, 50–55.
27. Davies, *The Cosmic Blueprint*, 106.

activity in which they are all located], then how is it that different cells implement different parts of that plan?[28] The relatively new field of evolutionary developmental biology addresses that issue from a scientific perspective. From a philosophical perspective, however, problems remain in understanding how genes can be selectively turned on and off rather than being always active and how the same "toolkit" genes can be at work in significantly different organisms to produce remarkably similar effects (e.g., eye formation in all animals). A revised understanding of Whitehead's categories of actual entity and society such as I have presented in this book, however, might help to explain the unexpected emergence of discontinuity in the midst of continuity or the emergence of continuity where one would expect discontinuity within evolutionary developmental biology. Let us presuppose that a cell as a mini-organism is a Whiteheadian structured society/field of activity that contains a specific set of genes as its common element of form. Each gene, however, as a DNA molecule is likewise a structured field of activity for its atoms. Each atom, once again from a Whiteheadian perspective, is still another subsociety or structured field of activity for the dynamic interrelation of its constituent actual entities (subatomic particles). What one thus encounters is a hierarchy of structured fields of activity for actual entities, momentary self-constituting subjects of experience, that alone make things happen in terms of the societies to which they belong. The governing structure of the various fields of activity, to be sure, acts as a constraint on each new set of constituent actual entities. Yet the constraints of a Whiteheadian society on its constituent actual entities are internal rather than external; that is, each constraint is a conditioning (though not controlling) factor in the self-constitution of the constituent actual entities.[29]

28. Ibid., 103.
29. Whitehead, *PR*, 34.

What results, then, is a form of top-down and bottom-up causation in which continuity and discontinuity can both be present in varying proportions, depending upon which stage of the evolutionary/developmental process is in question. The actual entities in their intrinsic self-constitution are the place where discontinuity is to be found, but it is a discontinuity heavily conditioned by the already-existing structure of the field(s) of activity in which it originates. Continuity, on the other hand, is to be sought in the prevailing structure of the structured field(s) of activity for a given set of actual entities in their dynamic interrelation. But discontinuity is also to be expected in the governing structure of each field of activity since, unlike a Thomistic-Aristotelian substantial form that never changes form, the governing structure of a Whiteheadian society, a structured field of activity for its constituent actual entities, will unquestionably change over time since it is heavily conditioned by the dynamic relations of its ever-changing constituent actual entities in their relations to one another and to the external environment.

This same philosophical construal of physical reality might also be available for making sense out of still another anomaly within natural science, in this case contemporary quantum theory. The question at issue here is the phenomenon of decoherence, the so-called "collapse" of the wave function. That is, the quantum state is described by a wave function or mathematical concept that calculates the relative probabilities of the location of a subatomic particle here and now along the trajectory of an energy-wave in a given field of activity. Yet the wave function itself as a mathematical concept evolves deterministically: "Knowing the state of the system at one time (in terms of the wave function), the state at a later time can be computed, and used to predict the relative probabilities of the values that various observables will possess on measurement. In this weaker form of determinism, the various probabilities evolve deterministically, but the observable quantities themselves do not."[30] That is, one cannot predict precisely where the "particle" will be found on the mathematically calculated trajectory of the energy-wave. But once its position has been experimentally observed and measured within the overall field of activity proper to the system as a whole, one can then ascertain once again in terms of the mathematical wave function where it is *likely* to be the next time the wave function "collapses."[31] This combination of mathematical determinism and empirical contingency in measuring the path of a "particle" through its encompassing field of activity is what accounts for much of the seeming mystery or "weirdness" of contemporary quantum theory.

Yet the theoretical scheme proposed above for dealing with issues in evolutionary developmental biology may likewise have some applicability here. The components of a Whiteheadian society are, as already noted, actual entities, momentary self-constituting subjects of experience. According to Whitehead, every actual entity is both subject of experience and objective superject as a result of its self-constituting decision.[32] As a subject of experience, it "prehends"/feels its immediate past world/encompassing field of activity, subjectively responds to the patterns to be found among past actual entities in that field of activity, and makes a conscious or, more often, unconscious "decision" as to its own pattern of existence and activity. Thereby it becomes a material reality, a superject. That is, it exhibits an empirical pattern of activity that is open to "prehension" by subsequent actual entities in the same society or structured field of activity. As a result, every actual entity is in very rapid succession first an observer and then something observed, a mini-subject that prehends and a mini-object that is or at least can be prehended

30. Davies, *The Cosmic Blueprint*, 166–67.
31. Ibid., 168.
32. Whitehead, *PR*, 26–28.

by subsequent actual entities in their process of self-constitution. Equivalently, then, there is a passage from potentiality to actuality, a "collapse of the wave function," in the self-constitution of every actual entity provided that it is understood in field-oriented terms as a mini-process within the overall structured field of activity for the society in which it arises and to which it contributes its own momentary pattern of existence and activity.

The problem with this explanation for the issue of decoherence in quantum physics, of course, is that electrons or other elementary components of the quantum system are not generally considered to be self-constituting like a Whiteheadian actual entity. But, if, as Whitehead claims, an electron is itself not an actual entity but an inanimate society of actual entities,[33] then an electron is not self-constituting; it is the objective byproduct or result of a series of electronic actual entities. Actual entities as the components of electrons from moment to moment are first observers and then objects observed as a result of their process of self-constitution. Their collective "decision" at any given moment determines the location of the electron within the field of activity broadly defined by the wave function in terms of its mathematical formula. In other words, an electron like every other "entity" in Whitehead's worldview is not a fixed reality but a process. An electron retains a "common element of form" or determinate pattern of existence and activity for its constituent actual entities from moment to moment; but it is a strictly time-bound reality, what Paul Davies described in *The Cosmic Blueprint* as a "disturbance" in an already-existent energy-field.[34] This might be a "hard sell" for many empirically oriented physicists. But it offers a plausible rational explanation for an otherwise puzzling

33. Ibid., 104.
34. Davies, *The Cosmic Blueprint*, 12.

phenomenon, the notion of decoherence or collapse of the wave function.

Admittedly, one has also to presuppose here with Whitehead that consciousness is not needed for a "decision" in the self-constitution of actual entities: "The principle that I am adopting is that consciousness presupposes experience, and not experience consciousness. . . . Thus an actual entity may or may not be conscious of some part of its experience."[35] In defense of Whitehead's position, one can point to varying degrees of self-awareness among organisms. Whitehead, after all, characterized his metaphysics as a "philosophy of organism."[36] So every actual entity is an organism with some minimal degree of self-awareness. Perhaps at the atomic level self-awareness is simply the ability to be an active subject of experience rather than simply an inert object of experience, that is, to relate or interact with other actual entities on a feeling-level within a given context. The more complex actual entities that are components of the mental activity of higher-order animal species are in some measure aware of themselves as selves distinct from other selves. Full self-consciousness, however, seems to be reserved to human beings, at least when they are alert to what is going on around them.

Furthermore, in the ongoing effort to justify the notion of decoherence, the counterclaim proposed by some physicists, that the actualization of possibilities within the cosmic process is necessarily dependent upon human beings or other higher-order animal species seems even less likely, given the billions of years that have passed in the development of the cosmic process before higher-order animal species possessing consciousness or at least sense awareness came on the scene. Still more contrary to common sense, it seems to me, is the "many worlds" theory first espoused by Hugh Everett and

35. Whitehead, *PR*, 53.
36. Ibid., 18.

then even more dramatically proposed by Bryce de Witt, that with every collapse of the wave function and the actualization of a new possibility within quantum mechanics a new universe emerges to take its place alongside those already existing.[37] So in one way or another one has to set aside the deliverances of common sense to focus on what is conceptually plausible rather than what can be empirically verified here and now.

This is, of course, not to claim that my revision of the categories of actual entity and society in Whitehead's metaphysics solves all the conceptual problems in contemporary quantum mechanics. My basic argument in this and the preceding chapter has only been to claim that a consistent process- or systems-oriented approach to physical reality—in which the notion of a sequential series of actual entities as momentary self-constituting subjects of experience within hierarchically ordered fields of existence and activity in nature replaces the older Aristotelian/Thomistic categories of substance and accident—is a suitable contemporary model or symbolic representation of the world in which we live. That is, the notion of society or system replaces the Aristotelian concept of substance as the necessary principle of continuity within this ever-changing world, since a society by definition allows for gradual evolution of its governing structure, whereas in Aristotelian-Thomistic metaphysics a substantial form cannot evolve in its intelligibility so as to become over time something else. Actual entities as momentary self-constituting subjects of experience are the equivalent of "accidents" in classical metaphysics. But, unlike accidents they are not relatively passive realities, simply contingent qualifications of the substance as a self-defined reality, but instead active agents of change that by their dynamic interrelation with one another and with

---

37. Barbour, *Religion and Science*, 173.

the external environment over time produce a significant change in the governing structure for the society to which they belong. For both these reasons, a process- or systems-oriented approach to reality seems to be a more suitable model or symbolic representation of the world in which we live than classical metaphysics.

Yet in the end it is only a model, not a blueprint, of physical reality. Like all other models, it takes note of certain features of reality but inevitably overlooks or ignores others. Thus as Ian Barbour comments in *Religion and Science,* "Models and theories are abstract symbol systems, which inadequately and selectively represent particular aspects of the world for specific purposes. . . . Models, on this reading, are to be taken seriously but not literally; they are neither literal pictures nor useful fictions but limited and inadequate ways of imagining what is not observable."[38] So this model of physical reality as constituted by interrelated actual entities and hierarchically ordered fields of existence and activity for events taking place within them deserves a rational hearing but certainly is not definitive. I use the word "events" because actual entities as momentary self-constituting subjects of experience are from moment to moment passing events within broader and more comprehensive processes or systems rather than enduring mini-things like material atoms. Whitehead himself also used the term "actual occasion" to make clear that an actual entity is something that happens and is gone, a mere "drop of experience" in a long sequence of such events, rather than something that comes into existence and is relatively permanent in its ongoing existence and activity.[39]

38. Ibid., 117.
39. Whitehead, *PR*, 18.

Lothar Schäfer and Ervin Laszlo

To bring this chapter to a close, I will briefly review the work of two contemporary philosophers of science who basically agree with Whitehead that early modern classical physics was mistaken in assuming that physical reality is solely constituted by material atoms in various combinations as a result of external forces. This purely mechanistic approach to nature lent itself readily to mathematically calculated physical laws that were quite predictable in terms of conventional cause-and-effect relationships. But physical reality as a result was seen simply as matter-in-motion with no reference to the reality of spirit as necessary counterpart to matter for the workings of nature. Both of these contemporary authors have essays in a single past issue of *Zygon*, a religion and science journal, titled "Quantum Reality and the Consciousness of the Universe."

In his essay, "Quantum Reality, the Emergence of Complex Order from Virtual States, and the Importance of Consciousness in the Universe,"[40] Lothar Schäfer lists the following characteristic aspects of quantum reality: the basis of the material world is nonmaterial; the nature of reality is that of an indivisible wholeness; quantum entities possess aspects of consciousness in a rudimentary way. As a consequence of the last point he claims: "When a quantum entity makes a transition from one state to another in a quantum jump, it does so spontaneously and seemingly without any cause . . . a mind is the only thing that we know that can act in this way."[41] Hence, quantum entities are psychic as well as physical entities. He also argues that what he calls "virtual states" are necessary for this quantum jump. Virtual states are not in themselves actualities, nor are they simply mental concepts or ideas of a future state. They exist between

---

40. Lothar Schäfer, "Quantum Reality: The Emergence of Complex Order from Virtual States," *Zygon* 41, no. 3 (September 2006): 505–32.
41. Ibid., 510.

the mere possibility of an actual state and its de facto reality. Much like Platonic ideas, virtual states for Schäfer are part of a transcendent cosmic order that exists as an all-encompassing immaterial reality apart from physical reality. The actualization of a virtual state by a subatomic particle indicates that the material world is derivative from "the wholeness of the transcendent order of the universe."[42]

In his response to Schäfer, Ervin Laszlo agrees that reality has an indivisible wholeness and that quantum entities possess aspects of consciousness in a rudimentary way. But he disagrees with Schäfer's assumption that as a result the underlying basis of the physical world is nonmaterial. For Laszlo this assumption implies a dualism between spirit and matter, that is, the opposition of an immaterial reality (a cosmic order) to the partial actualization of that immaterial cosmic order in a material reality via a "quantum jump" of a particle into one of many conceivable virtual states. He himself prefers a nondual approach to the interrelation of spirit and matter. That is, in line with Teilhard de Chardin and Whitehead, Laszlo claims that all of empirical reality is simultaneously both spirit and matter, albeit in different ways. For Teilhard de Chardin, for example, spirit and matter are the "Within" and the "Without" of physical reality; for Whitehead, as we have already seen, it is the notion of the immaterial subject of experience and its material superject as co-constitutive of any given material thing.[43] Likewise, within the human mind there is as a result no opposition between two different kinds of events (mental and physical) occurring at the same time as Schäfer presupposes, but instead two closely interrelated "chains of events" that together produce one and the same empirical reality, namely, human consciousness at any given moment.[44]

42. Ibid., 512.
43. Ervin Laszlo, "Quantum and Consciousness: In Search of a New Paradigm," *Zygon* 41, no. 3 (September 2006): 533–41, 539–40.
44. Ibid., 539.

Even though the difference between "virtual states" for Schäfer and what Laszlo calls "potential states" may seem to be minimal, from my perspective as a Whiteheadian Laszlo has the better argument. That is, rather than presuppose a preexisting immaterial order that is the immediate source of the virtual states of all physical entities, it makes more sense simply to think of the potentialities available to physical entities at any given moment. For, the existence of such a transcendent cosmic order cannot be empirically verified; but a set of potentialities for a physical entity here and now is something that can be mathematically determined through the wave function that is descriptive of the behavior and activity of a given set of quantum particles. What both Schäfer and Laszlo both fail to explain, however, is how this "jump" from a virtual to an actualized state for Schäfer and from potentiality to actuality for Laszlo takes place. What is needed to make it happen? Here Whitehead's notion of an actual entity that is a momentary self-constituting subject of experience within an encompassing process or system seems to fill the gap. The actual entity makes a "decision" for one possibility rather than another. As already noted, in most cases the "decision" is not conscious because the entity in question (e.g., a subatomic particle within an atom, a molecule, or a living cell) has no consciousness but only a primitive ability to respond on a feeling-level to changes in its immediate environment. But the "decision," however made, is still the reason for the actuality of the actual entity here and now. Furthermore, if the actual entity is not only an immaterial subject of experience but also a material reality, namely, a specific pattern of self-constitution for the actual entity that is integrated into the overall pattern or common element of form for the society to which it belongs, then the alleged mystery surrounding the spontaneous move from a potential or virtual state of a system to an actual state at any given moment disappears.

There is, however, still another difference between the theories of Schäfer and Laszlo, on the one hand, and Whitehead's metaphysics on the other. According to Whitehead, individual actual entities don't move in space. One actual entity transfers its energy and pattern of self-constitution to the next actual entity in the society to which both belong but that second actual entity often exists at a different location in space. A photon emitted by the sun, for example does not as a mini-substance travel at a speed of 186,000 miles a second so as to reach the earth in roughly eight minutes. A photon in Whitehead's scheme is rather a series of photonic actual entities that covers the huge distance between the sun and the earth in a series of quantum jumps from one location in space to another until the last photonic actual entity impacts upon the earth so as to provide heat and light to its inhabitants. Schäfer, however, speaks about quantum waves as being part of the transcendent immaterial order and thus different from matter waves (i.e., water waves, sound waves, and light waves) in that they need no medium and carry no energy.[45] Here I side with Laszlo in the belief that waves at the quantum level of existence and activity convey energy as well as information since they emanate from and eventually return to a preexisting quantum vacuum or structured field of activity that is the energy-source of the ongoing cosmic process.[46] So a transcendent source of energy and information is not needed to keep the cosmic process going from moment to moment.

Yet I would side with Schäfer in his contention that there must be a transcendent source or ultimate ground of physical reality. That is, the quantum vacuum itself must be derivative from a higher-order, strictly transcendent reality. As I see it, the invisible quantum vacuum

45. Lothar Schäfer, *In Search of Divine Reality: Science as a Source of Inspiration* (Fayetteville: University of Arkansas Press, 1997), 28.
46. Laszlo, "Quantum Consciousness," 537.

in Laszlo's scheme is derivative from the all-comprehensive field of activity for the three divine persons of the Christian doctrine of the Trinity in their ongoing dynamic interrelation.[47] This structured field of activity for the divine persons, accordingly, is what all the material entities of this world originally come forth from, exist for a while, and eventually recede back into at the moment they cease to exist in creation. But what first comes into existence within this structured field of activity proper to the divine persons is the quantum vacuum or the quantum plenum. The quantum plenum, in other words, as an all-comprehensive but still finite field of activity is intermediate between the infinite field of activity proper to the divine persons and all the more limited fields of activity proper to the material entities of this world.

Hence, I find myself agreeing with both Laszlo and Schäfer in their respective theories about how this world of ours came into existence, albeit for different reasons: Laszlo for his proposal of a non-transcendent immediate source of the material world in terms of an all-encompassing quantum plenum, and Schäfer for the belief that a transcendent source is still ultimately responsible for the existence and activity of this same quantum plenum. In this way, I respect the legitimate boundaries of reason and revelation in their ongoing interrelation. Reason should govern our human understanding of the natural order taken by itself; revelation is needed for understanding the invisible impact of the supernatural order upon the natural order whenever and wherever it seems to have occurred (e.g., an alleged

47. Cf. my analysis of Wolfhart Pannenberg's proposal that Spirit is both a divine person and the nature of the triune God, namely, an underlying energy- or force field for the ongoing co-existence of the divine persons, in chapter 6 of this book. I only differ from Pannenberg in claiming that "force-field" in this context is not to be identified with any of the four fundamental forces of nature in contemporary physics. "Field" like "substance" in classical metaphysics is an analogical concept that always needs to be further specified when it is employed in different areas of academic investigation (e.g., in the natural sciences, the social sciences, the humanities).

miracle such as God become human in Jesus of Nazareth, life after death, etc.). If these boundaries are respected and carefully maintained, then there should be no enduring conflict between religion and science; temporary skirmishes due to mutual misunderstanding will presumably take place, but nothing more.

In these first two chapters, then, I have laid the groundwork for a systems-oriented understanding of the generic God-world relationship. That is, I have in various ways questioned the deliverances of commonsense experience that allow us to believe that we live in a world populated by semi-permanent things. Rather, we live in a world constituted by interrelated processes or systems (including ourselves as a hierarchically ordered set of physical and psychic systems). In the next two chapters, I will take up in rapid succession various theories *pro* and *con* with respect to panentheism. Then in the second part of this book, I use my own systems-oriented approach to panentheism so as to rethink the traditional understanding of several key doctrines of the Christian faith.

3

———

Panentheism

Hierarchically Ordered Systems of Existence and Activity

Readers of the *Summa Theologiae* by the celebrated medieval theologian Thomas Aquinas are sometimes startled to read in one of the opening chapters, titled "Does God Exist?" the initial answer: "it would seem not to be so."[1] Reassurance comes shortly with the recognition that Aquinas is employing the style of argument in the public academic disputations of his day: namely, first with various arguments to deny the truth of the proposition at issue, then to offer counterarguments for its truth, and afterwards to state one's own position along with an answer to each of the initial objections. As I shall explain below, Aquinas establishes the existence of God on the basis of Aristotle's understanding of causality in terms of efficient, formal, final, and material causality. This means, however, that the

---

1. Thomas Aquinas, *Summa Theologiae* (Madrid: Biblioteca de Autores Cristianos, 1951), I, Q. 2, art. 2.

God whose existence and activity in this world is thereby "proved" is not so much the God of biblical revelation but the God of a philosophical cosmology originally put forth by a non-Christian. For example, at the end of each of the proofs Aquinas concludes, "This is what everyone knows to be God." More precisely, he should have said that the First Efficient, Formal, and Final Cause of this world is what everyone of his day assumes to be God, given the all-pervasive influence of Christianity on the medieval worldview. But over the centuries since Aquinas wrote his *Summa*, others have contested this assumption. If, as Aristotle says, there must logically be an Uncaused Cause to cause everything else in this world, why not stipulate that the Universe itself is its own sufficient reason, hence, is the Uncaused Cause proven by Aristotle's and Aquinas's understanding of causality?

I raise this issue only to make clear that Christian theology is indeed heavily dependent upon God's self-revelation in the Sacred Scriptures but that it also is generally based upon an accepted philosophical system for explanation of reality (equivalently, a metaphysics). Aquinas, for example, encountered no little opposition in academic and ecclesiastical circles for using the philosophy of Aristotle, a pre-Christian pagan, for this purpose. But his opponents were consciously or unconsciously using the philosophical worldview of other ancient philosophers—Plato or one of his disciples like Plotinus, the leading thinker in the tradition of neo-Platonism—to articulate their own Christian worldview. St. Augustine, for example, was heavily influenced by the philosophy of Plato and neo-Platonism: for example, the doctrine of the primacy of immaterial spirit in the form of unchanging transcendental Ideas over material reality as the contingent self-expression of those Ideas. Plato's Idea or Form of the Good was for these early Christian philosophers and theologians a much more attractive option for a philosophical understanding of God than the Unmoved Mover in

Aristotle's cosmology. But Aquinas relied upon Aristotle, not exclusively, but certainly more than Plato and neo-Platonists like Plotinus for articulation of his own position on the God-world relationship. Eventually Aquinas's views prevailed, so that he became for later medieval and then many modern philosophers and theologians the champion of Christian orthodoxy in defending the various articles of Christian belief. But this only makes clear what I said above, that Christian theology is almost inevitably dependent upon a finite and thus fallible philosophical system for articulation of Christian beliefs over and above their initial grounding in Sacred Scripture.

Thus one should be careful not to "baptize" an accepted philosophical understanding of reality as the necessary rational counterpart to Christian belief.[2] That philosophical system (e.g., classical Aristotelian/Thomistic metaphysics) may eventually be challenged for its continuing validity by new empirical discoveries in the natural and social sciences. For example, this is what seems to have been the bone of contention in the celebrated trial and later condemnation of the views of Galileo Galilei as heresy by the Catholic Church in the seventeenth century. Galileo was in his mind a faithful Christian who believed in the basic truth-claims of biblical revelation when properly understood. As he said in a celebrated letter to an Italian noblewoman, "the Bible teaches us how to go to heaven, not how the heavens go."[3] In this view, he was supported by many churchmen, including the Jesuit Cardinal Robert Bellarmine, provided that he recognized that his own theory of heliocentrism as opposed to geocentrism was still a hypothesis, not an empirically established fact.[4] But here Galileo in his enthusiasm for heliocentrism

2. Granville Henry, *Christianity and the Images of Science* (Macon, GA: Smyth &Helwys, 1988), 21–28.
3. Richard J. Blackwell, "Galileo Galilei," in *Science and Religion: A Historical Introduction*, ed. Gary B. Ferngren (Baltimore: Johns Hopkins University Press, 2002), 110.

affirmed what even on strictly scientific grounds was still an unproven hypothesis and claimed instead that heliocentrism was definitively proven on the basis of his empirical observation and research. So, while mistakes were made both by Galileo and the Vatican authorities, the Vatican authorities and their theological advisers inadvertently "baptized" Aristotelian/Thomistic metaphysics and thereby confused the legitimate defense of the Christian faith with the defense of a fallible philosophical cosmology open to broad revision on scientific grounds.

God-World Relationship in Thomistic Metaphysics

What then would be a suitable philosophical underpinning for contemporary Christian understanding of the God-World relationship? Many Christian philosophers and theologians today argue that the classical Aristotelian/Thomistic understanding of the God-world relationship in terms of efficient, formal, and final causality is still preferable to other alternatives, if properly understood and explained to others. But many others, especially those in the religion-and-science dialogue, propose instead what has come to be called panentheism, namely, that the world exists in God but operates according to its own God-given laws and principles. Hence, within a panentheistic scheme, the world has its own ontological integrity and the influence of God on the cosmic process is more indirect than direct. God provides a directionality to the cosmic process but does not control its day-to-day operation in terms of its own laws and mode of operation.[5] The expression "in whom we live and move and

---

4. Ibid., 111–12.
5. Arthur Peacocke, "Introduction," in *In Whom We Live and Move and Have Our Being: Panentheistic Reflections on God's Presence in a Scientific World*, ed. Philip Clayton and Arthur Peacocke (Grand Rapids: Eerdmans, 2004), xviii–xxii.

have our being" is found in St. Paul's speech to Greek philosophers on the Areopagus near the acropolisat Athens (Acts 17:28), as he was talking to them about the Unknown God to which they had erected a statue. Paul's intent, of course, was to proclaim to them salvation through Christ who is the public revelation of this Unknown God, the invisible Creator of Heaven and Earth. Hence, he was teaching from a theological, not a specifically philosophical perspective, at that moment. In contemporary theology, however, it has definitely become a philosophical issue.

For example, given that God is infinite, where else can the world of creation exist except somehow in God? Yet classical metaphysics has always claimed that the God of the Bible is pure Spirit with no admixture of matter.[6] How then does creation as a material reality live and move and have its being within a purely spiritual being? Aquinas lists three ways in which God as Pure Spirit is present to the world of creation: namely, as first cause of everything finite that exists, through God's intellectual knowledge and love of all finite things, and through God's power to make things happen in creation.[7] In a related article, Aquinas notes that, unlike a material reality, God does not take up space, that is, exclude other entities from a given spatial location, by being present in a certain place.[8] As a purely spiritual being, God can be spiritually present to a material reality in the very same space, as noted above, through God's essence as Subsistent Being, through God's presence in terms of knowledge and love, and through the divine power to bring all things into being and sustain them in their created existence.

But questions can still be raised about this line of argument, all dealing with the precise relation between matter and spirit. For

---

6. Aquinas, ST, I, Q. 3, art. 1 resp.
7. Ibid., Q. 8, art. 3 resp.
8. Ibid., Q. 8, art. 2 resp.

example, God's knowledge and love of creatures is contained within God and does not immediately affect the world of creation. For example, if I know and love you as a fellow human being, this knowledge and love affects my relationship to you but not necessarily your relation to me. You may be ignorant of my knowledge and love of you or, if aware of it, choose to ignore it. Knowledge and love, in other words, have to be mutually exchanged if they are to affect both parties. With reference to God's presence to creation as the first cause of their existence and the sustaining cause of their continuing to exist, one can philosophically counterargue that this kind of presence, like the presence of the soul in the body, could be due to the workings of an activity, but not an entity as such. Alfred North Whitehead argues in *Process and Reality*, for example, that creativity as the principle of novelty for the cosmic process is indeed Ultimate Reality,[9] but that it "is actual only in its instantiations,"[10] which include God and all finite entities. So, while creativity (like God for Aquinas) can coexist with or, better said, spatially exist within a given entity as its principle of activity, it is in itself an activity, not an entity as Aquinas maintains with respect to God. One could counterargue, of course, that in Whitehead's own terms, creativity only becomes actual, concretely exists, in entities, all of which in some way have to be bodily or material. So in this sense entities are required for activities to exist. Yet creativity for Whitehead is not God but the principle of process for the cosmic process as a whole. As Whitehead notes in his concluding chapter in *Process and Reality* on the God-world relationship: "God and the world are the contrasted opposites in terms of which Creativity achieves its supreme task of transforming disjoined multiplicity, with its diversities in opposition,

---

9. Alfred North Whitehead, *Process and Reality: An Essay in Cosmology*, corrected edition, ed. David Ray Griffin and Donald W. Sherburne (New York: Free Press, 1978), 21. Hereafter: *PR*.

10. Ibid., 7.

into concrescent unity, with its diversities in contrast."[11] So for Whitehead, not God but the cosmic process as a whole is the ontological origin and ongoing ground of creativity. God is creativity's "primordial, non-temporal accident" or principal instantiation within the cosmic process.[12]

These remarks are not intended to show the superiority of the process theology inspired by the philosophy of Whitehead to the classical understanding of the God-world relationship as articulated by Aquinas and his successors through the centuries. Quite the contrary, these remarks are intended to show the limitations of both Aristotelian/Thomistic metaphysics and Whitehead's metaphysical scheme for adequately explaining the God-world relationship as given in the Bible. Aristotelian/Thomistic metaphysics, as noted above, does not provide a fully satisfactory explanation of God's immanence within the world, and Whitehead's metaphysics does not make clear God's transcendence of the cosmic process. For, if God like finite entities is "a creature transcended by the creativity which it qualifies,"[13] then God is a component rather than the transcendent source of the cosmic process. Once again, we are reminded not to "baptize" any philosophically or scientifically grounded explanation of the God-world relationship, that is, declare it a fact on the basis of its alleged compatibility with divine revelation. Philosophy and science as human achievements rather than divine revelation will inevitably change as new philosophical theories and new scientific discoveries appear on the scene. Theology should not be left "holding the bag," defending an outdated philosophy/scientific understanding of the world as part of divinely revealed truth found in Sacred Scripture. As Granville Henry comments in *Christianity and the Images*

11. Ibid., 348.
12. Ibid., 7.
13. Ibid., 88.

of Science, "Conflict between science and religion occurs when religion, after accepting science into its theology, engages a new and different science when it arises."[14]

Panentheism for Hartshorne and McFague

To return to the theme of panentheism as a model for the God-world relationship in Christian theology, it seems to offer a new option for that relationship which is perhaps more compatible with both biblical revelation and contemporary natural science than the metaphysics of either Aquinas or Whitehead. That is, as already noted, Aquinas has trouble explaining the immanence of God as Pure Spirit in the world of creation, and Whitehead has the opposite problem in explaining the transcendence of God as Creator to the cosmic process as a finite, created reality. Panentheism, however, seems to provide both for the immanence and the transcendence of God; the world is in God but distinct from God in its mode of operation. Yet one must be cautious here since, as might be expected, there are many different models for explaining what is meant by the term "panentheism." It is defined in the *Oxford Dictionary of the Christian Church* as follows: "The belief that the Being of God includes and penetrates the whole universe, so that every part of it exists in Him, but (as against Pantheism) that His Being is more than, and is not exhausted by, the universe."[15] But philosophical models to explain that belief vary.

Perhaps the best-known and most widely accepted model is that originally proposed by Charles Hartshorne, perhaps Whitehead's best-known disciple, namely, that the cosmos is to be understood as God's body. God, in other words, is the "soul" of the cosmos and

---

14. Henry, *Christianity and the Images of Science*, 28; see also Ian G. Barbour, *Religion and Science: Historical and Contemporary Issues* (San Francisco: HarperCollins 1997), 117.
15. Peacocke, "Introduction," xviii.

the cosmos is the "body" of God. "God is the compound individual who at all times has embraced or will embrace the fullness of all other individuals existing at those times. He is the only eternal individual."[16] With the term "compound individual," Hartshorne has in mind the soul-body relation for those organisms endowed with a central nervous system as opposed to more primitive organisms without a central nervous system and nonliving things such as rocks and other inanimate objects that are simply aggregates or "composite individuals."[17] This model has strong appeal for the affirmation of God's presence in every part of the cosmos, much as the soul is thought to be present everywhere in the body as its animating principle. But there are also obvious limitations to its use without qualification.

Sallie McFague, for example, in her well-known book *Models of God: Theology for an Ecological, Nuclear Age* likes the image of God as present to creatures in their suffering and pain and thereby helping them to achieve something worthwhile during their brief time on earth. Contrasting the classical picture of God as Absolute Monarch over creation with the more contemporary picture of the world as God's body, she notes:

> The monarchical model encourages attitudes of militarism, dualism, and escapism. It condones control through violence and oppression; it has nothing to say about the non-human world. The model of the world as God's body encourages holistic attitudes of responsibility and care of the vulnerable and oppressed; it is nonhierarchical and acts through persuasion and attraction; it has a great deal to say about the body and nature.[18]

16. Charles Hartshorne, "The Compound Individual," in *Philosophical Essays for Alfred North Whitehead* (New York: Russell & Russell, 1936), 218.
17. Ibid., 215.
18. Sallie McFague, *Models of God: Theology for an Ecological, Nuclear Age* (Philadelphia: Fortress Press, 1987), 78.

McFague's depiction of the classical God-world relationship is perhaps biased against the classical "monarchical" model. But the popularity of the book since its first appearance in 1987 testifies to the fact that contemporary Christians are uneasy with the further implications of the classical model even when it is more sympathetically presented by Thomas Aquinas and his successors.

Yet McFague also sees limitations in the soul-body metaphor for depiction of the God-world relationship: "[W]e have to ask whether we are reduced to being mere parts of [God's] body? What is our freedom? How is sin understood here?"[19] So she substitutes a more interpersonal metaphor for understanding our human relationship to God: the image of God as simultaneously Mother, Lover, and Friend.[20] There are Trinitarian overtones here: God the Mother rather than the Father, Jesus as Divine Lover, the Holy Spirit as intimate friend. As she comments, "[T]o think of God as personal in no sense implies a being separate from other beings who relates externally and distantly to them in the way that the king-realm personal model suggests. On the contrary, it suggests, I believe, that God is present in and to the world as the kind of other, the kind of Thou, much closer to a mother, lover, or friend than to a king or lord."[21] Given that the title of her book is *Models of God*, McFague is obviously comfortable with "switching metaphors in mid-stream." But if still another model for explanation of panentheism could be found that combines the sense of intimacy expressed in the soul-body metaphor and the sense of ongoing interpersonal communication located in the threefold image of God as Parent, Lover, and Friend, then one may have hit upon something close to the ideal model of the panentheistic God-world relationship.

19. Ibid., 75.
20. Ibid., 78–87.
21. Ibid., 83–84.

A Systems-Oriented Approach to Panentheism

To begin my exposition, I note that within most explanations of panentheism the God-world relationship is pictured as hierarchically ordered with different levels of creaturely existence and activity. Each level of existence and activity exists for itself and in its mode of operation even as it simultaneously contributes to an even greater corporate reality, ultimately the corporate reality of the God-world relationship as an all-comprehensive community of entities (in scriptural terms, the kingdom of God). What often does not get explained, however, is how this is possible within a world of "things" that have external but not internal relations to one another. That is, within the world of "things," one entity can incorporate another entity into its own self-constitution only by destroying the independent self-identity of the other entity. The most obvious example of what I mean here is the ingestion of food (lower-order animal and plant life) by ourselves and other higher-order creatures so as to survive and prosper in our own more complex form of existence and activity. Within the proposed systems-oriented understanding of Whiteheadian societies, however, there is a limited principle of self-organization even within atoms and molecules so that they can maintain their ontological identity as a mini-system that constitutes from moment to moment a certain kind of atom or molecule. Then, while still remaining themselves as specific kinds of atoms and molecules, they can become functioning parts of the higher-order reality of a cell or mini-organism. This is what philosophers of science refer to as "strong emergence" versus "weak emergence." That is, "strong emergentists maintain that evolution in the cosmos produces new, ontologically distinct levels, which are characterized by their own distinct laws or regularities and causal forces. By contrast, weak emergentists insist that, as new patterns emerge, the fundamental causal processes remain those of physics."[22] So, at least in terms of the notion of "strong emergence," atoms and molecules become part of a higher-order form of existence and activity (e.g., the life proper to a cell) without losing their ontological identity as atoms and molecules.

Virtually all theistic theories on panentheism favor this notion of strong rather than weak emergence to explain the hierarchically ordered character of the world in which we live. But do they understand strong emergence in terms of progressively higher forms of processes or systems or simply as progressively higher levels of existence and activity for individual things, both nonliving and living, ending with God as the supreme individual entity? This is the decisive question. Is the world composed of individual things in various combinations, or is the world instead composed of higher-order and lower-order systems? From my own neo-Whiteheadian perspective the world is composed of higher-order and lower-order systems within the all-comprehensive system of the divine life, the kingdom of God. God is thus neither a transcendent individual entity (as in classical metaphysics) nor simply the necessary principle of unity within the cosmic process as in Whitehead's cosmology,[23] but the all-inclusive system within a world composed of hierarchically ordered systems.

The Problem of the One and the Many

Admittedly, this move from "things" to systems is a "hard sell" to traditional theists. For, belief in monotheism seems to demand that God be an individual entity. Yet paradoxically Christians profess

---

22. Philip Clayton, *Mind & Emergence: From Quantum to Consciousness* (New York: Oxford University Press, 2004), 9.
23. Whitehead, *PR*, 348.

God as Trinity, one God who "subsists" in three Persons. So there is some ambiguity here. As might be expected, there have always been different ways to explain how God is simultaneously three and one. In the West, this cherished Christian belief led Augustine to the so-called psychological model of the Trinity. God as an individual entity manifests "himself" to us human beings in terms of three psychological functions: memory, understanding, and will. To the Father is appropriated the function of memory; to the Son the function of intellect (the divine Logos); and to the Spirit the function of love as the personalized Love of the Father and the Son for one another.[24] Yet, just as all these different functions are active within a human being as an individual entity, so God remains an individual entity, albeit with three functions exercised by three distinct (but not separate) persons.[25] Thomas Aquinas in turn described the persons as "subsistent relations,"[26] even though he like Augustine is thereby quite close to modalism, that is, one divine entity progressively revealed in three different ways.[27]

The Eastern Orthodox tradition, however, took a different tack in explaining the Trinity. The three divine persons are linked with one another in terms of *perichoresis*, literally a moving around of the Persons vis-à-vis one another but more popularly imagined as the divine dance involving all three Persons at the same time. Yet the Greek Fathers of the Church, even though in this way clearly affirming the plurality of the divine Persons as the starting-point for their explanation of the Trinity, still (in my judgment) thought of God as in the first place three individual entities and only in the second place as performing a corporate activity (e.g., a dance

24. Augustine, *The Trinity*, trans. Stephen McKenna (Washington, DC: Catholic University of America Press, 1963), Bk. 15, chap. 3, n. 5.
25. Joseph A. Bracken, S. J., *God: Three Who Are One* (Collegeville, MN: Liturgical, 2008), 16–17.
26. Aquinas, *ST* I, Q. 29, art. 4.
27. Bracken, *God: Three Who Are One*, 19–21.

together). For almost without exception they gave priority to the Father among the Persons of the Trinity. The Father is the origin of the divine life, equivalently the originating principle of the Godhead from which the Son and the Spirit derive their existence and intelligibility within the divine life.[28] All participants in a dance, however, are equally involved in performing the dance, even if in different ways. So both the Western and Eastern understanding of the Trinity seem to give priority to the Persons as individual entities over their corporate identity as an indissoluble divine community or higher-order system.

Reference to the Eastern Orthodox doctrine on *perichoresis* as the bond of unity among the divine persons has become quite popular among contemporary Christian theologians in the West who endorse a basically social or communitarian model of the Trinity as the basis for their understanding of the God-world relationship. Elizabeth Johnson, for example, titles her book *She Who Is*, but stresses that all three divine persons are self-expressions or manifestations of *Sophia* (divine wisdom), namely, "the creative, relational power of being who enlivens, suffers with, sustains, and enfolds the universe."[29] But when she refers to God as the creative, relational power of being *who* [emphasis mine] enlivens and suffers with the creatures of this world, is "being" here a verb or a noun? This may seem to be a trivial point, but in fact it is crucial for her prior understanding of the doctrine of God. Is she basically repeating here in a different idiom Aquinas's proposal in his *Summa Theologiae* that God's essence is his existence?[30] But then what does Aquinas mean in affirming that God is "to-be," the act of existing without further determination? Is God thus

---

28. Ibid., 22–26.
29. Elizabeth A. Johnson, *She Who Is: The Mystery of God in Feminist Theological Discourse* (New York: Crossroad, 1992), 13.
30. Aquinas, *ST*, I, Q. 3, art. 4.

described a verb or a noun? For Aquinas, God's "to-be" is apparently both noun and verb, but his focus is on God as Supreme Being, an entity rather an activity. Likewise, Johnson's describing God as the creative, relational power of being who (rather than which) enlivens and suffers with creation, results in her thinking of God more as an entity than as an activity. Yet, if she had put the focus on being as an activity, then it would have been relatively easy for her to claim that this divine power or activity of be–ing (*Sophia*) dynamically links Spirit, Jesus, and Mother[31] as its three dynamically interrelated ways of existing as a divine person. That is, like Whitehead's notion of creativity in *Process and Reality*,[32] Sophia passes from potentiality as an activity to actuality as an entity in each of the divine persons. In this way, *Sophia* would be the personalized name for the divine being as a dynamic system of three interrelated persons, the uppermost system of existence and activity in a hierarchically ordered universe, which includes within itself all the finite systems of this world without endangering their own ontological identity as systems in their own right.

Systems Too Impersonal?

But here one might object that the term "system" is too impersonal and deterministic to be applicable to belief in the tripersonal God. Isn't one thereby sacrificing the interpersonal reality of the divine persons to the theoretical unity of the Godhead or the divine being as a system? Yet "system" is not a univocal but an analogical term with different connotations, depending upon the reality thereby being described. With reference to the mode of existence proper to atoms and molecules the system is clearly non–personal or, in some cases,

31. Johnson, *She Who Is*, 124–87.
32. Whitehead, *PR*, 7.

pre-personal. That is, some systems of atoms and molecules serve as the necessary subsystems within the bodies of human persons. There are also a wide variety of living systems in the physical world, some of which once again end up as subsystems at work within the body of a human person: for example, systems coordinating the physical activity of breathing, moving one's arms and legs, digesting food and excreting waste material, and so on. Likewise mental activities (sensing, thinking, decision-making) are subordinate systems within a human being who alone is personal in the full sense of the word. Furthermore, from such intra-personal systems, one can then move to interpersonal relations between friends and lovers, within families, local communities, political organizations, economic systems, international relations. In each of these cases the system in question deals with differing relations between human beings in achieving common goals and values. Finally, there exist what might be called supra-personal systems, that is, systems that involve human beings but are not limited to interpersonal exchange between human beings, for example, the physical environment as an ecological system, the movement of the earth and the other planets around the sun in the solar system, the role of our solar system within the system proper to the Milky Way galaxy, the role of galaxies vis-à-vis a super-system of galaxies within the universe as a whole. In each case, the term "system" is a strictly generic term requiring further specification in order to pertain to one physical reality rather than another.

Looked at in this way, "system" is just as much an analogous term as "substance" in classical metaphysics. In fact, it is even more comprehensive since "system" is applicable to the analysis of social realities as well as of individual entities. That is, families, human communities of various sizes, governments, and businesses are not substances or individual things. We commonly refer to such socially organized entities as "corporate persons" because individual entities seem more real to us than socially organized groups. But in fact the reverse is true. The reality of life for each of us human beings and for all other organisms on the earth is that we are born into and sustained by participation in various social systems: the family, the local community, the national and international communities, the physical environment, and so forth. To consider oneself an individual entity is in fact a mental abstraction from the concrete reality of life in this world.[33] It is what Whitehead called in *Science and the Modern World* the fallacy of misplaced concreteness, "mistaking the abstract for the concrete."[34]

Admittedly, thinking of ourselves as separate individual entities serves a useful purpose in day-to-day living. We can much better manage our thinking and behavior with other human beings and all the other creatures of this world if we tacitly ignore the complex socially organized character of the world in which we live and simply focus on how to deal with this individual entity in abstraction from other individual entities and the systems that allow us and all of them to exist here and now. The dangers of uncritically accepting this commonsense experience of a world populated by individual things have only manifested themselves in the nineteenth century with the origin and growth of the social sciences, and in the twentieth century with the shift of attention among many scientists to the life-sciences where interaction with the physical environment is crucial to understanding what is going on in the world around us. Even in the historically "thing-oriented" natural sciences, like physics and chemistry with their preoccupation with the activity of atoms and molecules, the discovery of the world of subatomic particles in

---

33. J. Scott Turner, "Biology's Second Law: Homeostasis, Purpose and Desire," in *Beyond Mechanism: Putting Life Back into Biology*, ed. Brian G. Henning and Adam C. Scarfe (Lanham, MD: Rowman & Littlefield, 2013), 808–31.
34. Alfred North Whitehead, *Science and the Modern World* (New York: Free Press, 1967), 51.

quantum mechanics has led scientists in these disciplines to question whether they are dealing with mini-things (subatomic particles) or dynamically interrelated energy-events within a system or internally structured field of activity.[35] Furthermore, in the life-sciences, the mechanistic gene-oriented understanding of Darwinian natural selection through random mutation is under pressure from a "new understanding of gene expression and its relation to the cellular milieu in which it operates" so that "a gene is more a process than an object, which makes it part of the broader physiological—homeostatic—system in which it resides."[36]

Open-Ended Systems

But, even if systems are not necessarily impersonal, are they not by definition completely deterministic in their mode of existence and activity? If so, how is one to account for the seemingly unmistakable contingency of events in the physical world around us and, above all, for the reality of free choice among human beings and to some extent even among other higher-order animal species? Almost twenty years ago, working with Boolean networks and other mathematical models with computer-generated results, Stuart Kauffman of the Santa Fe Institute in New Mexico proposed that natural selection with its basis in chance rather than design is only part of the workings of nature. "Another source—self-organization—is the root source of order. The order of the biological world . . . is not merely tinkered, but arises naturally and spontaneously because of these principles of self-organization—laws of complexity that we are just beginning to

35. Paul Davies, *The Cosmic Blueprint: New Discoveries in Nature's Creative Ability to Order the Universe* (Philadelphia: Templeton Foundation Press, 2004), 12.
36. Léon Turner, "Individuality in Theological Anthropology and Theories of Embodied Cognition," *Zygon* 48, no. 3 (September 2013): 194.

uncover and understand."[37] Life, in other words, "is a natural property of complex chemical systems, that when the number of different kinds of molecules in a chemical soup passes a certain threshold, a self-sustaining network of reactions—an autocatalytic metabolism—will suddenly appear."[38] Kauffman's proposal is possibly overstated. Order, after all, is also presupposed in the workings of the law of natural selection. Moreover, at this level of existence and activity in nature, it appears to be quite determinate, even mechanistic in its mode of operation; for the same reason it is more predictable in its likely outcome. Likewise, many other evolutionary biologists would question Kauffman's claim that life is a natural property of complex chemical systems. It is "natural" in the sense that it seemingly requires no special divine intervention. But it is not "natural" if by that term is meant that it happens with any great frequency. Finally, as Terrence Deacon and Tyrone Cashman comment, "self-organizing processes are not sufficient to explain the coming-to-be of life-forms."[39] There are also nonliving autocatalytic processes with an inbuilt principle of self-organization.

Yet Kauffman and others in evolutionary biology are doing important work in questioning the classical mechanistic approach to physical reality that is implicit in many forms of neo-Darwinism.[40] The unanswered philosophical question in this groundbreaking scientific research, however, is how one can move from a mechanistic approach to the workings of the natural world at the level of individual atoms and molecules to an organismic approach in which

---

37. Stuart Kauffman, *At Home in the Universe: The Search for the Laws of Self-Organization and Complexity* (New York: Oxford University Press, 1995), vii.
38. Ibid., 47.
39. Terrence Deacon and Tyrone Cashman, "Teleology versus Mechanism in Biology: Beyond Self-Organization," in *Beyond Mechanism*, 303.
40. Gernot Faulkner and Renate Faulkner, "On the Incompatibility of the Neo-Darwinian Hypothesis with Systems-Theoretical Explanations of Biological Development," in *Beyond Mechanism*, 93–114.

closely organized groups of component parts seem spontaneously to move from nonlife to life. In my judgment, Whitehead rightly argues that, to avoid the anomaly of a "quantum jump" in our human understanding of the workings of nature, there must be some primitive form of vitality, an inbuilt responsiveness to the workings of the external environment, among entities at the atomic and even subatomic level of existence and activity within nature. From that systematic starting-point, one can account for a slow but still predictable growth in size and complexity among these "building blocks" so as in the end to produce what Whitehead calls "structured societies," societies composed of subsocieties, one of which is "regnant" over all the others[41] and thus serves as the equivalent of a soul or spontaneous life-principle in classical metaphysics.

Soul-Body Relation

But does the regnant society of actual entities exercise agency vis-à-vis the various subsocieties within the structured society in the same way that the soul or life-principle exercises agency vis-à-vis the body in classical metaphysics? The answer to that question is "no," since the agency proper to the regnant society within a Whiteheadian structured society is a collective agency rather than an individual agency as in the understanding of the soul in classical metaphysics. That is, the collective agency proper to the regnant society is ontologically derivative from the individual agencies of its constituent actual entities even though different from them in that it is a collective or corporate agency rather than an agency exercised by an individual entity. At the level of consciousness in higher-order animal species and even more so at the level of self-consciousness

41. Whitehead, *PR*, 99.

within human beings as persons, of course, there is the reality of mind over and above the reality of the soul. But even here the mind exercises agency not for itself alone but for the sake of the animal organism as a whole. In this sense, it exercises a corporate rather than an individual agency. It only works in dynamic interrelation with all the subsocieties/subsystems within the body for the good of the organism as a whole.

Thus understood, the human mind is quite different from the traditional understanding of the rational soul within classical metaphysics, which distinguishes sharply between physical faculties proper to the body (e.g., sensing, nutrition, local motion, etc.) and the spiritual faculties proper to the mind or rational soul (imagining, thinking, deciding on a course of action, etc.). But the inevitable consequence of this line of thought is ontological dualism, the opposition of matter and spirit, that logically implies an intervention by God the Creator into the normal workings of the natural order so as to make possible the independence of finite mind or soul from its material conditions of origin and continued survival within the evolutionary process. How then can one maintain the basic premise of panentheism that all finite reality exists within God and yet is ontologically independent of God in its normal mode of operation? In his book *Mind and Emergence*, Philip Clayton rejects the mind-body dualism of classical metaphysics but he still endorses a theological dualism that distinguishes between God and human beings in terms of personhood and agency. On the one hand, "A God who carries out actions has to be conceived not just as a ground or force but also as an agent, which means that the divine must be somehow analogous to human agents."[42] On the other hand, he claims that human personhood and agency must be different from

---

42. Philip Clayton, *Mind and Emergence: From Quantum to Consciousness* (New York: Oxford University Press, 2004), 185.

the personhood and agency of God both in itself and in dealing with the world of creation. Human personhood he defines as "that level [of existence and activity within the cosmic process] that emerges when an integrated state is established between a person and her body, her environment, other persons, and her overall mental state, including her interpretation of her social, cultural, historical, and religious context."[43] Since God is not emergent out of the cosmic process but is conceived by Christians and other theists as the transcendent origin of the cosmic process, such a definition of personhood does not apply to God. The personhood and agency of God thus becomes simply a matter of philosophical speculation and religious belief.

But, if one adopts a systems-oriented approach to the notion of panentheism, then one can still think of human personhood and divine personhood in analogical terms. That is, if human personhood is based on an integration of various conditioning factors both within and outside the self, then it is clearly not a "thing" or Aristotelian substance but an ongoing process or system. Within the systems-oriented approach to panentheism that I have advocated in this chapter, the triune God of Christian belief is also an ongoing process or system, the process whereby the three divine persons as subprocesses or subsystems are fully integrated within the higher-order process or system of the divine community which in its own way is paradigmatic for the understanding of human communities and other socially organized realities within the cosmic process. In other words, instead of an analogy of being between God and creatures as in classical metaphysics, one can set up an analogy of becoming between God and creatures based on the foundational metaphor of process or system. In this way, as Whitehead claims in

43. Ibid., 195.

Process and Reality, the concept of God is not an exception to the categories of the metaphysical system but its chief exemplification.[44] This is not to deny, of course, Christian belief in the necessary transcendence of God to any metaphysical system, but only to claim that within one's chosen metaphysical system the concept of God has to be compatible with what is said about finite entities.

Bottom-up or Top-down Causation?

One last feature of this process-oriented understanding of panentheism still needs to be elaborated. As Clayton comments in *Mind and Emergence*, the notion of downward causation "is the most important defining characteristic of emergence."[45] Predictably there are many different approaches to this crucial topic. The two most important approaches would be part-whole constraint and top-down causation. "Whole-part constraint, which correlates with weak emergence, tends to treat emergent wholes as constraining factors rather than as active originators of causal activity."[46] Top-down causation is in some ways akin to the notion of substantial form in classical metaphysics although it differs from it in that unlike the substantial form in classical metaphysics, no dualism of matter and spirit is involved. Instead, a more complex and higher-order physical entity like a cell in its specific mode of operation acts as a constraint on the interrelated activity of its constituent atoms and molecules. Yet, unlike the substantial form in classical metaphysics, it thus exercises its causal activity from within the physical order; it is not introduced from outside the physical order by God as in the case of the substantial form. Furthermore, as I see it, top-down

---

44. Whitehead, *PR*, 18, 343.
45. Clayton, *Mind and Emergence*, 49.
46. Ibid., 51.

causation does not work apart from, but only in conjunction with, bottom-up causality to be co-constitutive of the mode of operation of the organism as a whole. It is, in other words, an artificial or purely rational distinction to maintain the difference between the efficient causality proper to bottom-up causation and the formal or informational causality proper to top-down causation. Both coexist and modify one another's existence and activity within the organism as a whole.[47] Here too, then, what is important is a proper focus on the ongoing reality of the whole over and above the role of the constituent parts in making up the whole.

Looking Back

To sum up, then, in this chapter I first reviewed the understanding of the God-world relationship in classical Thomistic metaphysics and Whiteheadian process theology. Thomism defends the transcendence of God at the expense of God's immanence within the world as a material reality, and process theology defends the immanence of God in the cosmic process at the expense of God's transcendence of that process as its Creator and Ultimate End. I then turned to Charles Hartshorne and Sallie McFague with their contention that God is the "soul" of the universe and the universe is the "body" of God. Given the problems associated with too close an application of that analogy for the God-world relationship, I set forth in the rest of the chapter my own systems-oriented approach to the God-world relationship. Its chief theoretical value is that, while lower-order entities or "things" cannot be integrated into higher-order entities without loss of their ontological identity as entities in their own right, lower-order systems can be readily integrated into higher-order

---

47. Evan Thompson, *Mind in Life: Biology, Phenomenology, and the Sciences of Mind* (Cambridge, MA: Harvard University Press, 2007), 216.

systems and still retain their separate identity as systems in their own right. Atoms are integral parts of molecules; molecules are integral parts of cells; cells are the components of organs and entire organisms. I then suggested that a systems-oriented approach to the doctrine of the Trinity might also solve the problem of three distinct persons and yet only one God. In the rest of the chapter, I addressed problems that inevitably arise in thinking of the God-world relationship from a systems perspective. Is the idea of system too impersonal to serve as an analogical concept applicable to both God and creatures in different ways? Is system by definition so deterministic that it does not allow for spontaneity and (in some cases) freedom of choice in the workings of the God-world relationship? Finally, how is agency operative within a systems-oriented approach to the God-world relationship? Is it grounded in bottom-up or top-down causation?

To all these questions I gave a preliminary answer defending a systems-oriented approach to the God-world relationship. In the next chapter I will review other contemporary approaches to the notion of panentheism and, in evaluating them in terms of my own approach in this chapter, thereby further explain my own position. Then in the second part of the book, I will use this systems-oriented approach to the God-world relationship to offer a new interpretation of key doctrines of Christian belief (e.g., Trinity, Incarnation, Church, and Eschatology) in the light of contemporary understanding of reality from an evolutionary perspective.

4

Other Approaches to Panentheism in the Current Religion-and-Science Debate

In 2004 Philip Clayton and Arthur Peacocke published the papers of an academic conference on panentheism that brought together many prominent natural scientists, philosophers, and Christian systematic theologians.[1] Given their large number (eighteen), in this chapter I will primarily focus on the essays of the systematic theologians in preference to those written by natural scientists and philosophers since in the chapters to follow I will be addressing various theological issues related to a number of classical Christian beliefs. The first essay to be considered, titled "God Immanent yet Transcendent: The Divine Energies according to Saint Gregory Palamas," was written by Kallistos (Timothy) Ware, titular bishop of Diokleia in Anatolia

---

1. In *Whom We Live and Move and Have Our Being*, ed. Philip Clayton and Arthur Peacocke (Grand Rapids: Eerdmans, 2004).

in Asia Minor and longtime lecturer in Eastern Orthodox Studies at Oxford University. He begins by emphasizing the omnipresence of God in creation: "Creation is not something upon which God acts from the exterior, but something through which he expresses himself from within. . . . Much more profoundly, it means that without the active and uninterrupted presence of God in every part of the cosmos, nothing would remain in existence for a single moment."[2] A distinction between the divine essence and the divine energies, however, is necessary to keep God from being identified with the world or vice versa (pantheism). Ware cites Saint Gregory Palamas, archbishop of Thessalonika in the late thirteenth and early fourteenth century, in claiming that those privileged to attain union with God "are not united to God with respect to his essence since all the theologians testify that with respect to his essence God undergoes no participation. Moreover, the hypostatic union is fulfilled only in the case of the Logos, the God-man. Thus those privileged to attain union with God are united to him with respect to his energy."[3]

The energy of God, however, is love, which can only exist between two or more persons; love is thus necessarily intersubjective in its existence and activity. Hence, human beings who attain close personal union with God retain their finite identity as creatures even as they enter into an I-Thou relation with the three divine persons.[4] Palamas, to be sure, has been severely criticized for thereby undermining the ontological unity of God. But, as Ware notes, "Christianity envisages God not just as an undifferentiated monad, but as a Trinity of three hypostases [persons] dwelling in each other through an unceasing movement of mutual love."[5] So including

---

2. Kallistos Ware, "God Immanent yet Transcendent: The Divine Energies according to Saint Gregory Palamas," in *In Whom We Live and Move and Have Our Being*, 159.

3. Ibid., 163.

4. Ibid., 164.

5. Ibid.

human beings in the movement of mutual love between the divine persons does not endanger the ontological unity of God. Furthermore, I might add, ancient and medieval belief in unity as strictly indivisible was actually derived from Pythagorean number theory in which "one" was not itself a number but "the means by which we establish and measure the other numbers."[6] So, even from a mathematical/philosophical perspective, thinking of unity as a unity-in-diversity of parts or numbers is an advance beyond the notion of unity as indivisible and strictly homogeneous.

From the perspective of my own understanding of Whiteheadian metaphysics, however, one can in my judgment improve upon the distinction between divine essence and divine energy made by Palamas and Ware if one concedes that the essence or nature of God is not in the first place an entity but an activity. That is, for God to be a Trinity or corporate unity-in-diversity of parts or members requires that the nature or essence of God be in the first place a unifying activity. God is a community of co-equal divine persons only as a consequence of these three persons perfectly sharing a principle of activity that brings them together as "subsistent relations,"[7] that is, three intrinsically interrelated but still radically different ways of being the one God. This activity of creating unity out of multiplicity, which is in the first place the nature of God, can then by a free decision of the divine persons likewise become the principle of activity or essence of every finite entity within creation. Everything created has a multiplicity of parts or members, whether it be an atom composed of subatomic parts, an organism, or a corporate entity (an environment or community). Divine creativity lent to the creature enables this multiplicity of parts to become a unity

---

6. Granville Henry, *Christianity and the Images of Science* (Macon, GA: Smith & Helwys, 1984), 41.
7. Thomas Aquinas, *Summa Theologiae* (Madrid: Biblioteca de Autores Cristianos, 1951), Q. 29, art. 4. Hereafter: *ST*.

in diversity much akin to the dynamic unity in diversity present among the divine persons in the Christian doctrine of the Trinity. Whitehead, to be sure, claims that God and every finite (actual) entity is a "creature of creativity."[8] This is an unfortunate mistake on his part. For, elsewhere in *Process and Reality*, he describes creativity as "that ultimate principle by which the many, which are the universe disjunctively, become the one actual occasion [actual entity], which is the universe conjunctively."[9] Saying that God as well as every finite entity is a "creature" of creativity effectively converts creativity into the Supreme Being, that entity upon which all other entities depend for their existence and activity. Aquinas, of course, made much the same mistake when he identified being as the nature of God with God as an entity, namely, the Supreme Being.[10]

Panentheism from a Thomistic Perspective

One of the Western Christian theologians writing on the topic of panentheism is Denis Edwards, senior lecturer in systematic theology at Flinders University in Adelaide, Australia, and a frequent visitor to theological gatherings in the United States. He begins his essay by citing the cosmologist William Stoeger to the effect that "an entity's constitutive relationships make it what it is."[11] By constitutive relationships Stoeger means "those interactions among components and with the larger context which jointly effect the composition of a given system and establish its functional characteristic within the larger whole of which it is a part, and thereby enable it to manifest

---

8. Alfred North Whitehead, *Process and Reality: An Essay in Cosmology*, corrected edition, ed. David Ray Griffin and Donald W. Sherburne (New York: Free Press, 1978), 88. Hereafter: *PR*.
9. Ibid., 21.
10. Aquinas, *ST*, Q. 3, art. 4.
11. Denis Edwards, "A Relational and Evolving Universe Unfolding within the Dynamism of the Divine Communion," in *In Whom We Live and Move and Have Our Being*, 203.

the particular properties and behavior it does."[12] These relationships may be physical, biological, or social in character, but the most important constitutive relationship is that of the creator Spirit to each creature to enable it to be itself and develop accordingly.[13] The reference to creator Spirit allows Edwards to explain that his model or symbolic representation of panentheism is grounded in the Christian doctrine of the Trinity. That is, if the Trinity is a community of divine persons, then the Trinity is a relational reality with the consequence that creation as made in the image of God is constituted by finite entities in dynamic interrelation. Yet each of these individual entities has its own integrity. "Individual entities have a degree of self-directedness—whether we think of human beings with their experience of being free agents, of birds with their glorious freedom in flight, or of particles like photons whose individual motion cannot be predetermined."[14]

Admittedly, not all relationships among finite entities are productive; some are destructive, resulting in pain, violence, and death.[15] Hence, focusing on the mutual and equal love among the divine persons is necessary to resolve the inevitable ambiguity about the value and purpose of relationships drawn from studying empirical data showing the de facto interconnectedness of everything with everything else within the cosmic process. Likewise, it allows a Christian to hope that the ultimate eschatological goal of the divine creative process will be the communion of all created entities with one another through full incorporation into the divine life, active participation in the relationships of "absolutely equal and mutual love" among the divine persons.[16] Edwards further notes that "time

12. Ibid.
13. Ibid.
14. Ibid., 205.
15. Ibid., 206.
16. Ibid.

is a fundamental dimension of the way things are in the universe."[17] First of all, entities are "in relationship with all the creatures that preceded them, and with all the unknown creatures that will follow."[18] Secondly, change and growth in complexity of organic life within the universe takes place largely through a process of trial and error, that is, as Darwin pointed out, through random mutation and natural selection.[19] Accordingly, a new understanding of God the Creator is needed in which God is viewed "not simply as the dynamic cause of the *existence* of creatures, but as the dynamic ground of their *becoming*."[20] He concludes: "The creator Spirit is immanent in a time-bound universe, deeply involved with its becoming. But the Spirit is also the eschatological Spirit, the Spirit of the divine eternal communion."[21]

Edwards's conclusions regarding a panentheistic approach to the God-world are remarkably like my own. So I have no negative comments about the content of his approach. My only reservation is with his methodology. In my judgment, he does not present a fully consistent metaphysical scheme to support his position. For example in his "Conclusion," he reflects that the starting-point for his understanding of a panentheistic God-world relationship is "a key insight of the theology of creation of Thomas Aquinas," namely, the classical distinction between the primary causality of God and the secondary causality of finite agents within the evolutionary process.[22] But how does this linkage of primary and secondary causality work? If the primary causality of God lies in giving existence to creatures, thus empowering them to be themselves, then God would seem

17. Ibid., 207.
18. Ibid.
19. Ibid., 207–8.
20. Ibid., 208.
21. Ibid., 209.
22. Ibid., 209.

to be responsible for everything that exists, both the good and the bad.[23] Moreover, if this is the case, how is the primary causality of God different from the "primary causality" of the universe as a self-organizing system? If one responds that God is prior to the universe as its Uncaused Cause, then I could respond that this is a faith-statement, not a logical inference from empirical data. I could just as easily claim that the universe as a self-organizing system is my faith-based version of an Uncaused Cause. Furthermore, if the universe as a self-organizing system appears to operate via a process of trial and error, can the same *modus operandi* be attributed to God who is thought to be both omnipotent and omniscient in classical metaphysics and, if so, how can God both know and not know, predetermine and leave undetermined, what happens in creation? How can God, for example, as the Absolute Future, in the words of Karl Rahner,[24] guide the creative process to a predetermined eschatological outcome and still respect the autonomy and integrity of individual creatures to choose their own destiny? None of these questions is unanswerable. But they do not seem to be answered either in this essay or in his later book, *How God Acts: Creation, Redemption, and Special Divine Action.*[25]

I do not mean to scold Edwards here for inconsistency in failing to think through the metaphysical implications of his otherwise admirable understanding of the God-world relationship. As I see it, his position on a more dynamic understanding of the God-world relationship only reflects what seems to be the *status quo* in much of contemporary Roman Catholic systematic theology. That is, among many (if not most) of the Roman Catholic authors cited by Edwards

23. Joseph A. Bracken, *Does God Roll Dice? Divine Providence for a World in the Making* (Collegeville, MN: Liturgical, 2012), 50–51.
24. Edwards, "A Relational and Evolving Universe," 208.
25. Denis Edwards, *How God Acts: Creation, Redemption, and Special Divine Action* (Minneapolis: Fortress Press, 2010); see also Bracken, *Does God Roll Dice?*, 47–58.

in his essay, there is the same ambivalence about the continuing validity of traditional scholastic metaphysics to serve as the theoretical underpinning of a theology of creation from an evolutionary perspective. For example, as Edwards also notes, Karl Rahner, perhaps the most highly regarded Roman Catholic theologian of the twentieth century, "insists that the discovery that we are part of an evolving world demands a new understanding of reality, a new metaphysics."[26] But simply stating that God is not only the cause of the existence of creatures but the dynamic ground of their becoming[27] does not establish how God can be both at the same time. That is, how can God be both a transcendent entity existing in and for itself and the immanent dynamic ground of being for other entities at the same time? Is that ground of being for creation, in other words, to be found in the personhood of God or in God's nature, the ongoing creative activity of God whereby both the three divine persons of the Christian doctrine of the Trinity and all their creatures coexist in a symbiotic relationship and yet remain distinct from one another? But, if the latter alternative is more likely, then how does one sort out the different kinds of causality necessarily at work here and the way they work together to produce the same empirically verifiable effect?

Ruth Page and Pansyntheism

Two other contributors to the volume on panentheism are Ruth Page and Celia Deane-Drummond. Ruth Page is a retired principal of New College at the University of Edinburgh. Previously she acquired

---

26. Edwards, "A Relational and Evolving Universe," 208; cf. also Karl Rahner, "Evolution," in *Sacramentum Mundi: Vol. 2*, ed. Karl Rahner, Cornelius Ernst, and Kevin Smyth (London: Burns & Oates, 1968), 289–97.
27. Edwards, "A Relational and Evolving Universe," 208.

advanced degrees in theology in New Zealand and England before becoming a lecturer in systematic theology at Otago University in Dunedin, New Zealand. In this essay she both praises and critiques various forms of process-oriented theology for their contemporary understanding of the God-world relationship. For example, she recognizes that Whiteheadian process theology nicely accounts for the immanence of God in the cosmic process without being totally identified with it. Yet she critiques the anthropomorphism implicit in describing the gradual emergence of levels of complexity leading up to self-consciousness in human beings as the divinely intended climax of cosmic evolution. "Increasing complexity in one direction decreases flexibility in another."[28] Humans are small, slow creatures in comparison with other animal species who excel in speed or size. Likewise, self-consciousness enables human beings to transcend their immediate situation and needs, but also is a source of anxiety and frustration in that human beings can remember the past and anticipate the future.[29] Finally, human self-consciousness is achieved only at the cost of the gradual extinction of over 90% of other life forms in the course of the evolutionary process.[30] Arguments that human beings have a richness of experience which justifies the extinction of so many other life-forms so as to provide room for the emergence of *homo sapiens* seem to involve a favoritism on God's part which reflects negatively on divine impartiality and proper regard for all of God's creatures.[31] Furthermore, it carries the consequence that "God would have spent ages without real pleasure in creation if all that was happening was influence toward future qualities."[32] Finally,

---

28. Ruth Page, "Panentheism and Pansyntheism: God in Relation," in *In Whom We Live and Move and Have Our Being*, 223.
29. Ibid.
30. Ibid.
31. Ibid., 226.
32. Ibid.

given the notion of divine initial aims in Whitehead's metaphysical scheme, one has to wonder whether these same initial aims were responsible for the predator-prey relationship in the animal kingdom with all the pain and suffering to the victims that it inevitably involved.[33]

Page's own position is what she calls "pansyntheism," wherein God's contribution to the creative process is the provision of "the possibility of possibilities without designing any particular forms, including the human, to be aimed at."[34] By her own admission, this comes dangerously close to deism in which God simply set up the possibility of creaturely choice "but then abandoned creation to its own success and failure."[35] Yet "God who gave the freedom of possibility in the first place, is in relationship with every diverse creature which uses possibility to come into being—thereby responding to the Creator's gift."[36] So God's giving of possibility to the creature is conditioned here and now by the creature's "decision" re past possibilities. This keeps God active at every moment in the creature's existence, thus assuring an ongoing intersubjective relationship. Moreover, God knows the creature from the inside, so to speak, what it feels like "to be a tree frog or a jaguar" not just in general but in terms of its de facto situation here and now.[37] In this way, God "transcends the species barrier" in a way that would be impossible for even the most sensitive human animal lover. She then adds that the "decision" or choice of possibilities for the creature is more a question of attention to particular circumstances than anything else. It does not require a conscious decision on the creature's part but only "a new perception of the situation leading

33. Ibid., 227.
34. Ibid., 228.
35. Ibid.
36. Ibid.
37. Ibid., 229.

to consequent action."[38] Thus God through a divinely intended attraction to one possibility rather than others does not move the creature toward greater complexity and eventual self-consciousness but only to more enjoyment of what is possible to it here and now. The creature, of course, could find some other possibility open to it to be more attractive and thus do long-term harm to itself and other creatures as a result.[39] But that, after all, is the risk of a genuine intersubjective relationship; the Other must remain free to be itself even when it is doing harm to itself and the relationship.

Much of Page's critique of process-oriented forms of panentheism impresses me as correct, although some of it might more properly be directed at the theological use of Whitehead's cosmology than at Whitehead's scheme in itself. For example, in *Process and Reality*, Whitehead does claim that "the growth of a complex structured society exemplifies the general purpose pervading nature."[40] But he does not see the overall focus of the evolutionary process as leading to a definitive end, the emergence of human beings as a result of the progressive growth of self-consciousness. "God's purpose in the creative advance is the evocation of intensities. The evocation of societies is purely subsidiary to this absolute end [the evocation of intensities of experience in actual entities]."[41] The society, in other words, is a governing structure for the type of togetherness that gives added intensity to the experience of its constituent actual entities. Larger and more complex societies of actual entities allow for a quality of experience for their constituent actual entities that is impossible for the actual entities taken individually apart from their togetherness as members of a given society. The enjoyment of actual entities in an atom, for example, is less than their enjoyment as

38. Ibid., 230.
39. Ibid., 231.
40. Whitehead, *PR*, 100.
41. Ibid., 105.

constituent members of a molecule and even less enjoyable for themselves as atoms if they are also constituents in the life of a cell or an entire organism. Naturally, his overriding emphasis on the good of the parts as opposed to the good of the whole can be critiqued on other grounds, for example, as an example of "metaphysical atomism."[42] But taken by itself, his cosmological scheme is in no sense of the word anthropocentric. As already noted, Whitehead is a philosopher setting out the most general principles of a process-oriented world view, not a Christian theologian preoccupied with the proper relation of human beings to self, God, and the world.

For example, Whitehead simply notes the predator-prey relationship among animal organisms: "[A]ll societies require interplay with their environment; and in the case of living societies this interplay takes the form of robbery. The living society may, or may not, be a higher type of organism than the food which it disintegrates. But whether or not it be for the general good, life is robbery. It is at this point that with life morals become acute. The robber requires justification."[43] Thus the taking of life to preserve one's own is not in itself immoral provided that it is done with awareness of the intrinsic value of the quality of experience enjoyed by the actual entities constitutive of the other organism and with no other alternative to preserve the shared quality of experience for one's own constituent actual entities. This is, to be sure, an ontological argument, but it is not opposed to the argument from "ecological fitness in interrelationship, which would suit the planet better."[44] Rather ecological fitness in interrelationship demands the regular taking of life for the right reasons simply as a way to sustain the cosmic process in its entirety. Without the proportionate taking

---

42. Ibid., 35.
43. Ibid., 105.
44. Page, "Panentheism and Pansyntheism," 226.

of life, there would be no life at all either on earth or presumably anywhere else in the universe.

Page, however, is in my judgment correct in her critique of the way the notion of divine initial aim in *Process and Reality*[45] has been used by many process theologians. As she correctly notes, it is not divine inspiration to choose one possibility over many others available to an actual entity,[46] but simply the awareness of multiple possibilities from which the creature can choose what suits it best here and now.[47] Whitehead's focus in this passage out of *Process and Reality* is primarily not on the divine initial aim but on the subjective aim that guides the concrescence (process of self-constitution) of the actual entity. The divine initial aim comes into question when he says, "But the initial stage of its [subjective aim] is an endowment which the subject inherits from the inevitable ordering of things, conceptually realized in the [primordial] nature of God."[48] As I have emphasized in my own rethinking of Whitehead's metaphysical scheme, the divine initial aim is more an empowerment of the actual entity to make a choice (thus equivalently an actual grace in classical Christian theology) than to make one choice over many others. So God is not thereby responsible for natural evil, as Page argues.[49] On the contrary, God simply empowers the actual entity to make a choice within a wide range of objective possibilities and then, if needed, to do "damage control" in terms of the effects on the cosmic process as a whole if the choice turns out to be disastrous for the actual entity itself and for all the other actual entities with which it is in contact. As Whitehead notes in the final chapter of *Process and Reality*,

45. Whitehead, *PR*, 244.
46. Page, "Panentheism and Pansyntheism," 227.
47. Ibid., 229.
48. Whitehead, *PR*, 244.
49. Page, "Panentheism and Pansyntheism," 227.

> The revolts of destructive evil, purely self-regarding, are dismissed into their triviality of merely individual facts; and yet the good they did achieve in individual joy, in individual sorrow, in the introduction of needed contrast, is yet saved by its relation to the completed whole. The image—and it is but an image under which this operative growth of God's nature is best conceived, is that of a tender care that nothing be lost.[50]

These remarks by Whitehead would seem to be quite compatible with Page's belief in "pansyntheism" as the proper understanding of the God-world relationship at the end of her essay: "The whole of creation is companioned by God, not on the basis of hierarchy, but according to what is proper and necessary for the creature in its circumstances."[51]

Along the same lines, Page is in my judgment justified in saying that God is *with* creation rather than *in* creation as the term "panentheism" mighty otherwise seem to imply. "A relationship is close, but not so close that one is overwhelmed by the other. Thus relationship is not fusion; rather it preserves some space between participants, a to-and-fro even in the coming together."[52] In my own revision of Whitehead's metaphysics in the service of a Trinitarian process-oriented God-world relationship, I too have emphasized that a genuine I-Thou relationship involves a common space that participants to the dialogue share and by their ongoing interrelationship progressively structure.[53] This space is what Martin Buber in his celebrated book *I and Thou* describes as "the Between."[54] But unlike Buber's version of the Between, such a space between interrelated subjects of experience does not dissipate with further

50. Whitehead, *PR*, 346.
51. Page, "Panentheism and Pansyntheism," 229.
52. Ibid., 231.
53. Joseph A. Bracken, *Subjectivity, Objectivity, and Intersubjectivity: A New Paradigm for Religion and Science* (West Conshohocken, PA: Templeton Foundation Press, 2009), 100–106.
54. Martin Buber, *I and Thou*, trans. Walter Kaufmann (New York: Scribner's, 1970), 71–72.

experience of life in a basically I-It world but remains as a permanent feature of a metaphysics of universal intersubjectivity. Buber's Between, in other words, corresponds to my own understanding of Whitehead's category of society. A Whiteheadian society is not simply a genetically linked set of actual entities with a "common element of form" or defining characteristic" found within each constituent actual entity.[55] Rather, in my view a Whiteheadian society is a progressively structured field of activity for successive generations of these dynamically interrelated subjects of experience. In terms of Page's description of pansyntheism, it is the space between God and creatures that allows both God and the individual creature to be free in their response to one another. In this sense, as Page comments, God "companions" creation rather than presides over it.[56] Furthermore, as Page likewise points out, this notion of God "with" rather than "in" or "over" creation goes a long way to solve the issue of God's relationship to natural and moral evil: "God, being freedom and love, desired the possibility of finite freedom and love, and took the attendant risk of constraint and evil [in empowering creatures to be themselves], without which freedom and love are not possible in this world."[57]

Sophianic Panentheism

Celia Deane-Drummond is currently professor of theology at the University of Notre Dame in South Bend, Indiana, and the author or editor of nine books. The title of her contribution to the volume on panentheism is "The Logos as Wisdom: A Starting-Point for a Sophianic Theology of Creation." Hence, her focus is on

---

55. Whitehead, *PR*, 34.
56. Page, "Panentheism and Pansyntheism," 229.
57. Ibid., 232.

panentheism from an explicitly Christian perspective with attention to the Wisdom or Sophianic tradition within Christianity. At the same time she regards the Logos and Wisdom traditions within Christianity as interrelated ways in which God is present to the world without being identified with it as in pantheism.[58] That is, not Logos or Wisdom alone but only Logos and Wisdom in combination accurately describe the work of God in creation as both creative and redemptive, both rational and affective, based on the cultivation of close relationships between God and creation as well as a divinely designed plan or blueprint for the workings of the cosmic process.[59] This leads naturally into the notion of the Incarnation as the manifestation in Christ of God's compassionate love for creation in the face of adversity as well as the reestablishment of order over chaos in creation as a result of human sin.[60] Understood in these terms, the glory of God is to be found at least as much, if not more so, in the Cross than in the Resurrection. This violates, of course, the conventional wisdom of the world in favor of a divine wisdom that only finds full rational justification in eschatology where the wisdom of the cultivation of relationships through the sharing of suffering is vindicated.[61] Deane-Drummond commends Ruth Page for her notion of pansyntheism, the co-working of the divine and the creaturely in the works of creation. But she feels that divine and creaturely collaboration as thus envisioned by Page does not sufficiently emphasize God's participation in the pain and suffering as well as the joy and creativity inevitably present in the creative process. In addition, this focus on God sharing the pain and suffering of creation allows one to introduce practical ethical issues into an

58. Celia Deane-Drummond, "The Logos as Wisdom: A Starting-Point for a Sophianic Theology of Creation," in *In Whom We Live and Move and Have Our Being*, 238.

59. Ibid., 239–41.

60. Ibid., 240–41.

61. Ibid., 242.

otherwise purely speculative understanding of the God-world relationship.[62] Here she equates Sophia with practical wisdom or prudence, that is, finding the mean between opposing alternatives.[63] Science, of course, is often just as guilty as theology in presenting only a one-sided version of a controversial ethical issue. She concludes: "Suffice it to say that bringing back Sophia into our understanding of panentheism rattles any sense of complacency in the quest for relating science and religion, since she [Sophia] forces us to address where our wisdom is to be found, and in doing so, reaches to the heart of the moral vacuum of much secular philosophy."[64]

There are many interesting points to be raised in evaluating Deane-Drummond's essay in terms of a panentheistic understanding of the God-world relationship. First of all, her conscious focus is on a Christian rather than a more generic theistic understanding of the God-world relationship: "[I]f a panentheistic model of the relationship between God and the world is to be *Christian*, rather than simply *theist*, it requires proper reflection on the radical particularity of Christ as the revelation of God expressed in the mystery of the incarnation."[65] While this move does not necessarily exclude use of her hypothesis by Jews and Muslims to defend their own understanding of panentheism as the appropriate model for the God-world relationship, it inevitably makes it more difficult. For, the notion of incarnation would have to be somehow likewise available in the Hebrew Bible and in the Qur'an. Along the same lines, she also resists "the dominance of process philosophy in panentheistic thinking, where the total receptivity of God to all events in the world seems to be implied."[66] She is partially in error here. Whitehead

62. Ibid., 243.
63. Ibid., 244.
64. Ibid., 245.
65. Ibid., 233.
66. Ibid., 234.

himself was not a panentheist. Unlike his first disciple Charles Hartshorne, he did not favor the mind-body metaphor to describe the God-world relationship. In the final chapter of *Process and Reality*, for example, he says: "God and the world are the contrasted opposites in terms of which Creativity achieves its supreme task of transforming disjointed multiplicity, with its diversities in opposition, into concrescent unity, with its diversities in contrast."[67] Thus for Whitehead, God and the World are opposite poles in a dialectical process empowered by creativity as a principle of activity. He was, moreover, a philosopher of science more interested in cosmology than in theology. But even as a philosopher he had within his reach the possibility of a metaphysics of universal intersubjectivity which, as I see it, would suit very well Deane-Drummond's proposal of a friendship relation between God and creatures, a sharing in their pain and suffering as well as their passing joys and sense of creativity.

Furthermore, with the conscious adoption of a metaphysics of intersubjectivity, which is implicit in Whitehead's presupposition that "the final real things of which the world is made up are actual entities [momentary self-constituting subjects of experience],"[68] new links could be established with the Muslim and Jewish communities in the effort to come up with a satisfactory ecumenical model of the God-world relationship. Finally, a panentheistic understanding of the God-world relationship in terms of a metaphysics of universal intersubjectivity would allow for the "space" in which God and creatures can interact with one another while remaining distinct from one another, so as to co-create the kingdom of God on earth through a common venture.[69] In brief, only a combination of the down-to-earth concerns of practical theology with a metaphysically

67. Whitehead, *PR*, 348.
68. Ibid., 18.
69. Bracken, *Subjectivity, Objectivity, and Intersubjectivity*, 53–64.

grounded metaphysics of universal intersubjectivity will provide the theoretical structure for an equitable resolution of controversial ethical issues.

System rather than Structured Field of Activity

In my own essay for the volume edited by Clayton and Peacocke, I proposed a field-oriented approach to panentheism based upon a revised understanding of Whitehead's notion of society in *Process and Reality*. That is, if a Whiteheadian society has a "common element of form" or "defining characteristic"[70] for its constituent actual entities at any given moment over an extended period of time, then it makes sense to claim that the society is in effect a structured field of activity within which each new set of constituent actual entities arises and to which they contribute their individual pattern of existence and activity before passing out of existence.[71] Thus while constituent actual entities come into and go out of existence, the society as a structured field of activity for the next set of actual entities survives the passage of time relatively unchanged in its governing structure. That common element of form for the society, however, will itself over time evolve as successive sets of constituent actual entities readjust their relation to one another and to their external environment and thereby impact upon the structure of their common field of activity for the next set of actual entities.[72]

In this way, there is both bottom-up and top-down causation at work in Whiteheadian societies at every moment. The constituent actual entities of the moment exercise efficient causality by

---

70. Whitehead, *PR*, 34.
71. Joseph A. Bracken, "Panentheism: A Field-Oriented Approach," in *In Whom We Live and Move and Have Our Being*, 212–14.
72. Ibid., 214.

reaffirming or slightly revising the "common element of form" already present within the society to which they belong. The society in virtue of that same common element of form, however, exercises formal causality by imposing necessary constraints upon the activity of each new set of actual entities. As I see it, this understanding of the interplay between a Whiteheadian society and its constituent actual entities legitimates a theory of emergent monism (as opposed to classical dualism) to govern a panentheistic approach to the God-world relationship. That is, over time progressively higher-order fields of existence and activity for constituent entities have emerged out of the dynamic interplay of constituent actual entities within antecedent lower-order fields of activity in the ongoing growth of the cosmic process. The cosmic process as a whole, however, was initially emergent out of the antecedently existing all-comprehensive field of existence and activity for the three divine persons of the Christian doctrine of the Trinity. This same field of activity for the divine persons even now serves as the context or environment for the interaction of the divine persons with all their creatures from moment to moment.[73] Yet, in line with the conventional understanding of panentheism, the entities at each level of existence and activity within the cosmic hierarchy have an independent individual identity even as they all contribute to the ongoing but ever-changing corporate reality of the God-world relationship. Thus within the framework of this philosophical scheme, one can give rational plausibility to a whole array of traditional Christian beliefs, for example, the doctrine of the Trinity, *creatio ex nihilo*, the kingdom of God on earth, and so on.

In his *Afterword* for all the essays on panentheism, Philip Clayton simply notes that I advocate a field-oriented approach to the defense

---

73. Ibid., 214–15.

of panentheism.[74] In the present book, I am concerned to present my understanding of panentheism in terms of contemporary systems theory. The term "system" better than "structured field of activity" makes clear that reality is socially organized. It is more obviously an objective reality over and above the dynamic interrelationship of its constituent parts or members. Whether one is referring to atoms as a dynamic unity of constituent subatomic particles, a living organism as constituted by vital organs, neural networks, bones and skin, or a community or natural environment as constituted by interrelated individual entities, the whole or the social totality is the deeper reason for the existence and activity of the parts, not vice versa. For the same reason, I realize now better than in the earlier essay that the community of the three divine persons as one God should not be conceived as akin to the interactions of three human beings in ongoing cooperation for the achievement of common goals and values. The divine persons are rather to be understood as dynamically interrelated subprocesses within the corporate process proper to the divine communitarian life. Accordingly, the agency of the triune God toward creation is always a unified corporate reality in which all three divine persons in different ways are fully engaged. The unity of the divine being is thus rightly restored to its proper place in our human understanding of God. But it is no longer a homogeneous unity in line with the alleged simplicity of God.[75] Instead, it is a much more complex diversified unity of interrelated existence and activity among the divine persons that brings to the fore the necessarily social character of reality, both for God and all of God's creatures. Nothing/no one exists alone; every individual entity finds its meaning and value in a reality bigger than itself that is not fixed or

---

74. Philip Clayton, "Panentheism Today: A Constructive Systematic Evaluation," in *In Whom We Live and Move and Have Our Being*, 258.
75. Aquinas, *ST*, I, Q. 3, art. 7.

static but continues to evolve in ongoing pursuit of a transcendent goal.

PART II

5

"Incarnation" as Key to the Argument for Panentheism

Part One of this book was basically philosophical in its orientation. In chapter 1, I proposed that our understanding of the world around us is at least partly conditioned by the language we habitually employ. Given our Western emphasis on the priority of nouns to verbs in sentence construction, we tend to see the world in terms of individual things with various contingent relationships to one another. An emphasis on verbs, however, might lead us to the belief that physical reality is in flux and seems to be constituted by coordinated processes or systems. Moreover, contemporary scientists tend to think in terms of processes or systems in their research and writing, even though outside the classroom or laboratory they too use the conventional language of things in their relations with family and friends. Then in chapter 2 I further claimed that within processes or systems that are open-ended and thus still evolving in terms of structure and complexity, their components should likewise be mini-organisms, momentary self-constituting subjects of experience with internal rather than purely external relations to one another. For only in this way can one guarantee that the processes or systems that are the objective result or ongoing byproduct of the interplay of their components will themselves be open-ended, capable of further development in structure and complexity of organization. Finally, in chapters 3 to 4, beginning with my own approach to the God-world relationship, I set forth various philosophically and theologically based arguments for panentheism (all things within God but still distinct from God in their own existence and activity) as the most suitable model for the God-world relationship within contemporary religion-and-science dialogue.

Now in Part Two of this book, I have to test out my hypothesis of a systems- or process-oriented approach to the God-world relationship with respect to key doctrines of Christian belief. I begin with a systems-oriented understanding of the doctrine of the Incarnation, that is, Christian belief that Jesus of Nazareth was a divine person with two natures, the one divine and the other human. For, as I see it, if a systems-oriented understanding of reality gives rational plausibility to traditional Christian belief in the doctrine of the Incarnation, it indirectly vindicates the more generic understanding of panentheism that I set forth in chapter 3. The doctrine of the Incarnation, in other words, is the test-case *par excellence* for a systems- or process-oriented understanding of the God-world relationship. The smooth working of the divine and human, the Infinite and the finite, in Jesus throughout his life is proof that what otherwise might seem logically impossible is in fact the case. The divine and the human interpenetrate one another without thereby reducing the divine to the human or the human to the divine. What is infinite and what is finite are not logical contradictories but

116

complementary realities that give richer meaning and value to one
another.

Overview of the Chapter

To make clear how this ongoing interplay between the natural and
the supernatural in the life of Jesus but also in all the other events
of this world illuminates the longstanding problem of the proper
relation between the Infinite and the finite, I analyze the argument of
the German philosopher G. W. F. Hegel regarding the Infinite and
the finite in his metaphysics of absolute idealism. My conclusion is
that, while Hegel clearly understands that the Infinite must somehow
include the finite if it is not to be limited by the presence and activity
of the finite and thereby become itself a finite reality, his conclusion
that the Infinite is God or Absolute Spirit which progressively
manifests itself in Nature and human history is really not applicable to
a fully Christian understanding of the God–world relationship. Finite
reality is thereby absorbed without remainder into the Infinite within
a conceptually closed or deterministic system of thought. Then, in
the second part of the chapter I analyze the process–oriented but
strictly monotheistic (as opposed to Trinitarian) understanding of
the God–world relationship espoused by Charles Hartshorne, perhaps
the most celebrated early disciple of Whitehead in the promotion
of process philosophy and theology. Even with his process–oriented
interpretation of the God–world relationship, Hartshorne seems to be
caught between the poles of pantheism and dualism in his depiction
of God as the soul of the universe and the universe as the body of
God. Then in the third and final part of the chapter, I set forth my
process– or systems–oriented explanation of how the divine and the
human were equally at work in everything that Jesus said and did.
What a secular understanding of Jesus' words and actions would say

is simply human can, from the perspective of my hypothesis, be seen as also revelatory of the triune God's intentions for human life and creation as a whole.

Hegel's Approach to the Infinite

As already noted, one of Hegel's major preoccupations was whether an Infinite Being can truly incorporate a finite reality into its own sphere of existence and activity without loss to the independent reality of the finite entity as a more limited form of existence and activity or without the Infinite itself thereby becoming a finite reality. He first distinguished between false and true Infinity. The true infinite is not simply an unending succession of finite states of being the same thing.[1] Likewise, the infinite is not in opposition to the finite since the infinite is thus put on a par with the finite, and the way in which they are one remains unclear.[2] The true infinite is realized only in Hegel's own philosophy of absolute idealism in which each of the constituent parts of the whole is the whole or totality from a different perspective. So the parts do not add up so as to become the whole; they reflect the whole as if each part is a mirror or reflection of the whole from a different angle. But, as a result, such a system or network of different images of the whole must be closed or completely determinate. Nothing new is learned by studying the different images. They all reflect the same determinate reality, God or Absolute Spirit, which in itself does not change. Otherwise, the Infinite would become finite; God or Absolute Spirit would be something new at every moment of the cosmic process in an endless progression of time-bound states of being.

---

1. *Hegel's Logic (being Part One of the Encyclopedia of the Philosophical Sciences)*, trans. William Wallace (Oxford: Clarendon, 1975), 137 n. 94.

2. Ibid., 140 n. 95.

Charles Taylor in his book *Hegel* seems to confirm this last remark.
That is, he first notes that for Hegel "the infinite as the whole system
of changing finite things is the unfolding of conceptual necessity."[3]
But he then adds:

> Because of this inner necessity, the infinite is not just the whole in the
> sense that it is a collection of finite things from which nothing has
> been left out, or a group of finite things which are in contingent causal
> interaction. It is a totality, a whole whose parts are intrinsically related
> to each other, that is, where each can only be understood by its relation
> to others. For these parts, or finite things, arise and succeed each other
> by conceptual necessity.[4]

Thus the Infinite as the unchanging totality of a predetermined
process of becoming among its finite self-determinations is likewise
subject to conceptual necessity. The Infinite cannot be anything
other than the totality of a fixed set of finite self-determinations. God
or Absolute Spirit has no more freedom to exist apart from the process
than any of its finite self-determinations.

In his lectures on the Philosophy of Religion, Hegel applies these
somewhat abstract reflections on the Infinite and the finite to the
God-world relationship. His aim is thereby to integrate the world as a
set of finite manifestations of Spirit into the unbounded reality of God
as Absolute Spirit, the culmination of his process-oriented philosophy
of Spirit (*Geist*):

> The Absolute, eternal Idea is, in its essential existence, in and for itself,
> God in His eternity before the creation of the world, and outside of the
> world. What is thus created, this otherness or other-Being, divides up
> within itself into two sides, physical Nature and finite Spirit. What is
> thus created is therefore an Other, and is placed at first outside of God. It
> belongs to God's essential nature, however, to reconcile to Himself this
> something which is foreign to Him, this special or particular element

---

3. Charles Taylor, *Hegel* (New York: Cambridge University Press, 1975), 243.
4. Ibid.

which comes into existence as something separated from Him, just as it is the nature of the Idea [the perfect unity of subjectivity and objectivity as the ideal or goal of philosophical reflection] which has separated itself from itself and fallen away from itself, to bring itself back from this lapse to its truth or true state.[5]

But, if Spirit is identified with thought or rational necessity, then its final, totally adequate form must be a form that is identical with its content (namely, thought thinking itself) that determines itself to be itself.[6] Hence, just as religion moves beyond art as a self-manifestation of Absolute Spirit, so philosophy (Hegel's philosophy of Spirit) "sublates" religion by providing it with rational content purified of externals like ritual, creeds, and so forth. In this way, as Taylor comments, Hegel reconciled traditional religion and the Enlightenment. Enlightenment thinkers tried to free themselves from the authority of the Church and to entrust themselves to reason alone. But they pursued clarity of thought for its own sake and lost "the dialectical truth in religion," the reconciliation of opposites to be found in the often paradoxical truth-claims of religion.[7] Hence, philosophy that uses dialectical thinking to reconcile with one another these paradoxical truth-claims (e.g., the ongoing dynamic interrelation of the Infinite and the finite), unites the aspirations and goals of the Enlightenment with those of religion. But it does so only by conceiving religion in fully rational terms, namely, as the progressive self-manifestation of Spirit in nature and history, ending in the concept of God as Absolute Spirit, the perfect identity of subjectivity and objectivity, the Infinite and the finite.[8]

---

5. G. W. F. Hegel, *Lectures on the Philosophy of Religion together with a Work on the Proofs of the Existence of God*, trans. Rev. E. B. Speirs and J. Burdon Sanderson (New York: Humanities Press, 1974), III:1.

6. Taylor, *Hegel*, 505–6.

7. Ibid., 506.

8. Ibid., 507.

But, as already mentioned, if God as Absolute Spirit is governed
by rational necessity, then God is no longer free to be God, an
ontological reality independent of the dialectical scheme designed by
Hegel to explain the God-world relationship. To his credit, Friedrich
Schelling, a classmate and friend of Hegel in their early years and
later his rival as a proponent of Transcendental Idealism in German
academic circles, realized that Hegel's system was a triumph of
speculative logic but for that same reason was without grounding
in empirical reality. Hegel, in effect, subordinated reality (what is de
facto the case) to the logic of his thought-system instead of modifying
his system to adjust to reality. Hence, beginning with his lectures
at the University of Munich in 1827 and culminating in his lectures
on mythology and revelation at the University of Berlin from 1841
to 1854, Schelling distinguished between "negative" and "positive"
philosophy. Negative philosophy is based on speculative logic or
rational necessity (e.g., Hegel's *Phenomenology of Spirit* in which.
Spirit devoid of all finite determinations or pure Being is the starting-
point of the *Phenomenology*, and Spirit as the totality of all finite
determinations is Absolute Spirit or God, the logical endpoint of
the *Phenomenology*).[9] On the contrary, positive philosophy or the
philosophy of revelation is based on an alleged free decision of God
as an objective reality totally independent of the dialectical process
or thought-system.[10] Thus whereas Hegel critiqued Schelling for his
reliance on feeling or intuition rather than pure thought,[11] Schelling
vindicated his positive philosophy through a religious intuition, the
experience of God as a free and independent subject of experience
rather than an impersonal object of thought.

9. G. W. F. Hegel, *The Phenomenology of Mind*, trans. J. B. Baillie (New York: Harper & Row, 1967), 81; 789–90.

10. Joseph A. Bracken, *Subjectivity, Objectivity, and Intersubjectivity: A New Paradigm for Religion and Science* (West Conshohocken, PA: Templeton Foundation Press, 2009), 87.

11. Taylor, *Hegel*, 532.

Schelling's vindication of empirically based thinking over purely speculative reflection, to be sure, was very limited. Once he had established the origin of God's self-revelation in a free divine choice without antecedent grounding in speculative logic, he then subjected the subsequent process of divine revelation in and through Salvation History to the same dialectical pattern (thesis–antithesis–synthesis) that had governed Hegel's philosophy and his own earlier attempts at a philosophical cosmology. But, to his credit, Schelling still called into question the entire movement of German Idealism based on abstract logic. After Schelling's death in 1854, Western European philosophers like Søren Kierkegaard more and more rejected systematic philosophical reflection in favor of reflection on concrete human experience so that the very idea of metaphysics as a systematic understanding of reality became subject to skepticism or outright rejection. Among natural scientists, to be sure, the need for systematic thinking remained constant simply as a result of adherence to scientific method: close attention to empirical data within the context of some antecedent hypothesis based on universal laws or principles. But then at the beginning of the twentieth century, given what seemed to be radical contingency in the workings of Nature at the quantum level, belief in such universally binding laws and principles became somewhat suspect even for natural scientists.

Whitehead and Hartshorne on Panentheism

It was with this surprising turn of events in natural science that philosophers of science like Whitehead and Bergson undertook a radical critique of the metaphysical presuppositions of early modern science. Is a heavily mechanistic approach to nature based on rigorous mathematical formulas and unvarying physical laws only a useful abstraction from the full details of what is going on in the world around us at every moment? Is the natural world instead more like a cosmic organism with dynamically interrelated parts or members that by their ongoing interaction evolve to more and more complex forms of organization? The response of Whitehead and Bergson, as already noted in Part One of this book, was to set up a new metaphysics based on principles of becoming or change rather than (as in classical metaphysics) based on enduring principles of being in a world otherwise threatened by chaos. But did these founders of process philosophy and their disciples succeed any better than Hegel and Schelling in reconciling the rival concepts of Infinite and finite, spirit and matter, within their philosophical schemes?

Whitehead himself, for example, can be interpreted either as an inadvertent advocate of pantheism or as a deliberate proponent of dialectical dualism. For example, in Whitehead's metaphysical scheme, God is "the primordial actual entity."[12] As such, God alone survives the passage of time with its "perpetual passing" or loss of immediate actuality.[13] Moreover, as the sole principle of unity and permanence within the ever-changing cosmic process, God "saves the world as it passes into the immediacy of his own life."[14] That is, God gives the world objective immortality from moment to moment by incorporating it into what Whitehead calls the divine consequent nature.[15] But this amounts to pantheism, since the world of finite actual entities has no enduring objective reality apart from God. Looked at from another perspective, however, Whitehead espouses dialectical dualism: "God and the world are the contrasted opposites in terms of which Creativity achieves its supreme task of transforming disjointed multiplicity, with its diversities in opposition

---

12. Alfred North Whitehead, *Process and Reality: An Essay in Cosmology*, corrected edition, ed. David Ray Griffin and Donald W. Sherburne (New York: Free Press, 1978), 65. Hereafter: *PR*.
13. Ibid., 346.
14. Ibid., 340.
15. Ibid., 345.

[the world of temporal actual entities], into concrescent unity, with its diversities in contrast [the divine consequent nature]."[16] There is a constant moving back and forth between diversity represented by all the temporal actual entities in their brief moment of independent existence and unity represented by the only nontemporal actual entity (God in terms of the divine consequent nature): "The revolts of destructive evil [within the world], purely self-regarding, are dismissed into their triviality of merely individual facts; and yet the good they did achieve in individual joy, in individual sorrow, in the introduction of needed contrast, is yet saved by its relation to the completed whole [the divine consequent nature]. The image—and it is but an image—the image under which this operative growth of God's nature is best conceived, is that of a tender care that nothing be lost."[17]

Presumably because he was uncomfortable with the vagueness of Whitehead's own position on the God-relationship, Charles Hartshorne devised a process-oriented understanding of panentheism: God is the soul of the universe; the universe is the body of God. "God is the compound individual who at all times has embraced or will embrace the fullness of all other individuals existing at those times. He is the only eternal individual."[18] With the generic term "compound individual," Hartshorne has in mind the soul-body relation for organisms endowed with a central nervous system as opposed both to more primitive organisms without a central nervous system and to nonliving things such as rocks and other inanimate objects that are simply aggregates of actual entities or "composite individuals."[19] Admittedly, this model of the God-world relationship

16. Ibid., 348.
17. Ibid., 346.
18. Charles Hartshorne, "The Compound Individual," in *Philosophical Essays for Alfred North Whitehead*, ed. F. S. C. Northrup (New York: Russell & Russell, 1936), 218.
19. Ibid., 215.

has strong appeal for the affirmation of God's presence in every part of the cosmos. God is present to the world much as the soul is thought to be present everywhere in the body as its animating principle. But in my judgment it still suffers from the same limitations as I just mentioned in connection with Whitehead's understanding of the God-world relationship. That is, Hartshorne's soul-body metaphor is likewise open to interpretation as either implicit pantheism or dualism.

That is, if God is "the only eternal individual," then the world has no enduring actuality. At every moment the world is a new reality, given that its ultimate constituents, actual entities, are new at every moment and the "societies" to which they belong are in some modest way also different from what they were a moment ago. Hence, if God alone survives the passage of time or "perpetual passing,"[20] then pantheism rather than panentheism (everything in God but distinct from God) seems to result. In the end, nothing finite survives except what has been incorporated without remainder into God. Likewise, Hartshorne's soul-body metaphor for the God-world relationship can be considered as implicitly dualist, in that God as the soul of the universe is radically different from the world as the body of God. Unlike Whitehead who conceives God as the sole nontemporal actual entity, Hartshorne claims that God is a unique society of divine personally ordered actual occasions. This society of personally ordered divine actual occasions never comes to an end. Unlike all the more limited societies of personally ordered actual occasions within the world of creation that ultimately come to an end, the society of personal ordered actual occasions proper to God as the soul of the universe never ends. But, as I see it, this understanding of the God-world relationship is just as dualistic in its philosophical

20. Whitehead, *PR*, 340.

implications as classical metaphysics. For Aquinas and other classical metaphysicians the soul is an immaterial reality and the body is a material reality.[21] The soul as an immaterial reality is naturally immortal whereas the body as a material reality only becomes immortal through the grace of God by way of resurrection.

The underlying problem here for the understanding of the God-world relationship offered by Hartshorne and Whitehead, as I see it, is that they both are so focused on God as the sole survivor in the cosmic process that they give scant attention to the objective reality of the world as an enduring network of subsocieties or subsystems existing in its own right. Within their metaphysical systems, the world exists to give "satisfaction" or pleasure to God as the sole nontemporal actual entity or as a trans-temporal or never-ending society of divine actual occasions. In itself, the world is characterized by "perpetual perishing," as Whitehead notes in *Process and Reality*.[22] One can counterargue, of course, that apart from the world God has no reason to exist. God exists to be the principle of unity within a cosmic process otherwise constituted by the quasi-infinite diversity of individually constituted actual entities at every moment. One can further counterargue that God gives objective immortality to the world even as from moment to moment it "perishes," ceases to exist as what it is here and now as a finite temporal reality distinct from God.[23] Yet in no sense is the world an objective reality in its own right, united with God but still distinct from God as is the case in a genuine panentheistic approach to the God-world relationship. The ultimate purpose of the world for Whitehead and Hartshorne is either to enhance the well-being of God (pantheism) or to stand in ongoing opposition to God within

---

21. Thomas Aquinas, *Summa Theologiae* (Madrid: Biblioteca de Autores Cristianos, 1951), I, Q. 76, art. 3–4.
22. Whitehead, *PR*, 340.
23. Ibid., 350–51.

the cosmic process (dualism). Perhaps on an even deeper level of reflection, for Whitehead (and by implication also for Hartshorne) both God and the world exist to sustain the cosmic process. Creativity, the principle of novelty within the cosmic process, requires both God and the world as dialectical opposites to justify its own existence.[24] Neither God nor the World but Creativity, the principle whereby "the many become one and are increased by one"[25] over and over again, is Ultimate Reality (explicitly for Whitehead, implicitly for Hartshorne).

A Systems-Oriented View of Panentheism

In this third and final section of the chapter on the Incarnation, I set forth my own approach to the dogma that is based not simply on an appeal to divine revelation in Sacred Scripture but on a new systems-oriented approach to the God-world relationship. In particular, I will focus on a new understanding of causality within a systems-approach to reality. That is, since systems in my scheme have as their component parts or members momentary self-constituting subjects of experience in dynamic interrelation, the causality between the subjects of experience within one system and the subjects of experience of another system is necessarily reciprocal, not unilateral as in classical metaphysics. Cause-and-effect relations within systems and between systems reciprocally act upon one another so that what results is simultaneous mutual causation. Martin Buber seems to have had in mind this new understanding of causality between interrelated subjects of experience in his classic work on interpersonal relations, *I and Thou*, when he says: "I require a You to become; becoming I, I say you."[26] Or, as Buber notes in distinguishing between I-You and

24. Ibid., 348.
25. Ibid., 21.

I–It relations, "There is no I as such but only the I of the basic word I–You and the I of the basic word I–It."[27] In either case, the "I" exists in relation to another, either another subject of experience as in the I–Thou relation or an object apart from oneself as in an I–It relation. Hence, to think of oneself as separate either from other human beings or from the world of things is an unconscious abstraction from concrete reality. Thus at least in the realm of interpersonal relations (as opposed to the realm of individual entities as objects of rational reflection) the unilateral causality of an antecedent cause upon a future intended effect is inoperative; in such an interpersonal context simultaneous mutual causality is the rule.

Furthermore, even among researchers in the life-sciences there is growing recognition that something like an inbuilt principle of self-organization at the molecular level of existence and activity as well as Darwinian natural selection is responsible for the transition from non-life to life.[28] This transit from non-life to life is not a regular but rather a relatively rare event. But, if it happens, then from a philosophical perspective something like simultaneous mutual causality rather than the unilateral causality of an antecedent cause upon a subsequent effect seems to be at work. That is, A acts upon B which then acts upon C which in turn acts upon A. This may not be strictly simultaneous causality of A, B, and C upon one another but there is evidently a "positive feedback loop" among them, which is called in the life-sciences "autocatalysis."[29] Robert Ulanowicz comments: "In this framework, agency exerted by configurations of processes takes precedence over universal laws

26. Martin Buber, *I and Thou*, trans. Walter Kaufmann (New York: Scribner's, 1970), 62.
27. Ibid., 54.
28. Robert E. Ulanowicz, "Process-First Ontology," in *Beyond Mechanism: Putting Life Back into Biology*, ed. Brian G. Henning and Adam C. Scarfe (Lanham, MD: Rowman & Littlefield, 2013), 115–31.
29. Ibid., 121.

acting on objects."[30] The universal laws of early modern natural science were governed by the classical understanding of cause and effect in which the cause precedes the effect, not vice versa. Configurations of processes all acting upon one another at the same time, however, presuppose the operation of simultaneous mutual causality.[31]

Two Dynamically Integrated Systems

So, given the likelihood of a shift from a mechanistic to a more organic approach to physical reality among researchers in the life-sciences, how would this apply to a new understanding of Christian belief in the doctrine of the Incarnation? Let us begin by quoting the classical text on the Christian doctrine of the Incarnation at the Council of Chalcedon in 451 C.E.:

> We confess one and the same Christ, the Son, the Lord, the Only-Begotten, in two natures unconfused, unchangeable, undivided and inseparable. The difference of natures will never be abolished by their being united, but rather the properties of each remain unimpaired, both coming together in one person and substance, not parted or divided among two persons, but in one and the same only-begotten Son, the divine Word, the Lord Jesus Christ.[32]

If, however, in place of "natures" one substituted "open-ended systems" in the formulation of the Chalcedonian decree, one might have a much more plausible rational explanation of this doctrine of the Incarnation. The divine and the human natures of Jesus as the Incarnate Word of God would then be "unconfused, unchangeable,

---

30. Ibid., 125.

31. Evan Thompson, *Mind in Life: Biology, Phenomenology, and the Sciences of Mind* (Cambridge, MA: Harvard University Press, 2007), 440–41.

32. *The Teaching of the Catholic Church*, ed. Josef Neuner, Heinrich Roos, and Karl Rahner, trans. Geoffrey Stevens (Staten Island, NY: Society of Saint Paul, 1967), 154 n. 302.

undivided and inseparable" open-ended systems, which in ongoing dynamic interrelation enable Jesus to be "one person and substance, not parted or divided among two persons," equivalently a "super-system," i.e., a harmonious synthesis of two interrelated subsystems.

Here one may object that this is simply a word-game, a nominal shift of terminology to describe in a somewhat different way what Christians have always believed about salvation in and through belief in Jesus as one's personal Lord and Savior. But the term "nature" seems to imply a self-sufficient and relatively unchanging reality, what is implied by the term "substance" in classical metaphysics. The term "system," on the contrary, implies an ever-changing reality, an ongoing activity rather than a fixed reality or "thing." Likewise, whereas one "thing" can be incorporated into another "thing" only through loss of its own identity (e.g., food and drink become part of me when I eat a meal), systems and other forms of internally or self-organized activity, however, are readily combined to produce a common effect (e.g., the coordinated activity of the nervous system, the circulatory system, and all the other subsystems within the human body from moment to moment). Thus Jesus in and through his human nature was constantly engaged in day-to-day activities, but in and through the workings of his divine nature he presumably performed those activities from a new and unconventional perspective. Consciously or unconsciously he was always responsive to the Will of his Father in heaven even as he retained the freedom to respond to the Father in his own way.

In other words, there was an ongoing reciprocal causality between the divine and the human in Jesus' experience. Jesus in his freedom as a human subject of experience thereby set certain limits to the workings of the divine nature within himself, and vice versa, the workings of the divine nature within himself set limits to his free choices in all the events of his life. Moreover, this reciprocal causation between the divine and the human in Jesus during his earthly life seems to be akin to what Terrance Deacon and Tyrone Cashman in their contribution to *Beyond Mechanism* call "autogenesis": "In autogenesis, it is not just constituents [two interacting processes or open-ended systems] that are joined in a reciprocally productive loop [autocatalysis], but the *constraints* that each process generates, because each of these processes generates boundary constraints that make the other process possible."[33] Accordingly, if the classical statement of the doctrine of the Incarnation at Chalcedon (two natures "unconfused, unchangeable, undivided and inseparable") seems to have at least some limited resemblance to the scientific understanding of autogenesis in living organisms, then the scientific understanding of autogenesis as offered by Deacon and Cashman in turn could be said to shed unexpected light on the classical understanding of the Christian doctrine of the Incarnation. That is, the doctrine of the Incarnation seems to be less paradoxical and more rationally plausible than the traditional understanding of the Incarnation in the decree of the Council of Chalcedon.

To further illustrate what I have in mind here, I now briefly evaluate and critique what I consider to be a good exposition of the classical theory to explain primary and secondary causality within the God-world relationship, namely, Thomas F. Tracy's article "Divine Purpose and Evolutionary Processes" in a recent issue of *Zygon*.[34] Tracy first asks about God's action in the world simply as its Creator: "[C]reation is an intentional divine action, not an involuntary emanation, as in some forms of Neo-Platonism. God could exist

---

33. Terrence Deacon and Tyrone Cashman, "Teleology versus Mechanism in Biology: Beyond Self-Organization," *Beyond Mechanism*, 299.
34. Thomas F. Tracy, "Divine Purpose and Evolutionary Processes," *Zygon* 48 (June 2013): 454–65.

without a world of created things, and the existence of such a world reflects God's loving generosity in giving being to creatures."[35] He also specifies that God grants to finite things causal powers of their own, namely, various capacities to affect and be affected by other finite things. Thus God empowers finite entities to exist and to exercise secondary causality vis-à-vis other things. Moreover, God acts indirectly in the created order by "establishing the causal laws and initial conditions of the universe."[36] This could result in a divinely predetermined universe down to the last detail, but it could also be understood to mean that God so constructs the world that "chance events conform to well-defined probabilistic laws and have a limited range of causal consequences in the events that follow from them."[37] God does not predetermine what happens but only what can happen, given the laws of nature. Finally, Tracy claims that God *acts* with natural causes. "But God does not act entirely *by means of* them."[38] Because this particular action of the creature is contingent or undetermined in its final outcome, God can further determine it without violation of the laws of nature and under the proper circumstances work a miracle that does not violate the laws of nature but certainly goes beyond what would otherwise be possible in terms of those same laws of nature. God, for example, could in a given case resolve an indeterminacy in the collapse of the "wave function" which would lead to an unexpected outcome.

From the perspective of my own theory of simultaneous mutual causality in the dynamic interrelation between the divine and the human subjectivities within the man Jesus, however, this leaves many unanswered questions. For, in terms of Tracy's understanding of primary and secondary causality, the effect of his divine nature or

35. Ibid., 456.
36. Ibid., 457.
37. Ibid., 458.
38. Ibid., 461.

divine causality upon the words and actions of the human Jesus would seem to be strictly unilateral on the part of the divine subjectivity of Jesus. Tracy says nothing about the response of the human subjectivity of Jesus to what his divine subjectivity is invisibly arranging for his life on earth. Admittedly, the Gospels make clear that Jesus saw his highest responsibility in life to be obedience to the Father's Will (e.g., John 6:38-39). But did Jesus in his human subjectivity then have any latitude in his interpretation of the Father's Will at any given moment? Was he free to change his mind and make a different choice? In dealing with the Syrophoenician woman (Mark 7:25-30) and in responding to his mother's request at the wedding feast of Cana (John 2:1-5), Jesus apparently had an unexpected change of heart. Was that change of heart simply due to a better understanding of what the Father wanted him to do or was it also due to a change of Jesus' feelings toward another human being in need and possibly a new assessment of the situation at hand, both of which came from his own human subjectivity?

Perhaps the Christian tradition has tended to so emphasize the divinity of Jesus as the primary cause in the events of his life that the humanity of Jesus appears to be simply the instrument of the divine will in the accomplishment of the work of salvation. In a genuinely intersubjective context where simultaneous mutual causation between two interrelated subjects of experience is at play, however, the divine subjectivity within Jesus empowers his human subjectivity and presumably influences the actual decision by Jesus in terms of what Whitehead referred to as a divine "initial aim."[39] But the divine subjectivity never fully controls the human subjectivity of Jesus. Persuasion rather than coercion is the only truly effective way for one subjectivity in an intersubjective context to move the other

---

39. Whitehead, *PR*, 244.

subjectivity to action. When overt force is used by the one subjectivity to compel the decision of the other subjectivity in a given direction, then in Buber's terminology the I-Thou relation has deteriorated into an I-It relation. This hardly seems to be in the spirit of the relation between the divine and human natures of Jesus as set forth in the above-cited decree of the Council of Chalcedon.

Admittedly, every explanation of the doctrine of the Incarnation will inevitably come up short; one is ultimately dealing with a divinely revealed truth beyond human comprehension. But in this chapter I have argued that thinking of the relation between the divine and the human natures of Jesus in the light of the classical understanding of cause and effect is harder to understand and confidently affirm than the notion of ongoing mutual causation or dialogue between the divine and the human subjectivities in the person of Jesus as the Incarnate Word of God. Furthermore, if this relatively new philosophical understanding of simultaneous mutual causation sheds light on what Deacon and Cashman understand by "autogenesis" in the ongoing interaction of open-ended systems in the life-sciences, then both scientists and theologians have something to think about and talk to one another about that otherwise would never have occurred to either party.

Postscript

In a pair of articles that appeared in print too late for inclusion in the original version of this book,[40] the Danish philosopher/theologian Niels Henrik Gregersen argued in much the same fashion as I have in this book that reality is socially constituted rather than based on

40. Niels Henrik Gregersen, "*Cur Deus Caro*: Jesus and the Cosmic Story" and "God, Information, and Complexity: From Descriptive to Explorative Metaphysics," *Theology and Science* 11 (2013), 370-93; 394-423.

the contingent interaction of individual entities with one another. That is, in the first article *Cur Deus Caro*, Gregersen proposed that in and through the incarnation of the Divine Word into Jesus of Nazareth God became incarnate, intimately involved, in creation as a cosmic totality. Hence, much akin to my argument in this chapter, in the person of Jesus the natural and the supernatural are intimately intertwined. Everything that Jesus said and did had both a natural and supernatural cause and a natural and supernatural effect in Salvation History and in the cosmic process as a whole. Then in the second article "God, Information and Complexity," Gregersen disputed the ancient and medieval understanding of God as Perfect Being or utterly simple, without constituent parts or members. God as Trinity is a complex unity of differences that make a difference for the divine persons in their life together as a transcendent corporate reality. The same notion of a complex unity of differences that make a difference governs the way that the evolutionary process is structured. Progressively more information-laden forms or structures both enable and at the same constrain the interrelated activity of individual entities within the ongoing history of the cosmic process. As I see it, Gregersen is here implicitly arguing for the equivalent of a systems-oriented approach to the God-world relationship. The triune God as the all-comprehensive system of the divine communitarian life is both the transcendent origin and ultimate goal of the cosmic process as a vast network of dynamically interrelated and hierarchically ordered finite systems whose progressive growth in order and complexity began with the Big Bang and will ultimately end with full incorporation into the divine life.

6

A Systems-Oriented Approach
to the Trinity

In the last chapter I outlined a systems-oriented understanding of the doctrine of the Incarnation. In this chapter I will use the same approach to present the doctrine of the Trinity in a new light. In both cases, the basic idea of a system as the byproduct or ongoing result of the dynamic interrelation of component parts or members remains the same. But the component parts or members are not the same in each case. With respect to the doctrine of the Incarnation, the system in question is the dynamic synthesis of the divine and human natures in Jesus as a divine person. The divine nature functions as a higher-order process and the human nature as a lower-order process within the overall system or mode of operation proper to Jesus as a divine person. Likewise, as noted earlier, the divine and the human natures constrain or limit one another in their conjoint existence and activity within the consciousness of Jesus. In virtue of his divine nature Jesus is always in contact with the Father and the Spirit in whatever he says and does. In virtue of his human nature, he enjoys a certain freedom of choice in deciding how to implement the purpose of the Father and the Spirit for each new situation in his life.

With respect to the doctrine of the Trinity, however, the system in question is the divine communitarian life to which each of the divine persons contributes by reason of "his" specific ongoing relation to the other two divine persons. Different from the workings of the divine and human natures in Jesus as an individual entity, therefore, in the workings of the divine communitarian life it is three fully constituted individual entities (the divine persons) that are joined together to produce the corporate reality of the divine communitarian life. Yet common to the mode of operation of the divine and human nature within Jesus as an individual entity and to the mode of operation of the three divine persons vis-à-vis one another within the divine communitarian life, the broader system or mode of operation that results is a logical consequence of simultaneous mutual causation between the divine and human natures within Jesus on the one hand, and simultaneous mutual causation between the divine persons within the divine communitarian life on the other hand. In other words, the classical cause-effect relationship with its sharp distinction between cause and effect as ontologically separate realities does not apply in either case. A classical cause-effect relationship between the divine and human natures in Jesus would mean the dominance of the divinity of Jesus over his humanity so that Docetism would result, that is, God using the humanity of Jesus as a tool for its own strictly divine mode of operation in this world. The classical cause-and-effect relationship, when applied to the relationship between the three divine persons, would result in the primacy of the Father over the Son and the Spirit in that the Father is the origin or source of the divine life and shares it with the Son and the Spirit, effectively denying their alleged equality as necessary co-participants in the divine communitarian life.

From a purely philosophical perspective, what I am urging here is a new model or paradigm for the relation between the One and the Many in which the Many through their dynamic interrelation from moment to moment co-produce the reality of the One as a higher-order corporate system or mode of operation for themselves as its participants and/or constituent parts. A living organism, for example, is a corporate system of interrelated processes (both bodily and mental) that are integral to its ongoing survival and prosperity. Within human beings, for example, the interrelated operations of the nervous system, the cardiovascular system, the respiratory system, and the neuronal system in the brain are all necessary to sustain life and continued growth. Similarly, at the level of socially organized realities like environments or communities, the One is a corporate reality that survives and prospers only if all the individual entities that constitute the parts or members of the environment or community are in harmonious working order vis-à-vis one another. In the rest of this chapter, accordingly, I will use this notion of systems within systems to resolve the otherwise logical contradiction in claiming that God is Trinity, one God and yet three distinct persons at the same time. This contradiction cannot be resolved if one is thinking in terms of ontologically separate entities in relation to one another, but only if one thinks of processes or systems in dynamic interrelation, what Whitehead calls a "structured society," a society or system composed of subsocieties or subsystems in ongoing interaction with one another.

Three Systems within One System

In the rest of this chapter, accordingly, I will indicate how this more dynamic paradigm for the One and the Many resolves the otherwise logical contradiction in claiming that God is for Christians both one entity and three entities at the same time. For example, if one focuses on the unity of the divine being and tries to explain how God is also three persons, one is tempted to modalism (one God with three self-manifestations). If one's primary focus is on the difference between the divine persons and then tries to explain that together they are one God, one is tempted to tritheism (belief in three gods in close collaboration). The medieval theologians in the West implicitly gave priority to the One over the Many.[1] God is one intelligent being but with three interrelated functions of memory, understanding, and will which correspond to Father, Son, and Holy Spirit as the divine persons. Eastern theologians, however, implicitly gave priority to the Many and found the oneness of God in the indissoluble community of life of the divine persons with one another since they are all linked together by *perichoresis*, the unifying activity proper to the divine essence.[2]

A much easier way to explain Christian belief in one God and three divine persons, however, is to think of the divine persons not as separate individual entities who together are a much bigger entity, but in terms of lower-order processes that are components of a higher-order process. That is, the lower-order activities proper to each of the divine persons (e.g., being Father rather than Son or Spirit, being Son rather than Father or Spirit, being Spirit rather than Father or Son) are integrated into the higher-order activity of the Trinity as a corporate whole or tightly knit interpersonal community.

1. Cf., e.g., Joseph A. Bracken, *God: Three Who Are One* (Collegeville, MN: Liturgical, 2008), 15–22.
2. Ibid., 22–27.

But that means that all three divine persons exist and are bound together by *perichoresis*, one and the same unifying activity which is constitutive of their existence as one God. Consequently, in dealing with the world of creation they act as a single corporate agency. They all create, redeem, and sanctify the human race and the rest of creation. Yet, because it is so hard for us human beings to think in these strictly corporate terms, we "appropriate" different roles to different persons.[3] The Father creates, the Son redeems, the Spirit sanctifies. But all these separate activities are in the end only one conjoint activity, the activity of being God both internally and in relation to creation. Yet, one may object, only the Son, the Divine Word, became incarnate as Jesus of Nazareth, not the Father or the Spirit. But how did the Son become incarnate, if not through the conjoint activity and participation of the Father and the Spirit in bringing it about (e.g., Luke 1:26-38)? Likewise, in his Last Supper discourse to the Apostles, Jesus stresses his unity with the Father and the work of the Spirit in his disciples that "all may be one, as you, Father, are in me and I in you, that they also may be in us, that the world may believe that you sent me" (John 17:21).

There is a movement in contemporary systematic theology away from the traditional emphasis on Logos-Christology to explain the God-world relationship to a new emphasis on a Spirit-Christology.[4] But unless this new strategy for doing systematic theology is carefully qualified, Spirit-Christology will be no more adequate to explain the doctrines of the Incarnation and the Trinity than its predecessor, Logos-Christology. The activity of the Trinity vis-à-vis the world of creation is always trifold or triune, not because the divine persons have freely decided to work together on the project of creation,

---

3. Thomas Aquinas, *Summa Theologiae* (Madrid: Biblioteca de Autores Cristianos, 1951), I, Q. 39, art. 7; Q. 41, art. 1. Hereafter: *ST*.
4. Joseph A. Bracken, "Trinitarian Spirit Christology: In Need of a New Metaphysics?," *Theological Studies* 72 (2011): 750–67.

redemption, and sanctification of the world of creation, but because otherwise they could not be one God. Their unity with one another is the unity of a higher-order corporate process that integrates the activity of the lower-order processes proper to each of the divine persons within itself so as to function as a corporate entity or system, a transcendent interpersonal community. In the *Summa Theologiae*, Aquinas seems to have had something like this in mind when he describes the divine persons as subsistent relations.[5] But because he was unconsciously thinking in the language of entities rather than activities, he used a noun (subsistent *relations*) rather than a verb or participle (subsistent *relatings*) to solve the problem of the One and the Many in terms of the doctrine of the Trinity. Yet, in fairness to him, such a shift in terminology would have meant him leaving the classical thought-world and moving into a new mental world in which interrelated activities or processes progressively constitute entities, not vice versa.

Yet, given this systems- or process-oriented understanding of divine personhood, what then should be said about the nature of human personhood? Are human persons entities or are they processes? Are they both entities and processes, that is, processes that from moment to moment have a transient entitative status, that is, are entities in evolution? Here I appeal to the metaphysics of Whitehead for guidance. In *Process and Reality* he uses the term "personally ordered society of actual entities" to describe a "nexus" or set of actual entities with basically the same "defining characteristic" or "common element of form."[6] This nexus of actual entities becomes a "society" when it endures over time with the same common element of form or defining characteristic as a group. In that case, it can be

---

5. Aquinas, *ST*, I, Q. 29, art. 4 .
6. Alfred North Whitehead, *Process and Reality: An Essay in Cosmology*, corrected edition, ed. David Ray Griffin and Donald W. Sherburne (New York: Free Press, 1978), 34. Hereafter: *PR*.

called a "personally ordered" society of actual entities. But, cautions Whitehead, it is most of the time not a person in the conventional sense, since personhood normally carries with it the connotation of consciousness. The human mind is such a personally ordered society of conscious actual entities, but all the actual entities constitutive of the societies/processes within the human body do not have consciousness. They function either unconsciously or in some cases subconsciously (with some kind of sense awareness but nothing more). In most cases these societies of unconscious or subconscious actual entities that retain a defining characteristic or common element of form are "enduring objects."[7] In commonsense experience they are material entities (e.g., atoms and molecules, the components of the physical things of this world).

Application to Controversial Moral Issues

In brief, then, for Whitehead a human person is a "structured society," a corporate process made up of interrelated subprocesses.[8] But one of those subprocesses is "regnant" over all the other subprocesses.[9] That one subprocess is equivalently the "soul" and all the other subprocesses are together the "body" of a human being within classical metaphysics. The one subprocess is regnant over all the others because it receives information from all the subprocesses making up the human body and gives some measure of order and direction to these other processes from moment to moment.[10] The mind or soul, in other words, is for Whitehead not an immaterial principle or substantial form within a material body as in classical metaphysics, but the key physical process in an integrated set of

7. Ibid., 35.
8. Ibid., 99.
9. Ibid., 103.
10. Ibid., 108–9.

physical processes constituting a human being. For Whitehead, then, a human being is a person, that is, a corporate reality or structured society with a defining characteristic or "common element of form" among its component subsocieties and their constituent actual entities from moment to moment.[11] But this human being/person is at the same time a strictly developmental reality, an ongoing corporate process with clearly defined stages of development. That is, a fertilized ovum is a person for Whitehead since it has a defining characteristic (in the language of science, a specified set of genes) that will heavily condition (though not totally control) its development first in the womb of the mother, then as an infant, a child, an adult human being, and finally a human being near death. But those different stages first of bodily development and then of bodily decline presumably also affect the spiritual identity or personhood of that human being, given the intimate bond between mind and body in human life. Accordingly, within a Whiteheadian context the morality and legality of beginning-of-life and end-of-life issues is not clear-cut and easily defined but quite complex and laden with qualifications. To be a person is both an indisputable fact and a still-unfinished process, a work in progress. Yet it would still seem to be an improvement over a dialogue-situation in which there is no common ground in analysis of such controversial ethical and legal issues.

Still another way in which a systems- or process-oriented understanding of the doctrine of the Trinity might be helpful in resolving controversial issues in contemporary medical ethics is available in reflecting on the way in which the three divine persons as interrelated personally ordered societies of actual entities equally contribute to their corporate existence as one God, the higher-order interpersonal process of the divine life. For, in the sometimes sharp

11. Ibid., 34.

exchanges between those representing different viewpoints on the beginning and end of human life, there is often little or no attention paid to the common good, the legitimate needs of the civil society in which all the disputing parties exist. The problem, of course, is in defining the common good under such circumstances. Is it, as John Locke maintained in his *Second Treatise on Civil Government*, simply the will of the majority over against the manifest resistance of minority groups?[12] Or is it, as Jean-Jacques Rousseau proposed in his book *The Social Contract*, the general will [*volonté générale*], presumably a consensus position based on a carefully worked-out compromise?[13] Clearly, to preserve the good order and long-lasting harmony of civil society, it should be Rousseau's *volonté générale* rather than simply Locke's will of the majority. The latter may de facto determine what is viewed as the common good of the civil society at any given moment, but the former is clearly the better choice, however difficult to achieve in actual practice.

Furthermore, thinking in terms of lower-order and higher-order individual processes within an even more comprehensive corporate system of interpersonal relations, such as can be said of a systems- or process-oriented understanding of the Christian doctrine of the Trinity, would possibly illuminate the otherwise elusive notion of *volonté générale.* If the higher-order process in a systems-oriented understanding of civil society represents the common good to be achieved through the conjoint activity of the lower-order processes, then just as the three divine persons together constitute and sustain their life as a divine community, so human beings should be willing to surrender some of their alleged rights as individual persons to

---

12. John Locke, *An Essay Concerning the True Original, Extent and End of Civil Government,* in The English Philosophers from Bacon to Mill, ed. Edwin Burtt (New York: Modern Library, 1939), ch. 8, n. 6.
13. Jean-Jacques Rousseau, *The Social Contract and Discourses,* trans. G. D. H. Cole (London: Everyman's Library, 1923), Bk. 2, ch. 3; Bk. 3, ch. 8.

a higher-order process constituting their life together within civil society. For the longer a stalemate over a disputed issue continues, the more damage it does to the likelihood of ever attaining a common good, that is, an acknowledged set of goals and values that all recognize as necessary for their life together. To put the matter even more broadly, within a systems-oriented understanding of reality, what ultimately counts in human life is the continued existence of the communities to which all human beings belong and on which they rely for their own individual existence. The rights of individual entities vis-à-vis one another are important but in the end subordinate to the common good in which all share. This, as I see it, is the deeper reality of Christian belief in God as Trinity. This is also the reality of human life in community insofar as human beings consciously or much more often unconsciously try to imitate in some small way the order and the harmony of the shared life of the three divine persons.

Review of Approaches to the Trinity

1. Karl Barth and Eberhard Jüngel

With this systems-oriented understanding of the doctrine of the Trinity in mind, I now address some of the multiple views on the doctrine of the Trinity that have emerged in the last one hundred years of Western systematic theology. I begin with Karl Barth's declaration in his *Church Dogmatics* that divine revelation has a specifically Trinitarian structure: God is the Revealer (God the Father), the One Revealed (God the Son), and the act of revealing (God the Holy Spirit), all at the same time. God is thus one God in three modes of being: "in the mode of the Father, in the mode of the Son, and in the mode of the Holy Ghost."[14] As Claude Welch comments, for Barth the doctrine of the Trinity is thus Christ-centered and revelation-grounded.[15] It cannot be justified by way of the Hegelian metaphysics of Absolute Spirit or by way of proof-texts from Sacred Scripture in Protestant fundamentalism or through the teaching authority of the Church in Roman Catholicism.[16] Revelation is to be found in the act of revealing, not in written propositions. For example, there is a threefoldness in the structure or pattern of the one act of God in Christ and therefore in the structure of all divine activity and of the Being of God.[17] Likewise, the direct experience of revelation in reading Scripture and through participation in Church life by the believer is more important than the explanation of its rational possibility for that Christian. "The word of God in revelation is not just a word *about* God but rather is God in the Godself . . . we find God on both sides of the revelatory equation. God is also on both sides of the eternity-time equation."[18] To quote Barth once again, "Without ceasing to be God, He has made Himself a worldly, human, temporal God in relation to this work of His."[19]

A generation later, Eberhard Jüngel published *The Doctrine of the Trinity: God's Being Is in Becoming.*[20] According to Jüngel, there exists a correspondence between the inner life of God and God's external relationship to creation.[21] The way in which God is related to the

14. Karl Barth, *Church Dogmatics* I/1, ed. G. W. Bromiley and T. F. Torrance, trans. G. W. Bromiley (Edinburgh: T. & T. Clark, 1975), 359.
15. Claude Welch, *In This Name: The Doctrine of the Trinity in Contemporary Theology* (New York: Scribner's, 1952), 119.
16. Ted Peters, *God as Trinity: Relationality and Temporality in Divine Life* (Louisville:Westminster John Knox, 1993), 84.
17. Ibid., 87.
18. Ibid., 90.
19. Barth, *Church Dogmatics* III/2, 457.
20. Eberhard Jüngel, *The Doctrine of the Trinity: God's Being Is in Becoming,* trans. Horton Harris (Grand Rapids: Eerdmans, 1976).
21. Ibid., 343.

world cannot be different from the way in which God is self-related.[22] But God is self-related in and through the *perichoresis* of the three divine persons vis-à-vis one another so as to be together one God: "Through this reciprocal participation the three modes of being [the divine persons] *become* concretely united. In this concrete unity they *are* God."[23] This means, however, that the unity of God is not a simple unity but a differentiated unity. But there is an underlying ambiguity here. Do the three divine persons first exist in their own right and only then join together via *perichoresis* to be one God? Or are they by nature thus joined together in a perichoretic unity and achieve their individual identity only as a consequence of the role that each plays in the ongoing divine life? As a way to resolve this problem one could say: "Why not just go all the way and affirm a God whose personhood is itself being constituted through God's ongoing relation to the creation?"[24] But this is a risky move since logically God then cannot be God apart from the world; God needs the world to be God: "What this implies is that the relationality God experiences through Christ's saving relationship to the world is constitutive of trinitarian relations proper. God's relations *ad extra* become God's relations *ad intra*."[25] Here one can appeal to what Karl Rahner says in his book on the Trinity: "God relates to us in a threefold manner, and this threefold, free and gratuitous relation to us is not merely a copy or an analogy of the inner Trinity, but this Trinity itself, albeit as freely and gratuitously communicated."[26] The key words here are "freely and gratuitously communicated" since that presupposes that "the three divine persons have an interrelated existence proper to themselves apart from their relation to us their

22. Peters, *God as Trinity*, 93.
23. Jüngel, *Doctrine of the Trinity*, 32.
24. Peters, *God as Trinity*, 95.
25. Ibid., 96.
26. Karl Rahner, *The Trinity*, trans. Joseph Donceel (New York: Herder & Herder, 1970), 35.

creatures."[27] This view is confirmed by Thomas Torrance in his understanding of the God-world relationship: "God in His transcendent freedom made the universe out of nothing [and gave it] a reality distinct from His own but dependent on it";[28] "the Son of God has become man without ceasing to be the God He ever was."[29] Torrance is basing his argument on traditional Church teaching re the God-world relationship. For me, it is simply the logical consequence of a systems-oriented approach to the doctrine of the Trinity. That is, the higher-order system in the God-world relationship is the divine communitarian life which functions apart from the world of creation. At a certain point in the history of the divine life, however, the three divine persons freely decided to bring into existence the lower-order system proper to creation and, moreover, to make it an integral even though subordinate part of their own communitarian life. Only at that point in the history of the divine life, in my judgment, did the time-bound economic Trinity become identical with the everlasting immanent Trinity.

2. Karl Rahner

Behind Karl Rahner's thinking on the God-world relationship is evidently a desire to remove the classical doctrine of the Trinity from the realm of speculative theology and to present it to the faithful in a more pastorally appealing way. After all, when we pray to the triune God, we normally pray to one of the divine persons, not to God in general. But he also recognized the danger of unconscious tritheism, belief in three gods, in this pastoral practice. God is one God, not three gods, in the creeds of the Church. Hence, he urged a change

27. Bracken, *Three Who Are One*, 47.
28. Thomas F. Torrance, *Space, Time and Incarnation* (London: Oxford University Press, 1969), 59.
29. Ibid., 53.

in the conventional understanding of person as applied to God so that each divine person is a "distinct manner of subsisting" in the one divine being (the one divine consciousness).[30] My own position, on the contrary, is that we should rather rethink what is meant by nature or essence. In a process- or systems-oriented metaphysics such as I propose in this book, nature or essence is an entity-constituting activity collectively exercised by closely interrelated subjects of experience. The entitative unity thus achieved is that of an objective system (in the case of the divine persons, an interpersonal system or community). The difference between the divine persons lies in the way each one contributes to the corporate activity constitutive of them all as an organized system/community. Each divine person achieves "his" individual identity in contributing something different to their corporate existence as an ongoing community. There is no danger of tritheism here since tritheism logically presupposes three individual divine persons who here and now work together but who are persons in their own right quite apart from their relations to one another. Within a systems-oriented approach to the doctrine of the Trinity, however, the divine persons have no individual identity or existence apart from co-constituting the divine community.

I wholeheartedly agree, however, with Rahner's understanding of the Trinity in his claim that the immanent Trinity is ontologically prior to the economic Trinity, not vice versa. The immanent Trinity, in other words, is the cause or ontological source of the economic Trinity, namely, the Trinity as operative in Salvation History.[31] Our Christian experience of the economic Trinity as three different divine persons at work in our lives does not determine the inner reality of the triune God apart from our experience. So, contrary to Peters's view that "the eternal or immanent Trinity finds its very identity in

30. Rahner, *The Trinity*, 107; 113-114.
31. Ibid., 76.

the economy of temporal salvation events,"[32] Rahner and I would presumably agree that the basic identity of the eternal or immanent Trinity is what it is quite apart from the way we experience it or think about it at this point in Salvation History. This is an important distinction since one otherwise unconsciously forfeits any rational ground for continuing to believe in the transcendence of God to the self and the world. God and the world then become co-constituents of a cosmic process that transcends both of them. Whitehead, for example, seems to have made that mistake in giving Creativity as the principle of process an ontological priority over both God and the World.[33] For Whitehead it was perhaps a pardonable error, since as a philosopher of science he was only interested in a new cosmology or purely philosophical worldview. But for a Christian theologian with strong belief in the transcendence of God to creation, it is a serious mistake.

3. Moltmann and Boff

In the final decades of the twentieth century, Christian systematic theologians tended more and more to favor a social or communitarian model of the Trinity, one that begins with the Threeness of the divine persons and argues to their Unity as an ongoing community. One of the earliest proponents of this social model of the Trinity was Jürgen Moltmann in his book *The Trinity and the Kingdom*: "Here we shall presuppose the unity of God neither as homogenous substance [Aquinas] nor as identical subject [Hegel]. . . . We are beginning with the trinity of the Persons and shall then go on to ask about the unity."[34] The unity of the divine persons is located in *perichoresis*, the term coined by the early

---

32. Peters, *God as Trinity*, 97.
33. Whitehead, *PR*, 348.

Greek Fathers of the Church.[35] But, as noted earlier, the notion of *perichoresis* is ambiguous in its implications. Do the three divine persons first exist in their own right and only then choose to engage in the perichoretic dance of life, or does their common perichoretic activity define their relation to one another as individual persons? The underlying presupposition of this book has been that activities define the entities that engage in them, not vice versa. Each of the divine persons is, of course, an individual entity, but "his" identity is defined by the role that "he" plays in the dance of the divine life, the ongoing system that defines their reality as one God, albeit in three distinctly different ways.

Still another proponent of the communitarian model of the Trinity is the Latin American theologian Leonardo Boff. In his book *Trinity and Society* he sees the perichoretic unity of the three divine persons as the model for human beings here and now in their life together in civil society.[36] He likewise claims that all of creation will be eventually incorporated into the communion of the divine life.[37] Boff's emphasis on the desire of the divine persons to share their communitarian life with all the creatures of this world is certainly commendable. But it inevitably raises still other metaphysical questions. How do human beings and the other creatures of this world participate in the divine life and yet retain their own finite identity both as individuals and, even more importantly, as members of various communities and environments? For, if entities are defined by the activities in which they are engaged, then human beings and all other creatures are primarily defined by the finite communities

34. Jürgen Moltmann, *The Trinity and the Kingdom: The Doctrine of God*, trans. Margaret Kohl (San Francisco: Harper & Row, 1981), 19.

35. Moltmann, *Trinity and the Kingdom*, 119. Cf. also J. N. D. Kelly, *Early Christian Doctrines*, 2nd ed. (New York: Harper & Row, 1960), 266.

36. Leonardo Boff, *Trinity and Society*, trans. Paul Burns (Maryknoll, NY: Orbis, 1988), 118–20.

37. Ibid., 147–48.

and environments to which they belong in this life. Only by the gracious invitation of the divine persons do they share in the divine life, both now and in eternity, but in both cases as members of a subsystem, a finite community or environment, within the more comprehensive system of the divine communitarian life. As I shall make clear in chapter 9, only rational creatures like us human beings will in full consciousness enjoy eternal life. Non-rational creatures will experience eternal life in their own limited way but not with full self-awareness.

4. Catherine LaCugna

If the basic problem in Boff's understanding of the Trinitarian God-world relationship is how finite entities can be themselves and still participate in the divine communitarian life, in Catherine LaCugna's book *God for Us* the problem is just the reverse. Following Karl Rahner's dictum that the "economic" Trinity is the "immanent" Trinity and the "immanent" Trinity is the "economic" Trinity,[38] LaCugna first claims that "what God has revealed and given in Christ and the Spirit *is* the reality of God as God is from all eternity. What is given in the economy of salvation, in other words, is the mystery of God which exists from all eternity as triune."[39] But she then adds immediately: "There are not two trinities, the Trinity of experience and a transeconomic Trinity. There is one God, one divine self-communication, manifested in the economy of creation, redemption, and consummation."[40] Here I disagree.

---

38. Rahner, *The Trinity*, 22.
39. Catherine Mowry LaCugna, *God for Us: The Trinity and Christian Life* (San Francisco: HarperSanFrancisco, 1991), 212.
40. Ibid.

Ontologically speaking, there is indeed only one Trinity. But phenomenologically speaking, there are two trinities: the Trinity of the divine persons as they exist in their own right apart from creation and the Trinity as experienced by human beings in and through divine revelation in Sacred Scripture and in their personal prayer life. Rahner and LaCugna would certainly resist my proposal here because it seems to put unreasonable distance between the divine persons and their creatures, above all, human beings. The inner life of God thus becomes an unfathomable mystery, the subject of endless and ultimately fruitless speculation on the part of systematic theologians. But in point of fact there is no way that human beings with strictly finite powers of intelligence can comprehend, first, what it means to be a divine person, and, secondly, the nature of their ongoing communion with one another from all eternity. All that I suggest in this book is that each of the divine persons is engaged in "his" own process of becoming and that these three subprocesses are linked together so as to constitute the system of the divine communitarian life, the perichoretic dance of being. More than that, I cannot say. From a commonsense perspective, however, I argue that the three divine persons cannot be "for us" without at the same time being different from us in their own existence and activity. The reality of intersubjective relations is that an "I" and a "Thou"' can become a "We" only if at the same time they remain distinct from one another precisely as "I" and "Thou."

5. Robert Jensen

Following the lead of Karl Barth, Robert Jenson proposes that "the threeness in God must . . . be understood not as three instances of one deity but as three events of one deity: God is God, and then *is God again, each time in a different way*."[41] But he then also claims: "Truly, the Trinity is simply the Father and the man Jesus and their Spirit as the Spirit of the believing community. Trinity is *eschatologically* God 'himself,' an 'immanent' Trinity. And that assertion is no problem, for God is himself only eschatologically, since he is Spirit."[42] Thus, in his effort to move from the classical understanding of God as timeless and thus existing apart from the world of creation, Jensen so closely identifies the immanent and economic senses of the doctrine of the Trinity that the cosmic process produces not only the reality of finite creatures but also the full eschatological reality of God as Spirit. He concedes that "God could have been also communal [triune?] without us, that in his eschatological immanence he would finally be 'we' with or without creatures."[43] But, for Jensen, this is a purely speculative issue. In the event of revelation, God is subject, Jesus is Object, and the Spirit witnesses to this self-revelation of God in Jesus of Nazareth.[44]

While I applaud Jensen's intention to substitute a modern process-oriented understanding of the Trinity for the relatively static classical understanding of the Trinity, I have serious reservations about his understanding of the relation between time and eternity. He should realize that the focus on the priority of the future over the past and the present is an inevitable consequence of thinking in purely time-bound categories. On the contrary, the future is for God real, but no more real than the present and the past. That is, in eternity past, present, and future simultaneously coexist for God. They are, however, not fixed or static realities for God as in the classical view of eternity, but dynamically interrelated dimensions of one and the same ongoing process of the divine life.[45] Robert Neville in his book *Eternity and Time's Flow* emphasizes the dynamic

41. Robert Jensen, *The Triune Identity* (Philadelphia: Fortress Press, 1982), 138.
42. Ibid., 141.
43. Ibid., 146.
44. Ibid., 148.

interrelatedness of past, present, and future within human consciousness: "Not only is something new always happening—the present is steadily moving on to new dates—but the past is always growing and the structure of future possibilities is constantly shifting in response to the decisions made in each moment of present actualization."[46] Within the context of a process-oriented approach to God, it makes sense to attribute to God the same awareness of the dynamic interrelation between past, present, and future that Neville ascribes to human beings in their time-awareness. That is, God does not see the future as an already-existing set of events predetermined by the divine will, but as an ever-changing set of possibilities for events that could happen in the future either because of the free decisions of human beings or in virtue of the spontaneity in the activities of nonhuman creatures. God is thus active in this cosmic process not to predetermine events in Salvation History and in the cosmic process as a whole, but to introduce new possibilities for something good to happen in the future.[47]

Hence, contrary to what Jensen (and others like Peters[48]) might claim, I do not endorse belief in the timelessness of the classical understanding of God. For, within my systems-oriented understanding of the God-world relationship, the system proper to the divine communitarian life is governed by space-time parameters that are different from the space-time parameters of our own cosmic system. So the divine persons can influence (but not predetermine) the course of events taking place within the world without being bound by the space-time parameters proper to our world. Their

45. Joseph A. Bracken, *Christianity and Process Thought: Spirituality for a Changing World* (Philadelphia: Templeton Foundation Press, 2006), 78–82.

46. Robert Cummings Neville, *Eternity and Time's Flow* (Albany: State University of New York Press, 1993), 111.

47. Bracken, *Christianity and Process Thought*, 78–86.

48. Peters, *God as Trinity*, 128–34.

present moment or "now" may very well embrace the entire cosmic process from the Big Bang to its final moment at some future date beyond our reckoning here and now. In effect, we finite creatures and the divine persons live in the same super-system, the God-world relationship as a dynamic totality, but inevitably in terms of different but interrelated systems, each with its own space-time parameters. What may seem timeless in terms of our own finite space-time parameters is in fact the result of our human inability to comprehend the space-time parameters of the higher-order ever-changing divine communitarian life.

6. Wolfhart Pannenberg

The last theologian that I cover in my brief review of twentieth-century Trinitarian theology is Wolfhart Pannenberg, whose understanding of the God-world relationship is remarkably like my own. For, as Pannenberg sees it, the Trinity has an eternal self-identity apart from the world, an identity that is confirmed and amplified by the events in the creation, redemption, and sanctification of human beings and the rest of the creation. The cosmic process has made a difference to the reality of God, but this difference is not constitutive of the very identity of the divine persons to one another.[49]

Admittedly, in the following passage from the first volume of his *Systematic Theology*, Pannenberg seems to say the opposite, namely, that God needs the world to be fully God:

> The rule or kingdom of the Father is not so external to his deity that he might be God without his kingdom. The world as the object of his lordship might not be necessary to his deity, since its existence owes

49. Wolfhart Pannenberg, *Systematic Theology*, Vol. I, trans. Geoffrey Bromiley (Grand Rapids: Eerdmans, 1991), 327–36.

its origin to his creative freedom, but the existence of a world is not compatible with his deity apart from his lordship over it. Hence lordship goes hand in hand with the deity of God.[50]

The existence of the triune God and the existence of the world thus seem to be mutually interdependent. Pannenberg is indeed somewhat ambiguous in the above-cited passage. But much of the ambiguity disappears if one reads the very next sentence in that same passage: "It [the lordship of the Father over creation] has its place already in the intratrinitarian life of God, in the reciprocity of the relation between the Son, who freely subjects himself to the lordship of the Father, and the Father, who hands over his lordship to the Son."[51] There is, in other words, already within the eternal life of the immanent Trinity a mutual handing-over of lordship between the Father and the Son. Hence, all that the passage really says is that the created world necessarily finds its place within relationships between the Father and the Son that have existed from all eternity. Otherwise, the created world could not fit into the already-existing pattern of existence and activity between the divine persons. So Pannenberg's Trinitarian theology should not be used as support for Jensen's thesis that the immanent Trinity is the eschatological fulfillment of the economic Trinity. For Pannenberg, the latter is only the time-bound manifestation of what has been true from the very beginning of the cosmic process, indeed from all eternity within the divine life.

Likewise, in his understanding of the role of the Spirit in the inner life of the triune God, Pannenberg's thinking is closely akin to my own:

> The two statements "God is Spirit" and "God is love" denote the same unity of essence by which Father, Son, and Spirit are united in the fellowship of the one God. . . . The Spirit is the power of love that

50. Ibid., 313.
51. Ibid.

lets the others be. This power can thus give existence to creaturely life because it is already at work in the reciprocity of the trinitarian life of God as in eternity each of the divine persons lets the others be what they are.[52]

Pannenberg seems to be saying here that Spirit is both an activity and an entity. That is, Spirit is the power of love that binds the divine persons to one another within the immanent Trinity and gives existence to creaturely life within the economic Trinity. But Spirit is also the name for one of the three divine persons. Furthermore, Spirit, when understood as the "essence" or innate principle of activity among the three divine persons, is much akin to a dynamic force-field within contemporary physics: "The idea of the divine life as a dynamic field sees the divine Spirit who unites the three persons as proceeding from the Father, received by the Son, and common to both, so that precisely in this way he is the force-field of their fellowship that is distinct from them both."[53] There is, to be sure, some ambiguity in this last citation. But Pannenberg clears it up immediately: "But the Spirit is not just the divine life that is common to both the Father and the Son. He also stands over against the Father and the Son as his own center of action. This makes sense if the Father and the Son have fellowship in the unity of the divine life only as they stand over against the person of the Spirit."[54]

Pannenberg's description of the inner life of the triune God is thus very similar to my own understanding of the Trinity and the God-world relationship from a systems- or process-oriented perspective. I too believe that the nature of God is Spirit or Love. The terms "Spirit" or "Love," however, only make full sense within a communitarian context. That is, Spirit and Love are the names

52. Ibid., 427.
53. Ibid., 383.
54. Ibid., 383–84.

for a principle of activity whereby parts or members are integrated into wholes, new corporate realities, on various levels of existence and activity within reality. Thus Spirit or Love as the underlying essence or principle of activity of the divine life is what enables the three divine persons to be one God, one corporate reality, rather than three gods that here and now choose to be closely related. The result of this unifying activity of Spirit or Love within the Trinity is a "force-field" or energy-source for the ongoing interaction of the three divine persons. The three divine persons are, of course, themselves ongoing Spirit- or Love-inspired processes, not individual entities. For only processes, not individual entities, can be so closely integrated with one another as to co-constitute a genuinely new corporate reality, that is, a community of life and love, equivalently a force-field or energy source for the ongoing interaction of the divine persons. Hence, my only difference from Pannenberg in explaining the doctrine of the Trinity is that I am more thoroughgoing than he is in offering a process-ordered understanding of the doctrine as solution to the paradox of three individual entities somehow becoming one corporate entity without losing their own ontological identity as individual entities. Likewise, profiting from the criticism Pannenberg received from scientists on his (mis)use of the notion of field,[55] I myself emphasize that the force-field proper to the divine persons is only one instantiation or exemplar of an analogous concept that needs to be further specified when employed in different contexts. "Field," in other words, is akin to "substance" in classical metaphysics, namely a generic concept denoting something that endures with a given structure or mode of operation in a world marked by constant change.

---

55. Cf., e.g., John Polkinghorne, *Belief in God in an Age of Science* (New Haven: Yale University Press, 1998), 82.

Governing Presuppositions in this Chapter

Looking back on the contents of this chapter dealing with the Christian doctrine of the Trinity, I realize that I have been working with a number of presuppositions that have governed my critique of the theories of other theologians and the formulation of my own systems-oriented approach to the doctrine. That is, I presuppose in the first place that the tension between the "conceptual traps" of modalism and tritheism in classical Trinitarian theology can only be truly eliminated by conceiving the divine persons as interrelated lower-order person-making processes that co-constitute a single higher-order process that is constitutive of their life together as a divine community. For, if individual entities constitute a community, they remain sufficiently separate from one another that one is tempted to say that the community is nothing more than the sum of its parts or members. This line of thinking, however, leads inevitably to either some form of modalism, one God in three different manifestations, or of tritheism, three gods engaged in a common activity. Secondly, while acknowledging the pastoral value of emphasis on the "economic" (as opposed to the "immanent") understanding of the doctrine of the Trinity, I believe that one must likewise guarantee the classical transcendence of the triune God to the world of creation. Furthermore, in my view, this can only be accomplished if one stipulates a higher-order process or system proper to the divine persons that serves both as the transcendent origin and the ultimate goal of the cosmic process. A process or system is, after all, a dynamic unity-in-diversity of parts or members, a patterned set of interrelated events. What could be more suitable to describe how the triune God works in Salvation History, and in the entire cosmic process? Finally, the Christian doctrine of the Trinity is for me not a proof but instead a stellar exemplar or illustration of a new philosophical paradigm for the complex relation between the One and the Many at various levels of existence and activity within reality. Given these presuppositions, I believe that I have developed in this chapter an understanding of the doctrine that is logically consistent and, even more importantly, internally consistent with the traditional teaching of the Church.

7

Tradition and Traditioning

Church as Both System and Institutional Entity?

Without question, the Roman Catholic Church and all other Christian denominations are longstanding institutional entities in the contemporary world. But is their reality as institutional entities here and now ultimately secondary to their deeper reality as historically grounded systems or processes for handing on a specific doctrinal and liturgical tradition from one generation to the next over hundreds or even thousands of years? In other words, is the Church primarily an institutional entity with a relatively fixed identity as a result of its longstanding doctrinal and liturgical heritage, or is the Church primarily a process or system for handing on a given doctrinal and liturgical tradition that demands the active participation of most of its lay members as well as its professional clergy and lay theologians? There is, of course, no quick answer to that rhetorical question. Everything depends upon what one takes for granted in critically reviewing the history of the Church. Many post-Vatican II ecclesiologists like Bernard Prusak implicitly stress the priority of the Church as a historical process to the Church as longstanding and relatively unchanging institutional entity. In the first chapter of his book *The Church Unfinished*, for example, Prusak states: "The emerging Church did not stress unchangeability or a fixity of structure by an immutable divine decision. . . . Open to God's universal presence, the early communities were tentative, provisional, and free to experiment in regard to their own order and structure, and in relation to the particularities of various moments and contexts. That was reflected in the diversity of their theological and structural expressions."[1] In later chapters, of course, he also makes clear that in response to various internal and external challenges the Church *perforce* rapidly took on a more fixed institutional structure, which largely remains in place even today. My purpose in this chapter, at least in part, is to support Prusak's hypothesis about the nature of the Church from a more philosophically oriented approach to ecclesiology based upon the basic thesis of this book, namely, that interrelated processes or systems rather than individual entities are the building-blocks of physical reality, including the reality of the Church.

In the first part of the chapter, I will spell out in more detail what I mean by the theoretical distinction between tradition and traditioning. Afterwards I will indicate the practical consequences of focusing on tradition as a historical process rather than on tradition as a virtually unchangeable reality in the life of the Church. In principle, this should allow Church leaders to be more flexible in balancing the memory of the past over against new possibilities for the future in making present-day decisions on church doctrine and practice. Likewise, it should encourage the faithful to discriminate

---

1. Bernard Prusak, *The Church Unfinished: Ecclesiology Through the Centuries* (New York: Paulist, 2004), 56.

more carefully between levels of belief and degrees of adherence to those beliefs in their personal assent to Church teaching. Then in the third part of the chapter I will defend the use of the notion of traditioning (as opposed to tradition in a fixed sense) for creatively rethinking the Church's relation to other Christian denominations in ecumenical discussions and to non-Christian religions in the context of interreligious dialogue. My basic reference point for this analysis of tradition and traditioning throughout the chapter, of course, will be the Roman Catholic Church since this Church tradition is the only one that I have experienced, so to speak, from the inside. But Christians who are members of other denominations will undoubtedly see some parallels in what I say about tradition and traditioning within the Roman Catholic Church in terms of their own institutional history, its received tradition, and its mode of operation as a *traditio* or process of traditioning.

Tradition and Traditioning

Reviewing the history of the early Church in his book *Ecclesiology for a Global Church*, Richard Gaillardetz comments that "an incipient theology of tradition developed out of the need for early Christian communities to affirm their identity as one in continuity with the faith of the apostles. This need to demonstrate a continuity of faith came in response to the emergence of new sects, particularly those associated with Gnosticism, that were believed to have broken with that faith and claimed a salvation available only to those in possession of an immediate and private revelation"[2] St. Irenaeus of Lyons, for example, wrote of a *paradosis* (tradition, in English) whereby the gospel message in its entirety was handed on in the local churches. At

2. Richard R. Gaillardetz, *Ecclesiology for a Global Church: A People Called and Sent* (Maryknoll, NY: Orbis, 2008), 211.

that point in early Church history, to be sure, no real distinction was made between the content of tradition and the way it was handed on from one generation to another. As a result it included not only the written Gospels, the letters of St. Paul, James, and John, but accounts of how the rituals of Baptism and the Eucharist were conducted in various local Christian communities, stories about the heroic death of martyrs to the faith, and so on. In short, it gave witness to "the whole living Gospel in all its various historical embodiments."[3]

At the same time, given the prevalence of a basically Platonic understanding of reality, that is, the sharp distinction between the perfect and imperfect, the eternal and the temporal, within the cultural context of the Greco-Roman world at that time, it was virtually inevitable that tradition understood as *tradita*, the unchanging contents of the gospel message, would sooner or later be set in contrast to *traditio*, the different culturally conditioned ways in which that unchanging gospel message had been transmitted and then shared in the local Christian communities scattered around the Mediterranean world. This distinction between tradition in the sense of the fixed "deposit of faith" and *traditio*, the process of handing on that faith to newcomers, in turn led to growth in the importance of the role of the overseer or bishop within the local community. That individual quickly became not just the community member who conducted the business of the community and often presided over the celebration of the Eucharist for the group but the one who provided leadership and guaranteed continuity in the *traditio*, the necessary handing-on of the authentic gospel message from one individual or small group of individuals in the community to another.[4] This community member, someone who either would have been directly

3. Ibid., 2008. See also Yves M.-J. Congar, *Tradition and Traditions: An Historical and a Theological Essay* (New York: Macmillan, 1967).
4. Prusak, *The Church Unfinished*, 107–19.

appointed by one of the Apostles or in later generations was seen as successor to those individuals appointed by the Apostles, would have the authority of the Apostles in settling disputes over doctrine and practice.

Tradition understood as *tradita*, doctrines to be believed, thus necessarily took precedence over *traditio*, the time-bound and culturally conditioned process of handing on that tradition. Likewise, while in the early days there was some ambiguity about the respective roles of bishop, deacons, and elders within different Christian communities,[5] by the time of Ignatius of Antioch at the beginning of the second century, leadership of the Christian community was vested in the bishop with the collaboration of the elders and the deacons in the community. Here too priority was given to the *tradita* over the *traditio*, since the bishop in virtue of his teaching office was the principal way in which the *traditio* functioned within the local community; he alone guaranteed that the *tradita* were properly communicated to the faithful. The earlier notion of the *traditio* as a corporate responsibility of everyone in the community, a byproduct of the ongoing life of the Christian community, thus receded into the background.

As Prusak notes, authority in the Church became more and more centralized as the centuries went on.[6] In each case, of course, it was justified by an internal or external challenge to the authority of the Pope as the head of the Church.[7] But the net effect was the virtual identification of *traditio*, the process of handing down the faith to later generations of Christians, with the teaching authority of the Pope and to a lesser extent the local bishop. Furthermore, the challenge to papal authority by Luther and other Protestant reformers only

5. Ibid., 103–6.
6. Ibid., 139–48.
7. Ibid., 179–84, 205–20.

confirmed the need for the Roman Catholic Church to maintain its institutional identity in terms of the magisterium, the teaching authority of the bishops but especially the authority of the Pope and Vatican bureaucracy.[8] The document *Pastor Aeternus* at Vatican I in 1870 was, accordingly, the highpoint of this move to centralization and uniformity of belief and practice in the Church. Yet, as Prusak points out, the decree on the personal infallibility of the Pope in matters of faith and morals was remarkably restrained in its specification of what constitutes infallible teaching by the Pope: "[T]he pope is not separated from the Church but is infallible only in union with it. . . . In other words, the Pope is endowed with the gift of personal infallibility not as a private person or teacher but only as a public person, exercising his charge of supreme *magisterium* as head of the church in relation to the universal church."[9] Equivalently, then, the Pope only formalizes or gives public expression to what Roman Catholics around the world already believe. Since the Church as a whole cannot be in error, the Pope in expressing the universal belief of the Church must be speaking infallibly.[10]

The Understanding of Tradition at Vatican II

The documents on the institutional structure of the Church at Vatican II (1962–65) embodied a different tone and used different language than *Pastor Aeternus* and the decrees of earlier ecumenical councils.[11] How far these conciliar documents differed in terms of content from their predecessors is a matter of scholarly debate to this day. What is in any case interesting is that two words bandied

8. Ibid., 247–54.
9. Ibid., 261.
10. Congar, *Tradition and Traditions*, 203–4.
11. John W. O'Malley, *Tradition and Transition: Historical Perspectives on Vatican II* (Wilmington, DE: Michael Glazier, 1989), 19-31.

about during the council that seemed to point in different directions—*aggiornamento* (in Italian, updating) and *ressourcement* (in French, return to the sources)—actually worked well in combination to give many of the conciliar documents at least a different tone and a new kind of official language. Both terms, moreover, make sense in terms of a process-oriented approach to church tradition. *Aggiornamento* looks to new possibilities for the reform of church life in the future; *ressourcement* looks to the past history of the Church, above all the early centuries of its existence, for the results of past experiments in living the Christian message. Both are needed to make a decision in the present for what must come next with respect to a specific issue or problem here and now. Prusak, relying on the work of the Jesuit theologian Avery Dulles, lists ten principles endorsed by the bishops at Vatican II that are key to understanding the new role of the Church in the modern world. Three principles "represent new horizons": religious freedom, ecumenism, and dialogue with non-Christian religions. Two, *aggorgiamento* and the reformability of the Church recapture "the early Church's readiness to adapt to new situations and cultures." The remaining five principles, "renewed attention to the Word of God, collegiality, the active role of the laity, regional and local variety, and the social mission of the Church with its emphasis on solidarity with the poor" would seem to be the product of *ressourcement*, returning to the mode of life of the early Church.[12]

Key to "the active role of the laity" in the life of the Church is what *Lumen Gentium*, one of the key documents of the council, describes as *sensus fidei*, the discrimination of what is a matter of faith by the whole body of the faithful: "The body of the faithful as a whole, anointed as they are by the Holy One (cf. John 2:20, 27), cannot

12. Prusak, *The Church Unfinished*, 273; see also Avery Dulles, *The Reshaping of Catholicism: Current Challenges in the Theology of the Church* (San Francisco, CA: Harper & Row, 1988), 20-33.

err in matters of belief. Thanks to a supernatural sense of the faith which characterizes the People as a whole, it manifests this unerring quality when, 'from the bishops down to the last member of the laity,' it shows universal agreement in matters of faith and morals."[13] This sense of the faith exercised by the People of God, of course, is quickly qualified in *Lumen Gentium* as being "under the lead of a sacred teaching authority to which it loyally defers." But even thus qualified, the term "sense of the faith" seems to take into account that the handing-on of the faith from one generation of Christians to another involves the conscious assent of the faithful to what the bishops and the Pope declare to be a matter of true belief and practice.[14] If this assent is not given by the faithful as a whole, then the process of handing on the faith and morals proper to church life, at least on the point at issue, is not fully effective and is in danger of either being ignored or for various reasons deliberately set aside.

At the beginning of this chapter, I proposed that the Church not only has a tradition dating back to the teachings of Jesus as reflected in the Gospel narratives, but that it is itself the process of traditioning, the handing-on of the contents of that tradition to later generations through its ongoing life as an actively engaged community of faith. The claim that the *sensus fidei* is a key principle for understanding what is meant by "the active role of the laity" in the life of the Church is thus fully consistent with my hypothesis that the Church not only has a tradition but is itself fully identified with that process of traditioning, the handing-on of the faith. As Prusak claims in the wording of the title of his book, the Church is unfinished. The process of handing on the faith is still going on not only through periodic decrees of the magisterium (the teaching office of the Pope

---

13. *Documents of Vatican II*, ed. Walter M. Abbott, S. J. (New York: Guild Press, 1966), "*Lumen Gentium*," n. 12.

14. Congar, *Tradition and Traditions*, 253–57.

and bishops) on various points of doctrine and practice, but through the compliance or active assent of the whole body of the faithful to what they are being taught. If either of these components of the traditioning process is not sufficiently involved in the process, then, as noted above, not only the mission of the Church to spread the gospel message, but the Church itself is at risk in its very identity as an actively engaged faith community. Chapter 2 of *Lumen Gentium* speaks of "the common priesthood of the faithful" in distinction from the ministerial priesthood of the clergy, but then adds: "Each of them in its own special way is a participation in the one priesthood of Christ."[15] This common priesthood of the laity is exercised by "receiving the sacraments, by prayer and thanksgiving, by the witness of a holy life, and by self-denial and active charity." I would add to these activities of the laity in the Church their active assent to and compliance with the decrees of the Pope and bishops in matters of faith and morals. Where this assent is not given but instead ignored or resisted, belief in the priesthood of the faithful as intimately involved in the process of handing on the faith from one generation to another is undermined, at least in terms of the point at issue.

This does not mean, of course, that every pronouncement of the Church's magisterium has to be given full assent by the faithful, no matter what the point in question happens to be. The active participation of the faithful in the process of traditioning, the handing-on of the faith from one generation of Christians to another, likewise implies in my view a careful discrimination on their part of required levels of belief or degrees of assent. Otherwise, one encounters in the life of the Church what Gaillardetz calls "creeping infallibility," a tendency on the part of church leaders to make every pronouncement of the magisterium a matter of strict adherence to

15. *Documents*, "*Lumen Gentium*," n. 10.

church teaching on faith and morals. But, as Gaillardetz wisely adds, the faithful should also be alert to the ever-present danger of "consumer Catholicism," choosing what one believes and is willing to put into practice simply on the basis of one's experience or personal convenience. So either in virtue of "creeping infallibility" or as a consequence of "consumer Catholicism," one is often not consciously involved in and responsible for the ongoing process of handing on the faith to one's children, one's students in the classroom, or to still others under one's supervision during their formative years.[16]

Consequences of the Process Approach to Tradition

Given these preliminary remarks on the distinction between tradition as *tradita*, the unchanging deposit of faith communicated to the Church by the Apostles and their immediate followers, and *traditio*, the historical process of handing on the faith to others by the membership of the Church, both clerical and lay, I now ask what would be the consequences of conceiving the Church primarily as a historically grounded corporate process with a provisional institutional structure at each stage of its growth and development rather than as a divinely established institutional reality with a timeless message based on the life and teachings of Jesus of Nazareth as contained in the gospel message. For both clergy and laity, it could be a liberating experience, freeing oneself from the "dead hand" of the past. That is, much as an individual, in reviewing the course of her life to the present moment, sees that she is the product of a number of contingent circumstances and decisions over which she had little or no control, so a person reviewing the history of the Church as an ongoing process would see much better how the Church came to be

16. Gaillardetz, *Ecclesiology for a Global Church*, 237.

what it is today.[17] This is not to deny the role of Divine Providence in guiding the Church through its two-thousand-year history since presumably Divine Providence is also at work in the lives of human beings from day to day. What it instead strongly affirms is that the Church is both a natural and supernatural reality at the same time. That is, the Church exists within the world of space and time and is constrained in its ongoing growth and development by the norms and values of the secular culture in which it finds itself even as it plays a pivotal role in Salvation History, the divine life as shared with other human beings, and in the overall directionality of the cosmic process as God's creation and handiwork. This should be a liberating experience since, as John O'Malley argues, it give us "a greater sense of security amid conflicting signals that come to [us] in the present from every side."[18]

More particularly for the Pope and bishops, however, this realization that the Church is still a work in progress should free them to experiment with significant structural change as well as with needed reforms within the current structure of Church government. This is not to call into question the legitimacy of the Pope as Supreme Pontiff or head of the worldwide Church, nor the role of the bishops in the administration of dioceses and archdioceses, nor finally the leadership role of the pastor in local Christian communities. It is only to say that the existing relationships between Pope, bishops, pastors, and the laypeople that all these clerics are supposed to serve are not engraved in stone as the one and only way for the Church to be organized. As I see it, this willingness to experiment with new structures or at least with new relationships within existing structures as a way to cope with recent changes in the secular order was the unexpected outcome of the working together of *ressourcement* and

17. O'Malley, *Tradition and Transition*, 34.
18. Ibid.

aggiornamento at Vatican II. Research on the early history of the Church made clear, as commented earlier in this chapter, that there was a fluidity in the organizational structure of the early Church: "Jesus had chosen the Twelve and had left an emphasis on service or 'pro-existence,' but he did not otherwise predetermine the development of his community."[19] This awareness of the strictly time-bound character of existing church structure in turn inspired many of the bishops at Vatican II in the spirit of *aggiornamento* to read "the signs of the times" in contemporary culture and to propose necessary reforms in the understanding of traditional Church doctrine, in the language of the liturgy in different parts of the world, and in the proposal to give greater autonomy to the local bishop and to bishops' conferences at the regional level of Church administration. At the same time, out of reverence for the long history of the Church, the bishops emphasized a continuity of their proposals for change and renewal with the decree of Vatican I on papal infallibility and with the traditional hierarchical order of the Church.[20] Admittedly, this confluence of *ressourcement* and *aggiornamento* at the council led sometimes to ambiguity in the interpretation of the documents of Vatican II. But compromise between rival options for decision is often deliberately ambiguous in its wording; only over time does it become clear that the proposed compromise really works or turns out to be either a failure or at best a very mixed success.[21]

O'Malley in *Tradition and Transition* proposed that Vatican II represented not just a reform of Church doctrine and practices within an already-existing Church structure but a reformation in church

---

19. Prusak, *The Church Unfinished*, 56.
20. *Documents*, "Lumen Gentium," n. *18*.
21. John E. Thiel, *Senses of Tradition: Continuity and Development in Catholic Faith* (New York:Oxford University Press, 2000), 153–56.

structure and pattern of life much akin to the sweeping reforms of Pope Gregory VII in the eleventh century as to the centralization of church government and the key role of the papacy in the appointment of bishops throughout the Western world. Likewise, in his mind, it has some affinity with Martin Luther's call in the sixteenth century for a radical decentralization of authority within the Church and for new emphasis on Scripture as the sole source of revelation for the individual.[22] Yet within a process-oriented understanding of the origin and development of the Church over the centuries, there is no way for the Church completely to change its direction and mode of operation. If one attempts such a radical change, either in the Church or in civil society, history has shown that the revolution in question will most likely end in failure and a paradoxical return to the *status quo ante* or something even worse. Whitehead in his little book *Symbolism: Its Meaning and Effect* underscores that point with his claim that "the English revolutions of the seventeenth century and the American revolution of the eighteenth century left the ordinary life of their respective communities nearly unchanged. When George Washington had replaced George III, and Congress had replaced the English Parliament, Americans were still carrying on a well-understood system so far as the general structure of their social life was concerned."[23] The French revolution in the late eighteenth century, on the contrary, was so radical that it did not last, producing instead a reign of terror that was far worse in its effects on the populace than the absolutist monarchy that preceded it. Only after a lengthy period of experimentation did the French finally arrive at a democratically

22. O'Malley, *Tradition and Transition*, 89–97.
23. Alfred North Whitehead, *Symbolism: Its Meaning and Effect* (New York: Fordham University Press, 1985), 76–77.

organized form of government that was achieved with relative ease in the English and American revolutions.

Generalizing even further on this point, one can point to the way in which the evolutionary process on planet earth has proceeded. After the Big Bang, billions of years passed before the earth came into existence within a newly formed solar system. In the beginning of the earth's history only inanimate forms of existence and activity (e.g., atoms and molecules) existed. But when primitive forms of life eventually emerged, they did not replace the existence and activity of those atoms and molecules but rather employed them as the necessary infrastructure for their own existence and activity as life-forms. Finally, several billion years passed before primitive forms of life became complex enough to support first sentient and then rational life. In each of these cases the previously existing structures were not set aside but remained as an integral part of a new and more advanced level of existence and activity within the evolutionary process. So the leaders of the Church, the Pope and the bishops, have no reason to uphold the structures and mode of operation of the Church in past centuries as a necessary safeguard against the challenge of change coming out of an uncertain future. Reading "the signs of the times" and responding to them creatively, on the contrary, is the best guarantee of the continued growth and prosperity of the Church in the future. As Whitehead says in the concluding paragraph of *Symbolism*:

> The art of free society consists first in the maintenance of the symbolic code [the key beliefs and practices of a society]; and secondly in fearlessness of revision, to secure that the code serves those purposes which satisfy an enlightened reason. Those societies which cannot combine reverence to their symbols with freedom of revision, must ultimately decay either from anarchy, or from the slow atrophy of a life stifled by useless shadows.[24]

One may counterclaim, of course, that what Whitehead says about the growth or decay of human societies does not take into account the workings of Divine Providence to keep the Church from either anarchy or a slow atrophy of enthusiasm and vitality among its members. But the basic thesis of this book is that the providential activity of the divine persons within the cosmic process is heavily conditioned by the existing laws of the natural order. As I will make clear in the next chapter, miracles in the sense of a special divine intervention into the normal workings of human life are theoretically always possible but normally speaking very rare.

Practical Implications of the Process Approach

Turning now to the relevance of this process-oriented approach to church life and church tradition for its members on a day-to-day basis, I first note that there are major differences in the respective roles of the clergy and the laity within the Church. That is, the Pope, bishops, and priests work in and for the Church full-time. Laypeople, apart from those in the employ of the Church in some capacity, have other jobs and as a result other responsibilities and interests. As Terrence Tilley notes in *Inventing Catholic Tradition*, "Christians do not live [and work] in the community of practice that is the Church. A person's social location is not determined by religion alone. . . . Conflicts affect the 'selves' we become in practice because we are constituted in multiple roles given by multiple practices. These conflicts often seem most painful when our role-specific duties and rights collide."[25] Handing on the tradition of the Church from one generation to the next succeeds or fails, therefore, not simply on the way that the clergy interpret the tradition and preach it to the

24. Ibid., 88.
25. Terrence W. Tilley, *Inventing Catholic Tradition* (Maryknoll, NY: Orbis, 2000), 183.

laity, but also on the way that the laity receive it and incorporate it into their lives as people that are living in the world and thus are heavily influenced by other practices, other traditions, important for survival and prosperity in that world. While the bishops at Vatican II in the Dogmatic Constitution on the Church at Vatican II, *Lumen Gentium*, have an entire chapter devoted to the role of the laity in the mission of the Church,[26] they may have underestimated the difficulty of fulfilling two vocations at the same time, one as a member of the Church and the other as a member of civil society.

For example, the bishops at the council lay heavy stress on the indispensable role that laypeople play in giving witness to the gospel message to the world: "[T]he laity are called in a special way to make the Church present and operative in those places and circumstances where only through them can she become the salt of the earth. Thus every layman . . . is a witness and a living instrument of the mission of the Church herself."[27] What this otherwise very laudable statement seems to overlook, however, is whether and to what degree those same laypeople are convinced that what the Pope, bishops, and priests are proclaiming makes sense in terms of their own experience of life in the world. They cannot effectively witness to what they themselves may have serious doubts about in terms of its practicality as an effective faith-response to secular practices and traditions that heavily influence the way they and other ordinary people live their lives in today's world. In a word, while most Christian laypeople do not in principle have trouble accepting the teaching authority of the Church in faith and morals, in practice at least some of them may have considerable difficulty in accepting without further question the Church's teaching on highly complex moral issues where people of good will can honestly differ. Here one comes face to face with the

---

26. *Documents*, "*Lumen Gentium*," nn. 30–38.
27. Ibid., n. 33.

tension in contemporary church life mentioned earlier in this chapter between the extremes of "creeping infallibility" on the part of some Church leaders and those laypeople who endorse their strong stand on controversial issues, and "consumer Catholicism" on the part of many other laypeople who feel torn, as Tilley comments, between rival commitments to traditions and practices with legitimate claim to their allegiance and in the end make a practical decision simply on the basis of personal preference.

It is crucially important for the continued growth and the prosperity of the Church in the contemporary world, however, that neither of these extremes in relation to authority be allowed to have the upper hand for an extended period of time. Tension between alternative choices on key moral issues is actually a sign of psychological health, not sickness, for those trying to deal with that tension in a sensible way. One is only experiencing a conflict of interests and expectations that should be present in such important decisions. To quote Tilley once again, "A theology of authority growing out of a practical account of tradition must both recognize the constancies in practice and in authorities that conservatives recognize and also acknowledge the contingency and multiple sites of authority within a tradition that liberals valorize."[28] The claim to the legitimate exercise of divine authority in a given controversial situation is, in other words, often more delicate than one might at first think.[29] The true exercise of authority should lead to a sense of spiritual freedom and inner peace for both the person in authority and for those subject to that person's authority. But an injudicious exercise of authority, even if otherwise well intentioned, will almost certainly lead to a loss of spiritual freedom and of inner peace once again on both sides. This being said, however, personal hardship

28. Tilley, *Inventing Catholic Tradition*, 183.
29. Thiel, *Senses of Tradition*, 102–9.

sometimes arises in complying reluctantly (though freely) with a given decision of church authorities when it impacts on one's customary behavior. What is important for the individual Christian at such a moment, of course, is to trust that Divine Providence will use one's current struggle to comply with church authority so as to achieve in the long run a higher goal or a greater value beyond what here and now can be humanly foreseen. To use a time-honored maxim, there are times when "God writes straight with crooked lines."

To sum up, the respective roles of the clergy and the laity in carrying out the Church's mission to the contemporary world can be understood in two quite different ways. If the Church is viewed primarily as an institutional entity with a relatively fixed historical identity, then it is clear that the clergy (the Pope, bishops, pastors of parishes, etc.) are in charge and that the laity are encouraged to assist the clergy in spreading the gospel message to the contemporary world. The following citation from *Lumen Gentium*, the Dogmatic Constitution on the Church at Vatican II, seems to bear this out: "Pastors of the Church, following the example of the Lord, should minister to one another and to the other faithful. The faithful in their turn should enthusiastically lend their corporate assistance to their pastors and teachers."[30] But, if the Church is viewed primarily as a system or process for handing on the faith to ever-new generations of Christians and non-Christians alike, then paradoxically the laity play a much greater role, whether they fully realize it or not. In that case, the chief responsibility of the clergy is to make sure that the laity spread the gospel message to the world properly. For, the laity by definition are intimately involved in contemporary society as well as in the life of the Church; thus they are in a unique position to give

---

30. *Documents*, "*Lumen Gentium*," n. 32.

powerful witness to what it means to be a Christian in the modern world.[31] To the credit of the bishops at Vatican II, many of them recognized the key role of the laity in the work of the Church and incorporated the following sentences into the chapter on the laity in *Lumen Gentium*: "[T]he laity are called in a special way to make the Church present and operative in those places and circumstances where only through them can she [the Church] become the salt of the earth. Thus every layman, by virtue of the very gifts bestowed upon him, is at the same time a witness and a living instrument of the mission of the Church herself."[32]

Implications for Ecumenical and Interreligious Dialogue

I end this chapter with some reflections on how this understanding of the Church as a system or corporate process for handing on the gospel message to the modern world could affect the Church's role first in ecumenical dialogue among the various Christian denominations and then within the context of interreligious dialogue—the dialogue of Christians with the proponents of the other major world religions. In advance, however, I restate the basic philosophical thesis of this book. While individual entities cannot be integrated into a higher-order individual entity without loss of their own ontological integrity, subordinate processes or systems can be incorporated into more comprehensive processes or systems quite easily. For individual entities are equivalently Aristotelian substances that by definition are self-sufficient in virtue of their substantial form, their own nature and intrinsic teleology. Organic processes

---

31. Cf. here Richard R. Gaillardetz, "How Does the Holy Spirit Assist the Church in Its Teaching?," *Duquesne University Eighth Annual Holy Spirit Lecture* (Pittsburgh: Duquesne University Press, 2014), 11–15.

32. *Documents*, "*Lumen Gentium*," n. 33.

or systems (as opposed to humanly contrived purely mechanical processes) are, on the contrary, transitional or time-bound realities with an ongoing entitative structure and mode of operation that itself keeps evolving both in response to their environment and as a consequence of the dynamic interrelation of their constituent parts or members. One need only think of how a human being changes not only in physical appearance but in psycho-physical organization and complexity as one moves through the various stages of life.

Applying this philosophical insight to the context of ecumenical dialogue among the various Christian denominations, one could propose that all of them be viewed as subprocesses of interpretation of the Christian tradition within an overall ecumenical process of handing on the message of the gospel both to the Christian and non-Christian world. Each denomination offers a unique interpretation of the broader meaning and value of Christianity from the perspective of its own institutional history. Furthermore, this more process-oriented conception of Christian tradition does not require any significant revision or consolidation of internal organizational structure or spheres of authority among the different denominations as a consequence of its acceptance since each denomination has to preserve its own basic mode of operation in order to survive as a privileged subprocess of interpretation of the Christian message within the mega-process of handing on the Christian tradition to the world at large in each new generation. Some higher-level organization like the World Council of Churches should exist, of course, to give Christians a more unified voice in the deliberations of secular organizations like the United Nations or the World Trade Organization for settlement of controversial issues in the contemporary world.[33]

Speaking personally, I would not be unsettled but instead pleased if the Roman Catholic Church became not simply an interested and sympathetic observer at the sessions of the World Council of Churches but a full participant. As noted above, such a decision on the part of the Pope and the bishops would not endanger the traditional institutional structures of the Catholic Church since, like all the other denominations within the World Council of Churches, those same institutional structures heavily condition, though obviously not fully control, the way that the Roman Catholic Church presents its own interpretation of the gospel message. At the same time, what might be called into question would be the assertion in the Decree on Ecumenism at Vatican II that "it is through Christ's Catholic Church alone, which is the all-embracing means of salvation, that the fullness of the means of salvation can be obtained."[34] Immediately preceding that statement, to be sure, the bishops at the Council noted that the other Christian denominations "have by no means been deprived of significance and importance in the mystery of salvation." Rather, "the Spirit of God has not refrained from using them as means of salvation which derive their efficacy from the very fullness of grace and truth entrusted to the Catholic Church."[35] On balance, then, the bishops at Vatican II are implicitly advocating a greater spirit of collaboration among the various Christian denominations in the spread of the gospel to the contemporary world. For such a spirit of collaboration would seem to be very much in line with God's plan for the salvation of the human race.[36]

Furthermore, it is conceivable that the institution of the Papacy within the Catholic Church could grow rather than diminish in

---

33. Cf., e.g., *Documents*, "*Gaudium et Spes*," nn. 4–10, in which the bishops at Vatican II talk about "the Church's" indispensable role in helping the peoples of the world better understand and adjust to a rapidly changing world order.

34. Ibid., "Decree on Ecumenism," n. 3.

35. Ibid.

36. Ibid., n. 4.

importance if the Catholic Church became a full participant in sessions of the World Council of Churches. As Richard Gaillardetz pointed out in *Eccclesiology for a Global Church*, the 1998 statement of the Commission on Faith and Order of the World Council of Churches "spoke cautiously of the value of a universal ministry of 'presidency' over the churches."[37] This ministry of presidency could presumably be exercised by the Pope if his role was understood to be the chosen spokesperson for all the Christian denominations in speaking to governments and other organizations holding the reins of power in the contemporary world. For example, the Pope even now speaks with some measure of authority in addressing contemporary political, economic, and social issues, as the attention given to his remarks on various issues in the secular news media again and again makes clear. That ability to speak with authority on important issues of the day, however, would be noticeably enhanced if the Pope spoke with the backing of all the participants in the deliberations of the World Council of Churches. In principle, then, this more limited exercise of the Papacy with the Pope as the chief spokesperson for the World Council of Churches could be a "win-win" situation for everyone. Moreover, in its own way, such an arrangement among the Christian denominations for the purpose of speaking with a more unified voice in addressing contemporary problems in the world at large would be still another triumph of *ressourcement*, a creative retrieval of how authority was exercised in the early years of the Christian tradition.

Could this more dialogical approach to ecumenical relations among the various Christian deonominations also apply to the relations of these same Christian denominations to the other major world religions? In its brief document on interreligious dialogue

37. Gaillardetz, *Ecclesiology for a Global Church*, 274.

at Vatican II, *Nostra Aetate*, the bishops first noted how important it is to look for areas of agreement instead of disagreement and then added: "From ancient times down to the present, there has existed among diverse peoples a certain perception of that hidden power which hovers over the course of things and over the events of human life; at times, indeed, recognition can be found of a Supreme Divinity and of a supreme Father too. Such a perception and such a recognition instill the lives of these peoples with a profound religious sense."[38] If the proponents of the various world religions in different ways acknowledge the invisible workings of a supernatural level of existence and activity within human life that is at the same time basically compatible with the natural order at all its various levels of existence and activity, then it makes sense to think of interreligious dialogue as a fruitful way for the representatives of these religions together to promote the value of spiritual as well as purely materialistic dimensions of human life.

An example of what I have in mind here is the comment of the well-known Japanese philosopher from the Kyoto School of Zen Buddhism, Keiji Nishitani, in the opening chapter of his book *Religion and Nothingness*:

> Religion has to do with life itself. Whether the life we are living will end up in extinction or in the attainment of eternal life is a matter of the utmost importance for life itself. In no sense is religion to be called a luxury. Indeed, this is why religion is an indispensable necessity for those very people who fail to see the need for it. . . . Religion should not be considered from the viewpoint of its *utility* any more than life should.[39]

---

38. *Documents*, "*Nostra Aetate*," n. 2.
39. Keiji Nishitani, *Religion and Nothingness*, trans. Jan Van Bragt (Berkeley: University of California Press, 1982), 2.

Nishitani was well acquainted with the history of Western philosophy and theology as a result of research for his doctoral dissertation on the notion of the Ideal and the Real in the philosophy of Schelling and Bergson. In addition, he had a strong interest in existentialism, specifically, the philosophy of Heidegger. Finally, he was familiar with the Western mystical tradition with special attention to Meister Eckhart, given the latter's understanding of the Godhead (*Gottheit*) as a transcendent reality beyond God as a personal entity. In any case, as Jan Van Bragt makes clear in his translator's introduction to the English version of *Religion and Nothingness*, "Nishitani came to see the conquest of nihilism as *the* task for himself as well as for contemporary philosophy and for future world culture in general."[40]

In dealing with a non-Christian philosopher of the caliber of Nishitani, Christian participants in interreligious dialogue would have nothing to lose and everything to gain from extended discussion both on the problem of materialistic nihilism in contemporary society and on the need for a new approach to the study of philosophy and theology. That is, for Nishitani and many of his followers in the Zen Buddhist tradition, religion and philosophy are studied with an eye to a concrete existential way of life rather than as strictly academic disciplines that all too often end up in pointless challenges to one another's truth-claims. Moreover, in still other ways interreligious dialogue can make clear to Roman Catholics and the members of other Christian denominations the necessarily perspectival character of their own religious traditions. The transcendent reality of God or the divine in its self-revelation through the workings of nature and human history demands that all participants to interreligious dialogue, but especially Western philosophers and theologians in

40. Ibid., xxxvi.

their normal preoccupation with differences rather than similarities, recognize the inevitable limitations in trying to define what is meant by the natural and the supernatural, the human and the divine. In the end, all parties to the dialogue should recognize that they are dealing with models or symbolic representations of a reality ultimately beyond human comprehension. As Ian Barbour pointed out years ago in *Religion and Science*, "models of the divine are crucial in the interpretation of human experience." But they should not be taken literally. "They are neither literal descriptions of reality nor useful fictions, but human constructs that help us to interpret [religious] experience by imaging what cannot be observed."[41] Perhaps the lasting fruit of interreligious dialogue, therefore, will be a new understanding of what Nicholas of Cusa called Learned Ignorance (*Docta Ignorantia*) and the representatives of many Eastern religions would call nonduality, the coincidence or, better said, higher-order integration of allegedly opposite realities in the conceptual order.[42]

41. Ian G, Barbour, *Religion and Science: Historical and Contemporary Issues* (San Francisco: HarperCollins, 1997), 119; see also Gordon D. Kaufman, *In Face of Mystery: A Constructive Theology* (Cambridge, MA: Harvard University Press, 1993), 3–17. N. B.: In the Conclusion, I offer further comments on Kaufman's understanding of the God-world relationship.
42. Joseph A. Bracken, *God: Three Who Are One* (Collegeville, MN: Liturgical, 2008), 37–38; see also David Loy, *Non-Duality: A Study in Comparative Philosophy* (New Haven: Yale University Press, 1988).

8

Miracles and the Problem of Evil

It might initially seem strange to link analysis of the possibility of miracles, that is, special divine interventions into the workings of the natural order, with the longstanding philosophical problem of evil in a book dedicated to a process-oriented understanding of the God-world relationship. For, if the symbiotic relationship between the natural and the supernatural order of events is working properly, then there should be no need for God to suspend or even to tinker with the normal workings of nature so as to help human beings to deal with some catastrophic series of events in the world of nature or in human history. But de facto catastrophic events do occur with some regularity in both cases. What does that mean either in terms of belief in Divine Providence or with respect to the workings of the natural order? In *The Future of an Illusion*, for example, Sigmund Freud defined what he meant by an illusion (as opposed to a factual error): "Thus we call a belief an illusion when a wish-fulfilment is a prominent factor in its motivation, and in doing so we disregard its relation to reality, just as the illusion itself sets no store by verification."[1] Then he applied the term "illusion" to traditional belief in God as a benevolent Father dealing with his wayward children and concluded that we human beings continue to cherish that belief because it helps us better to deal with the harsh realities of life in this world: God or the gods "must exorcize the terrors of nature, they must reconcile men to the cruelty of Fate, particularly as it is shown in death, and they must compensate them [human beings] for the sufferings and privations which a civilized life in common has imposed upon them."[2]

Yet, if Freud is correct in his judgment here, my argument for the rational plausibility of a symbiotic relationship between the triune God and the world of creation is, in Freud's words, an illusion, well intentioned perhaps but totally lacking in empirical verification. While I concede that there is no direct empirical verification for belief in God and the workings of Divine Providence in this world, I would argue that there is also no direct empirical evidence that belief in God and the workings of Divine Providence is false. From a strictly empirical point of view, neither belief can be vindicated as obviously true. In the end, as David Hume noted in his *Dialogues concerning Natural Religion*, everything depends upon what you are already believe and thus are looking for in judging how nature works.[3] But such a counterargument does not satisfy the deeper question why there is suffering and evil (both natural and moral) in our world. If, as I have consistently claimed in dealing with the God-world relationship, the set of processes proper to this universe are even now integrated into the ongoing process of the divine communitarian life,

---

1. Sigmund Freud, *The Future of an Illusion*, trans. James Strachey (New York: W. W. Norton, 1961), 31.
2. Ibid., 18.
3. Joseph F. Kelly, *The Problem of Evil in the Western Tradition: From the Book of Job to Modern Genetics* (Collegeville, MN: Liturgical, 2002), 140–41. Cf. also David Hume, *Dialogues Concerning Natural Religion* (Indianapolis: Bobbs-Merrill, 1970), Parts X–XI.

then why do we not experience as a result a pain- and suffering-free existence? For that matter, if in the person of Jesus the divine and the human were fully integrated so that he was both fully God and fully human at the same time, why did Jesus suffer as he did to redeem us? Should it not have been enough for him simply to tell us "I am the way, the truth and the life" (John 14:6) and then add "Go and do likewise"? There must then be a way that pain and suffering fit into the divine plan for the salvation of the world not simply as a challenge to be overcome with great effort or as a fitting chastisement by a just God for our past sins, but as a positive factor in the process of our own divinization in and through imitating the pattern of existence and activity exhibited by Jesus during his earthly life.

Suffering Even within God?

For some kind of suffering may well be present for human beings not only in this life but in eternal life if we human beings are to participate fully in the communitarian life of the three divine persons. That is, on the assumption of a dynamically interrelated process- or systems-oriented understanding of the God-world relationship, if Jesus suffered the pain of crucifixion and death in his humanity, he also must have suffered some form of pain and suffering in his divinity. But if Jesus in his divinity suffered the mental pain and physical suffering of the crucifixion, then the Father and the Spirit must have likewise felt pain and suffering as a consequence of Jesus' passion and death on the cross. For all three divine persons together constitute a single corporate process in which what happens to one person likewise happens to the other two persons. What one person does, the others likewise do since they co-constitute a single corporate agency vis-à-vis one another and with respect to the finite world of creation. Hence, if the divine persons experience some form of pain and suffering as a consequence of bringing into existence and sustaining the cosmic process, then we human beings through participation in the divine communitarian life will also experience pain and suffering as well as joy in becoming aware of the role we have played in Salvation History both as individuals and as members of the human race. I will explain all this in further detail in chapter 9 where I take up the issue of life after death and offer philosophical arguments for the rational plausibility of the traditional Christian belief in the resurrection of the body. But for now it should be clear from still another perspective how moving from a substance-oriented approach to a process- or systems-oriented approach to reality could well be a "game-changer" both for the understanding of traditional Christian doctrine and, even more, for the status of the religion-and-science dialogue.

In his youth during the Second World War, Jürgen Moltmann served briefly in the German army before being captured by the Allies and kept in an Allied detention camp for some time after the end of the war. As a result of these experiences, he was clearly influenced by the presence of evil in human life together with the pain and suffering that the presence of evil invariably brings with it. So, after writing *Theology of Hope* in response to the widespread sense of depression and futility in Western Europe after the Second World War, he produced a highly controversial book *The Crucified God*, describing how the experience of pain and suffering are the necessary context for a true understanding of eschatological hope in the redemption and resurrection of the human race and the transformation of the world of creation at the end of time: "*Theology of Hope* began with the *resurrection* of the crucified Christ, and I am now turning to look at the *cross* of the risen Christ. . . . The dominant theme then was that of *anticipations* of the future of God in the form of promises and hopes; here it is the understanding of the *incarnation* of that future, by way of the sufferings of Christ, in the world's suffering."[4]

The sufferings of Christ, however, are also the sufferings of the Father (and by implication the sufferings of the Spirit as well):

> God was not silent and uninvolved in the cross of Jesus. Nor was he absent in the godforsakenness of Jesus. He acted in Jesus, the Son of God: in that men betrayed him, handed him over, and delivered him up to death, God himself delivered him up. In the passion of his Son, the Father himself suffers the pains of abandonment. In the death of the Son, death comes upon God himself, and the Father suffers the death of his Son in his love for forsaken man.[5]

From a philosophical perspective, Moltmann is claiming here that to love is to suffer: "Were God incapable of suffering in any respect, then he would also be incapable of love. If love is the acceptance of the other without regard to one's own well-being, then it contains within itself the possibility of sharing in suffering and freedom to suffer as a result of the otherness of the other."[6] In a word, one feels "com-passion" for the other.

This is a provocative challenge to the classical teaching on the immutability of God. Following the teaching of Plato, Aristotle, and other philosophers in the ancient world, the early Church Fathers took for granted that to change is to be subject to corruption, to loss of one's share in the perfection of unchanging Being. So even though they believed that God is love (1 John 4:16), philosophically they still likened God to Aristotle's Unmoved Mover, that which changes everything else but itself remains unchanged, unaffected

---

4. Jürgen Moltmann, *The Crucified God: The Cross of Christ as the Foundation and Criticism of Christian Theology*, trans. R. A. Wilson and John Bowden (New York: Harper & Row, 1974), 5.
5. Ibid., 192.
6. Ibid., 230.

by anything or anyone else.[7] Moltmann, however, counterargues: "There is unwilling suffering, there is accepted suffering, and there is the suffering of love. Were God incapable of suffering in any respect, and therefore in an absolute sense, then he would also be incapable of love."[8] To love another is to be vulnerable to suffering because of the other. The suffering may come as a result of the unresponsiveness of the other to one's love, or it may come as one's sharing in the other's suffering, however that came about.

Moltmann's description of the suffering within the Trinity (the abandonment of the Son by the Father and the abandonment of the Father by the Son on the cross) and the suffering of the triune God in dealing with the unresponsiveness of creatures to their offer of life and love may be seen by some as overstated, much too dramatic. But in my view it makes unmistakably clear what I said earlier in this chapter, namely, that there is suffering as well as joy in eternal life. If one wishes to share the communitarian life of the three divine persons, a dramatic self-renunciation is required which is, after all, a form of voluntary suffering. If the divine persons fully give of themselves in order to constitute a perfect community or, as Aquinas claimed from a more abstract perspective, if the divine persons exist as themselves only in total self-donation to one another,[9] then any creature who shares that divine communitarian life must also be ready and willing to suffer for the sake of others, for the common good of the community. Over and above that special form of suffering as a participant in the divine communitarian life, there will also be for us fallible human beings the suffering that we will inevitably undergo in seeing "the big picture," the full history of our lives on earth with all its shortcomings as well as successes, when we pass

---

7. Aristotle, *Metaphysics,* trans. Hippocrates G. Apostle (Grinnel, IA: Peripatetic, 1979), 1072b.

8. Moltmann, *The Crucified God,* 230.

9. Thomas Aquinas, *Summa Theologiae* (Madrid:Biblioteca de Autores Cristianos, 1951), I, Q, 29, art. 4.

from this life to the next. Only if we at the same time recognize that we are still loved by the divine persons and likewise loved even by the people that we have wronged while in this life, will we be able to enjoy the blessings of eternal life. All that I would add in terms of my own systems- or process-oriented interpretation of Christian doctrine would be that the suffering love that Moltmann sees as characteristic of genuine human life both here on earth and even more so in heaven is necessarily intersubjective, something that only transpires between subjects of experience that are dynamically interrelated with one another within an ongoing system or process that is open-ended rather than completely determined in terms of its expected results. In other words, one has to move out of a relatively static thing-oriented world governed by classical cause-and-effect relations with others in which full reciprocity is seldom achieved, and become actively involved in a systems- or process-oriented world constituted by dynamically interrelated subjects of experience in ongoing simultaneous mutual causation. Everyone who participates in this kind of enduring intersubjective relationship finds herself both affecting and being affected by others, all at the same time, in ways that are hard to predict ahead of time. Likewise, it is precisely in this kind of free-flowing existential situation that both natural and moral evil are bound to occur and will somehow have to be dealt with. So, while this kind of world produces a lot of unwanted suffering, simply by the way that human beings are forced to deal with it, the existence of natural and moral evil in this world will indirectly produce a great deal of unselfish love that might otherwise not be there in terms of normal human relations. This is not to say that the end justifies the means, but only to realize the validity of the old adage, "no pain; no gain." To love is to suffer; not to love is to miss out on life's greatest challenge (and reward): "God is love, and whoever remains in love remains in God and God in him" (1 John 4:16).

Suffering and the Immutability of God

Writing shortly after the publication of Moltmann's *The Crucified God*, Karl Rahner in his own masterwork *Foundations of Christian Faith* tried to deal with the same issue of adjusting the classical understanding of the immutability of God to post–World War II sensibilities in Western Europe. "If we face squarely and uncompromisingly the fact of the Incarnation which our faith in the fundamental dogma of Christianity testifies to, then we have to say plainly: God can become something. He who is not subject to change in himself can *himself* be subject to change *in something else*."[10] By Rahner's own admission, this is a paradoxical statement. While there is no reason to deny that Jesus was born, lived the life of an itinerant preacher, was arrested and eventually executed by the Roman and Jewish authorities, the doctrine of the Incarnation actually says much more: "[T]his very event we are talking about, this process of becoming, this time, this beginning and this fulfillment is the event and the history of God himself."[11] So God's immutability "is by no means simply the only thing that characterizes God, but that in and in spite of his immutability he can truly become something: he himself, he in time."[12] Some pages later, he adds the following explanation for this restatement of the doctrine of the Incarnation:

> We must share the destiny of God in the world. We do this not by declaring with the fad of God-lessness that there is no God, or that we would have nothing to do with him. We do it rather by the fact that our "having" God must pass again and again through an abandonment to God in death, where God alone comes to meet us in a radical way. It passes through this because God surrendered himself in love and as

---

10. Karl Rahner, *Foundations of Christian Faith: An Introduction to the Idea of Christianity*, trans. William V. Dych (New York: Seabury/Crossroad, 1976), 220.
11. Ibid., 221.
12. Ibid.

love, and in his death this becomes real and manifest. The death of Jesus belongs to God's self-expression.[13]

This passage, in my judgment, sets forth both the depth of Rahner's reflection on the meaning and value of a key Christian belief and at the same time leaves the reader with lingering questions about how this is possible or even doubts that it could actually be true.

For, within the parameters of Thomistic metaphysics, even the revision of classical Thomism known as transcendental Thomism employed by Rahner in this book, one lives within a mental world populated by individual entities in dynamic relationship to one another. But for that same reason, how can one logically claim that God as Infinite Being empties himself into the finite reality of Jesus and that Jesus in response surrenders himself absolutely to the Father so as to become part of the Infinite Being of God? Elsewhere in *Foundations of Christian Faith*, Rahner talks about self-transcendence and "becoming *more*, the coming to be of more reality, as reaching and achieving a greater fullness of being."[14] But "if the metaphysical principle of causality is not to be violated, then this self-transcendence can only be understood as taking place by the power of the absolute fullness of being."[15] Yet a human being "does not simply receive this new reality passively and something caused only by God. On the other hand, the inner power of self-transcendence is to be understood at the same time as distinguished from this finite and active existent in such a way that the power of the dynamism which is intrinsic to the finite existent must nevertheless *not* be understood as constitutive of the *essence* of the finite existent."[16] This is the language of entities in dynamic interrelation, with the one entity having an

13. Ibid., 305.
14. Ibid., 184.
15. Ibid., 185.
16. Ibid.

impact on the other entity and the second entity in turn having an impact on the first entity. This makes sense on the level of finite entities in their dealings with one another, but does it still make sense in the context of the God-creature relationship?

If God is immutable, can God take on a new relationship with a creature and can the creature be so moved by the power of God as to transcend itself and yet still remain itself as a finite entity with a finite mode of operation? For that matter, is God as the power of absolute being an activity, presumably the nature of God communicated to a finite entity, or is God as the power of absolute being an entity, distinct from finite beings as the Supreme Being? As Hegel realized, the Infinite cannot enter into relationship with the finite without itself becoming finite.[17] So God when understood as the absolute Power of Being must be an activity, not an entity, something that can be shared by God and the creature without undermining the ontological difference between them. But is this logically possible within a metaphysics based on the interaction of entities with one another in various forms of contingent relation to one another?

As I pointed out above in chapter 5 on the doctrine of the Incarnation, it makes quite good sense within a systems- or process-oriented understanding of the God-world relationship. The system proper to the humanity of Jesus can be integrated within the system proper to the divine communitarian life that the Divine Word shares with the Father and the Spirit and yet retain its own ontological identity as a lower-order form of existence and activity within the higher-order level of existence and activity proper to the divine persons. The absolute power of being that Rahner seems to identify with God as the Supreme Being is instead in the first place the nature of God, empowering the three divine persons to become

---

17. G. W. F. Hegel, *Hegel's Logic (being Part One of the Encyclopedia of the Philosophical Sciences)*, trans. William Wallace (Oxford: Clarendon, 1975), 140 n. 95.

one corporate reality, a divine community. But in the second place, as the result of a free decision on the part of the divine persons from moment to moment, the absolute power of being or the divine nature is shared with creatures so as to empower each finite entity both to exist in its own right and yet to coexist in dynamic interrelation with Jesus as the Word Incarnate as well as with the Father and the Spirit. The finite creature must somehow choose to accept this offer of unending life with the divine persons. But in the case of human beings, it has to be a conscious choice made either during one's earthly life or at some point after death. Hence, with human beings there is, on the one hand, a real risk of making the wrong choice and yet, on the other hand, the special joy of having made the right choice (as I will explain at greater length in chapter 9).

Natural and Moral Evil
from a Whiteheadian Perspective

This last remark provides an opportunity for me not to solve the problem of evil, but to offer a rationally plausible explanation why it happens so often in a world that even now exists as a contingent but still important part of the ongoing communitarian life enjoyed by the three divine persons. As I see it, evil is invariably the result of a series of decisions, made by finite subjects of experience in their individual and collective response to an ever-changing environment. Whether one is dealing with moral evil consciously committed by human beings or natural evil produced by nonhuman creatures in ongoing competition with one another for satisfaction of deeply felt individual needs and desires, evil is the consequence of a series of decisions made by individual entities in terms of their own needs and desires in opposition to the felt needs and desires of other entities within the process or system of which all are co-participants. Evil, accordingly, is primarily a social or collective reality even though it only comes into being and is sustained in being by the individual decisions of finite subjects of experience. Individuals, in other words, either make the decision to satisfy their own immediate needs and desires at the expense of the other individuals within the process or system to which they all belong. Or they in different ways collectively decide to sustain the common good proper to the process or system by aligning their individual needs and desires to its ongoing mode of operation. Whitehead says much the same in his comments about the ongoing dialectical relationship between individual actual entities as momentary self-constituting subjects of experience and the society (system or process) within which they arose and to which they contribute the pattern of their individual self-constitution before ceasing to exist. "The antithesis between the general good and the individual interest can be abolished only when the individual is such that its interest is the general good, thus exemplifying the loss of the minor intensities [of its own immediate subjective experience] in order to find them again with finer composition in a wider sweep of interest."[18] One could object, of course, that Whitehead is still thinking here in terms of enlightened self-interest for the individual rather than *bona fide* concern for the common good and the good of other(s). But, for whatever reason the choice is made, evil is overcome only through sustained self-sacrifice on the part of individuals to achieve a common goal bigger than themselves as individuals. Evil as a collective reality is only overcome through conjoined effort to achieve a collective good that all can somehow enjoy.

Admittedly, the notion of the ultimate units of reality as being alive, that is, momentary subjects of experience co-sustaining an objective reality greater than themselves as individuals, rather than

18. Alfred North Whitehead, *Process and Reality: An Essay in Cosmology*, corrected edition, ed. David Ray Griffin and Donald W. Sherburne (New York: Free Press, 1978), 15. Hereafter: *PR*.

as being dead, that is, inert bits of matter linked together by chance through the influence of external forces of nature, is a "hard sell" for many natural scientists and other strongly empirical thinkers. But it explains so well how we human beings find ourselves in a world evidently governed by chance and necessity and how we are as a result capable of decisions for both good and evil whose effects are felt far beyond ourselves in terms of the communities and environments to which we belong. Consider, for example, the mini-process whereby an individual actual entity comes into being, makes a self-constituting decision, and passes out of existence after having contributed the structure of its self-constituting decision to the structure of the society out of which it emerged in the first place. Both chance and necessity are at work in this mini-process. That is, an actual entity comes into being within a pre-given field of activity already established in its basic structure and mode of operation by predecessor actual entities. So order is already present in the social context in which the actual entity arises. But the actual entity in making its self-constituting decision is not totally bound by the antecedent social order of the society to which it belongs. That decision is contingent upon the way the subject of experience reacts to its environment in its process of self-constitution. In the end it contributes its pattern of existence either to the ongoing maintenance of an existing social order or to some limited modification of that social order in a new direction. Yet by its contingent decision here and now, an individual actual entity will in some modest way influence the self-constitution of successor actual entities and the enduring structure of the society/process to which they all belong for good or for evil.

In this way, the self-constitution of an actual entity serves as a microcosm for the workings of the macrocosm of the evolutionary process as a whole. The corporate entities that constitute our world (inanimate things, organisms, communities, environments, etc.) have as their ultimate constituents momentary self-constituting subjects of experience in contingent dynamic interrelation with one another and with their surrounding environment. Yet the actual entities in each case are heavily conditioned (though not fully determined) by the preexisting structure of the system/process in which they originate and to which at any given moment they contribute their individual pattern of self-constitution. As Whitehead noted above, an actual entity can find its "satisfaction"[19] in an immediate or a long-range goal. It can seek its own intensity of subjective experience alone or it can widen that scope of its subjective experience so as to find a deeper satisfaction in the achievement of some higher-order goal or value. In general, evil (both natural and moral) arises when the individual actual entity makes its self-constituting decision in the light of an immediate rather than a long-range goal. I say "in general" because the anticipated higher-order "good" of a process/system (e.g., a totalitarian form of government) may actually be destructive rather than creative in its mode of operation. In that case, the immediate subjective experience of the actual entity should be revulsion at the order that it has inherited and to which it is expected to contribute by its own self-constitution. In this case, the really good decision for the actual entity would be to say no to the inherited order of the system and to initiate by its self-constituting decision a new more productive sequence of decisions by its successor actual entities so as to revise the mode of operation of the system or process to which they all belong, that is, to turn it from a destructive to a creative habitual mode of operation (a more just and democratically organized form of government).

19. Whitehead, *PR*, 40.

In brief, then, the decision-making process by which an actual entity achieves actuality and takes its place in a world constituted by dynamically interrelated actual entities is indicative of how both natural and moral evil come into existence and continue to have an impact on the overall cosmic process. Moral evil is simply natural evil at the level of existence and activity of human beings. The only difference is that the actual entities constitutive of human consciousness are much more complex in their process of self-constitution and thus are able to make a conscious choice for the realization of an immediate self-centered goal or for the achievement of a long-term other-centered or communal goal. Nonhuman animal species with sense awareness of their environment, as Joshua Moritz points out,[20] might well be premoral or "protomoral" in their decision-making process from moment to moment. But animal species lacking such sense awareness would be presumably even more constrained in the ongoing self-constitution of their constituent actual entities by the inherited order of the system or process that governs the mode of operation of the organism as a whole. Finally, the actual entities constitutive of plants and even more so of inanimate things like molecules and atoms would have the least amount of spontaneity to alter the order of the system/process to which they belong.

Because they have no evident spontaneity in their existence and activity, atoms and molecules are commonly thought to be non-living, hence constituted by inert bits of matter pushed around by external forces. But quantum physics tells us that subatomic particles exhibit unexpected contingency in their location along the mathematically determined pattern of a wave function. For a

---

20. Joshua Moritz, "Evolutionary Evil and Dawkins' Black Box: Changing the Parameters of the Problem," in *The Evolution of Evil*, ed. Gaymon Bennett, Martinez J. Hewlett, Ted Peters, and Robert John Russell (Göttingen: Vandenhoeck & Ruprecht, 2008), 182–86.

Whiteheadian, this contingency at the most inanimate level of existence and activity within nature is due to internal spontaneity within the subatomic particle rather than to pure chance. So from a Whiteheadian perspective, there is some minimal spontaneity, responsiveness of a momentary subject of experience to its environment, present at all levels of existence and activity within nature even though it is empirically obscured or "averaged out" at the atomic and molecular level of existence and activity by reason of the huge number of actual entities in dynamic interrelation sustaining the inherited order. But wherever there is spontaneity, however minimal, there is the option for good or evil in the self-constitution of constituent actual entities. At the nonhuman level of existence and activity, it is most often natural evil; at the human level of existence and activity it is much more often moral evil. In this way good and evil coexist and mutually condition one another's mode of operation.

A Systems-oriented Approach to Evil

This description of how an actual entity allows for a choice between good or evil in its self-constituting decision would seem to explain how good and evil can be everywhere present in a panentheistic understanding of the God-world relationship, in which the world as a very large but still finite system of interrelated and hierarchically ordered subsystems exists even now within the infinite system proper to the communitarian life of the three divine persons. But it does not explain why the triune God would allow for the existence and even the flourishing of evil (both natural and moral) within the world of creation. Moritz responds to this key question with what he calls the "free-process" defense of the inevitable existence of evil in a divine creation of a world that is fundamentally good, even "very good" (Gen. 1:31). Quoting John Polkinghorne here, he says that in the great act of creation, "'God allows the physical world to be itself, not in Manichean opposition to him, but in that independence which is Love's gift of freedom to the one beloved.'"[21] This is, of course, a theological explanation for the existence of evil in the world, based on the interpretation of Sacred Scripture. But a purely philosophical explanation of the existence of evil in the world is available in further analysis of my systems-oriented explanation of physical reality.

That is, open-ended systems in my view are specifically social or corporate realities that exist and continue to evolve in virtue of the interrelated activity of their constituent parts or members both with one another and in their communal response to the external environment. These parts or members, accordingly, must be self-constituting subjects of experience (actual entities) with the ability to choose either to seek individual subjective satisfaction in their self-constitution or to sustain with other constituent actual entities in the same society/system a long-term satisfaction in the ongoing achievement of a common good, the higher-order system to which they all belong. While in the short-term some of these coexisting subjects of experience can exist primarily for themselves without destroying the corporate reality of the higher-order system to which they belong, in the long-term the great bulk of them must work together, cooperate with one another, to sustain that higher-order system. Furthermore, the corporate agency or effectiveness of the higher-order system vis-à-vis other higher-order systems is intrinsically dependent upon the ongoing interrelated, cooperative activity of its own constituent parts or members. Thus cooperation rather than competition between the constituent actual entities of any given society, and cooperation rather than competition of societies with one another in the gradual emergence of an even

---

21. Moritz, "Evolutionary Evil and Dawkins' Black Box," 179; John Polkinghorne, *Science and Providence: God's Interaction with the World* (Boston: New Science Library, 1989), 66.

more comprehensive higher-order society in the hierarchy of societies, seems to be the way that Nature works.

As Moritz points out, Darwin's deterministic theory of natural selection of individual animal organisms and entire species based upon random mutations in their organic constitution has been challenged and subsequently modified by further empirical research in the field of evolutionary biology.[22] Cooperation between constituent parts or members rather than "winner-take-all" competition among the constituent parts or members of animal organisms is what in the long-term guarantees the survival of the individual organism and the propagation of its genetic inheritance to offspring. Presumably Darwin's theory of natural selection was heavily deterministic because he implicitly viewed the components of an organism as inert material entities related to one another by chance rather than self-constituting subjects of experience capable of influencing one another's process of self-constitution. But, if something more than pure chance is needed to explain the workings of natural selection, then only an open-ended systems-approach to evolutionary biology allows for the necessary symbiosis of parts or members of organisms with one another and symbiosis of organisms with one another for the co-creation and continued existence of communities of organisms and supportive environments (niches) needed to sustain an ecosystem. In other words, "loners are losers" in the long-term evolutionary process on this earth. Only organisms with parts or members that cooperate with one another rather than seek to destroy one another will survive to pass on their genetic inheritance to offspring. But such an understanding of evolutionary biology, in my view, demands for its full theoretical justification a metaphysics or worldview that is based on integrated systems of dynamically interrelated subjects of experience rather than on

22. Moritz, "Evolutionary Evil and Dawkins' Black Box," 165–86.

collections of individual material entities with purely contingent relations to one another.

Nevertheless, in addressing the problem of evil in this world, one still has to offer an explanation for why pain and suffering, even loss of life and extinction of entire species, seems to be a precondition for the possibility of genuine "winners" in the ongoing well-being and potential growth of the evolutionary process. On the human level, one can be sure that there will be more "winners" than "losers" in the workings of the cosmic process through appeal to miracles—periodic interventions of a loving God into the normal workings of the cosmic process—to set right a deplorable situation that Nature with its trial-and-error mode of operation has inadvertently brought about. But the claim to the working of a miracle raises theological questions about why God thus seems to favor some human beings but ignore the needs of others in performing the miracle in question and philosophical questions about whether a miracle could have taken place, given that the laws of nature seem to be rarely, if ever, suspended in their normal mode of operation. Underlying these questions is, of course the deeper question whether the triune God primarily had in mind the coming into being of rational creatures like ourselves as the primary goal of the cosmos process. Does it, in other words, make good sense to say that not only the course of evolution on earth but the entire cosmic process of the universe over the last 13 billion years was bought into existence by divine decision simply to make possible the existence and well-being of the human race? Within the remaining pages of this chapter, I indicate how in my judgment a systems-based approach to the God-world relationship can be helpful in trying to provide a rationally plausible answer to these very complex questions that arise in dealing with the coexistence of good and evil in our world.

First of all, within a hierarchically ordered systems view of the world, one must concede that, while lower-order systems have their own ontological value, yet in the broader scheme of things they exist to support the existence and well-being of the higher-order processes once the latter processes have come into being. That seems to be the price of progress in a world based on fully integrated and hierarchically ordered systems. Otherwise, as Michael Ruse commented in reflecting on how our world works, evolution "is a directionless process, going nowhere slowly."[23] At the same time, however, the system proper to human life does not as a result always have priority over the systems proper to animal, plant, and even inanimate creation within the system proper to this world as a whole. The common good to be achieved in the *symbiosis* of subsystems within the broader system proper to this world would seem ultimately to be to sustain the well-being and prosperity of continued existence of all of them on this earth insofar as that goal can be reasonably achieved without disproportionate suffering to any of them.

Jay McDaniel, for example, argues in *Of God and Pelicans: A Theology of Reverence for Life*: "Despite the possible justification of killing animals for food in certain circumstances, particularly if necessary for human survival, Christians in industrial societies whose lives do not depend on the eating of meat can and should choose vegetarianism. Given the appalling conditions under which most animals are raised for food and transported to slaughter, we are right to follow Peter Singer's advice and boycott the meat industry."[24] A compromise position, of course, would be for Christians and others

---

23. Michael Ruse, "A Darwinian Naturalist's Perspective on Altruism," in *Altruism and Altruistic Love: Science, Philosophy, and Religion in Dialogue*, ed. Stephen Post, Lynn G. Underwood, Jeffrey B. Schloss, and William Hurlbut (New York: Oxford University Press, 2002), 164.

24. Jay B. McDaniel, *Of God and Pelicans: A Theology of Reverence for Life* (Louisville: Westminster John Knox, 1989), 70–71.

who respect the rights of animals to live and die without unnecessary pain to seek a reform of the meat industry rather than to boycott it, namely, to insist that the current techniques employed in factory-farming be eliminated in favor of providing relatively peaceful existence for farm animals before they are killed for human consumption. McDaniel also claims that a concern for animal rights "must be complemented by a concern for land ethics: that is, for the well-being of biotic communities that serve as habitats for living beings."[25] Whether one fully agrees with McDaniel on these issues or not, he makes clear my own proposal that within the system proper to the workings of Nature as a whole the subsystem proper to human life plays a prominent role but not necessarily a proprietary role. We human beings need these other subsystems of existence and activity within Nature to survive and prosper; for, without their continued survival and well-being, we too will be doomed to ultimate extinction.

In brief, then, suffering and pain are part of what it means to be alive in a world of interdependent systems. As Nancey Murphy and George Ellis in their book *On the Moral Nature of the Universe* insist, "Self-renunciation for the sake of the other is humankind's highest good."[26] Such self-renunciation for the sake of others is especially important in our dealings with one another as human beings, but self-renunciation for the sake of others also extends to the nonhuman world, beginning with other higher-order animal species.

Yet, as Christopher Southgate and Robert John Russell point out, "the groaning of creation" (Rom. 8:22) that in some measure is found at all the levels of existence and activity within the cosmic process will only be satisfied for Christians by the scriptural promise of a "new

---

25. Ibid., 71.
26. Nancey Murphy and George F. R. Ellis, *On the Moral Nature of the Universe: Theology, Cosmology, and Ethics* (Minneapolis: Fortress Press, 1996), 118.

creation" in Christ at the end of the cosmic process (2 Cor. 5:17). Southgate, for example, says: "The rhythm of nature's birthing and dying, with all the creaturely suffering that we have seen necessarily attends it, awaited the ultimate self-transcendence of the humanity of Christ, whose dying and rising again inaugurated a new era of possibilities."[27] What Southgate means by "a new era of possibilities" is not only the redemption of the human race in terms of life after death but also the survival in some form or other of nonhuman animal species in the *eschaton*, the fullness of God's kingdom at the end of the world.[28] In similar fashion Russell claims:

> The only possibility for an adequate response to natural theodicy will be to relocate the problem of sin and evil beyond the theology of creation into a theology of redemption, and this will involve two theological moves: 1) The suffering of God with humanity through the cross of Christ must be extended to include the suffering of all life on earth, and 2) the eschatological hope for a New Creation that began proleptically at Easter with the bodily resurrection of Jesus must also be extended to include the participation of all life in the New Creation.[29]

In chapter 9, I offer a more strictly philosophical defense of Christian belief in a New Creation at the end of the cosmic process via my systems-oriented version of panentheism.

Miracles and the Problem of Evil

In the remaining pages of this chapter I first address the philosophical issue whether miracles in the sense of divine intervention into the normal workings of the evolutionary process are possible, given the

---

27. Christopher Southgate, *The Groaning of Creation: God, Evolution, and the Problem of Evil* (Louisville: Westminster John Knox, 2008), 94–95.
28. Ibid., 89.
29. Robert John Russell, "The Groaning of Creation: Does God Suffer with All Life?," in *The Evolution of Evil*, 139.

existing high degree of order in that process, or whether they are even recognizable, given the built-in contingency within those same workings of the evolutionary process through its normal trial-and-error mode of operation. Then I attempt an answer to the theological question of the meaning and value of miracles within the overall scope of Divine Providence so that the triune God may not be accused of favoring the needs and desires of some human beings but ignoring the equally worthy needs and desires of other human beings. There are many distinguished natural scientists who distance themselves from serious discussion of the possibility of miracles not only on methodological grounds (science should seek causes in the natural order for whatever happens in this world) but also because they are quite confident that in due time human reason will uncover all the laws of nature. Stephen Hawking, for example, at the end of his book *The Theory of Everything* asserts (whether seriously or as a parting tease to the reader): "[I]f we do discover a complete theory [of the workings of the universe], it should in time be understandable in broad principle by everyone, not just a few scientists. Then we should all be able to take part in the discussion of why the universe exists. If we find the answer to that, it would be the ultimate triumph of human reason. For then we would know the mind of God."[30]

Hawking seems to be more modest or restrained in his claims for the power of human reason when he comments: "Why does the universe go to all the bother of existing? Is the unified theory so compelling that it brings about its own existence? Or does it need a creator, and, if so, does He have any effect on the universe other than being responsible for its existence? And who created him?"[31] Hawking, of course, knows full well that every rational

---

30. Stephen W. Hawking, *The Theory of Everything: The Origin and Fate of the Universe* (Beverly Hills, CA: New Millennium, 2002), 166–67.
31. Ibid., 165.

system of thought begins with a reality whose origin and existence it cannot explain in terms of the system. It is the empirical "given" which has to be presupposed for the system to make sense. But his reference to a creator who "breathes fire into the equations and makes a universe for them to describe"[32] is worth pondering. Is God strictly bound by the laws that God has set up for creation? Even more to the point, how sure can we human beings be that we have full knowledge of the laws of nature so as to know in advance everything that can happen in this world as a result of these laws? As Keith Ward comments, "It is perfectly in accordance with science to see the laws of nature as primarily 'idealized models' of how things regularly happen, when all external factors are excluded."[33] Natural scientists, in other words, are only able to formulate the known laws of nature by abstracting from the full complexity of the situation under investigation so as to focus on what is here and now empirically measurable in a formal, idealized context.[34] As a result, it is always possible that there are further laws of nature at work in a given situation whose existence or in any case whose practical implications for the situation at hand are still unknown. People in the ancient and medieval world, for example, would have considered human flight through the air at several hundred miles an hour in a heavier-than-air machine a miracle or violation of the laws of nature. But it happens every day in our time because of human discovery of the laws of aerodynamics combined with the growth in technology needed to make use of those laws in the construction of aircraft.

With references to miracles as acts of divine intervention into the normal workings of nature, Ward proposes: "If there is divine causal influence, it must integrate with the law-like nature of physical

---

32. Ibid.
33. Keith Ward, *Pascal's Fire: Scientific Faith and Religious Understanding* (Oxford: Oneworld, 2006), 224.
34. Alfred North Whitehead, *Science and the Modern World* (New York: Free Press, 1967), 58–59.

reality in a rational way, and not be an arbitrary interference with an otherwise smoothly running system. There will be a divine influence for God that preserves the relative autonomy of nature and its probabilistic laws, and the freedom of creatures to accept or reject the invitation to respond to the divine presence."[35] Divine miracles, in other words, are not so much expressions of divine power but of divine wisdom, using unusual events in the natural order to manifest "in an extraordinary way in the physical realm the underlying spiritual basis and ultimate purpose of the cosmos."[36] Hence, the deeper purpose of a miracle such as acts of physical and mental healing by Jesus in the Gospel narratives is not simply to assist the individual in need of healing, but to awaken faith in the one healed and in those who witness the healing that the kingdom of God is at hand. By kingdom of God, of course, is meant the reconciliation of human beings with God their Creator, with one another, and with the circumambient world of nonhuman creation that must accompany full incorporation into the divine communitarian life after death. The writer of John's Gospel seems to have realized this inasmuch as he regularly referred to the miracles of Jesus as "signs" of the age to come (e.g., John 2:11; 20:30) rather than simply as proofs of Jesus' divinity through the exercise of divine power.

My own contribution to the discussion of miracles as manifestation of Divine Providence in the workings of the natural order is based on my overall thesis of a systems-oriented approach to reality. First of all, with respect to the philosophical possibility of miracles I would argue that in a systems-oriented approach to reality the components of a system do not have to be aware of the workings of the system in order to contribute to its proper functioning. The system is a higher-order objective reality, even though it originated in and is

---

35. Ward, *Pascal's Fire*, 226.
36. Ibid., 231.

even now sustained by the interrelated activity of its constituent parts or members. As such, it enjoys its own ontological integrity and mode of operation. From my perspective, this is what is meant by strong as opposed to weak emergence, as already noted in chapter 3 of this book. But if that is the case with systems in general, then presumably it is also true of the God-world relationship, albeit with proper qualifications. That is, God is not emergent out of the hierarchy of systems constituting the cosmic process as a whole; God is rather the transcendent source and ultimate goal of that cosmic process. Yet like higher-order systems vis-à-vis lower-order systems within the cosmic process, God enjoys an independence of those same finite lower-order systems for God's own existence and activity both in terms of the divine communitarian life and in view of God's long-term goals for the fulfillment of the cosmic process. As Ward noted above, God respects the law-like character of the world that God brought into being and now continually sustains. But God has purposes and goals for the final outcome of the cosmic process that are not empirically discernible within the domain of science: "Miracles are not entirely inexplicable; they are just not explicable by known scientific laws. They are not irreproducible, but, since only God can reproduce them, they are beyond the powers of science to reproduce."[37] Here, as I see it, is where religion and divine revelation through the Sacred Scriptures can add to what human beings through careful scientific research can learn about the meaning and value of the cosmic process. For example, as Stephen Hawking admitted at the end of his book *The Theory of Everything*, even if human beings eventually come up with a mathematical formula that fully explains how the world came into existence and even now continues to exist, they still need a Creator God to "breathe fire" into the equations so as

---

37. Ibid., 224.

to put them to work in a cosmic process that really exists (as opposed to one that only exists in the mind of the mathematician or theoretical physicist).

Secondly, a systems-oriented approach to reality implicitly gives priority to systems as socially organized realities to their ultimate components as individual (actual) entities. Admittedly, in *Process and Reality* Whitehead affirms the priority of actual entities to the societies into which they aggregate.[38] But in a later work, *Adventures of Ideas*, he apparently had second thoughts on the matter: "A society, as such, has an essential character, whereby it is the society that it is, and it has also accidental qualities which vary as circumstances alter. But an actual occasion has no such history. It never changes. It only becomes and perishes."[39] In any case, I argue that the priority of systems to their component parts or members reinforces the notion that the miracles of Jesus and other alleged miracles in virtue of divine intervention into the natural order over the centuries have a broader meaning and value than simply giving assistance to a individual in need, however worthy of divine protection he or she may be. There are spiritual goals and values being pursued by God in this miraculous event that transcend the needs of the individual and look to the overall workings of Salvation History within the cosmic process as a whole. A case in point from the New Testament would be that, when Jesus cured ten lepers and only one returned to express his thanks, he told the man who had knelt at his feet: "Stand up and go; your faith has saved you" (Luke 17:19). Presumably for the other nine their leprosy did not come back again by way of divine punishment for their ingratitude. Rather, only the one leper realized that Jesus was doing something far more important for him than curing him of a personally painful and a socially embarrassing debility. That is, Jesus

---

38. Whitehead, *PR*, 18, 35.
39. Alfred North Whitehead, *Adventures of Ideas* (New York: Free Press, 1967), 204.

was giving him on the occasion of a healing miracle a much deeper faith in the long-term Providence of God for himself and for others whom he knew and loved.

9

Resurrection and Eternal Life

Some years ago a collection of essays written by natural scientists and Christian theologians on the projected end of the world was published with the title *The End of the World and the Ends of God: Science and Theology on Eschatology*. It began with the following grim assessment of the projected end of the world from a purely scientific perspective:

> Not only our individual life but also the universe is doomed to physical decay. This scientific insight of the twentieth century poses a great threat to theology and the faith of all religions. How can we believe in God and think of God and God's intentions with the world when human remembrance and history will finally come to an end? . . . If the universe is finite, then there is only silence in the end. In the long run, everything will be in vain.[1]

Yet one of the editors of the volume, John Polkinghorne, in a subsequent book on the same subject sums up his own approach

1. John Polkinghorne and Michael Welker, eds., T*he End of the World and the Ends of God: Science and Theology on Eschatology* (Harrisburg, PA: Trinity Press International, 2002), 1.

to eschatology from both a scientific and theological perspective in terms of four propositions: (1) If the universe is created by God, then it makes sense to believe it will ultimately be redeemed by God from transience and decay. (2) If human beings are creatures loved by their Creator, they must have a destiny beyond their deaths in which all hurts will be healed and God's purpose in creation will be fulfilled. (3) There must be sufficient continuity in the transition from time to eternity to ensure that individuals truly share in the life to come as their resurrected selves and not as new beings simply given the old names. Yet there must be sufficient discontinuity to ensure that the life to come is free from the suffering and mortality of the old creation. (4) The only ground for such a hope lies in the steadfast love and faithfulness of God that is testified to by the resurrection of Jesus Christ.[2]

With all these propositions except the last, I am in basic agreement with Polkinghorne. I disagree that the only ground for such a hope in resurrection and eternal life for human beings is faith in God's love and faithfulness as testified to by the resurrection of Jesus. For, the basic project of this book has been to argue that there should be rational grounds for Christian beliefs, here hope in future resurrection and eternal life, other than simply faith in God's love for us and belief in the bodily resurrection of Jesus on Easter Sunday. Admittedly, there is no direct evidence for these religious beliefs in the current scientific understanding of the laws of nature. But, when confirmed laws of nature are integrated into a philosophical cosmology based on a contemporary evolutionary metaphysics such as I have proposed in this book, traditional Christian belief can be said to be based on both faith and reason, not on faith alone.

---

2. John Polkinghorne, *The God of Hope and the End of the World* (New Haven: Yale University Press, 2002), 148–49.

This is not natural theology in the sense described by John Hedley Brooke: "the attempt to construct rational 'proofs' for God's existence and attributes—a project drawing on the natural sciences, but vulnerable to philosophical critiques and to changes in scientific sensibility."[3] Rather, what I have in mind is a theology of nature: "A theology of nature does not start from science, as some versions of natural theology do. Instead it starts from a religious tradition based on religious experience and historical revelation. But it holds that some traditional doctrines need to be reformulated in the light of current science."[4] This is why I proposed at the beginning of this book that "system" and "process" should replace terms like "nature" and "substance" in our understanding of the creedal statements of the Church. But, to keep this change of terms from being considered pure nominalism, I have also claimed that a new evolutionary metaphysics is required to make sense of the terms "process" and "system," which are increasingly used in both the natural and social sciences. Equivalently, then, I am also aiming in this book at what Ian Barbour calls "systematic synthesis" where "both science and religion contribute to a coherent worldview elaborated in a comprehensive metaphysics."[5] Furthermore, with Barbour I argue that some form of process philosophy is presumably the best candidate for mediating between the rival truth-claims of religion and science "because it was itself formulated under the influence of both scientific and religious thought, even as it responded to persistent problems in the history of Western philosophy (for example, the mind/body problem)."[6] Thus if Aquinas gambled in using Aristotle's secular metaphysics and

---

3. John Hedley Brooke, "Natural Theology," in *Science and Religion: A Historical Introduction*, ed. Gary Ferngren (Baltimore: Johns Hopkins University Press, 2002), 163–64.
4. Ian G. Barbour, *Religion and Science: Historical and Contemporary Issues* (San Francisco: HarperCollins, 1997), 100.
5. Ibid., 103.
6. Ibid., 104.

philosophy of nature to undergird the explanation of the truths of faith in his *Summa Theologiae* in the thirteenth century, now in the twenty-first century perhaps it is time to gamble on process philosophy in some form or other to be the basis for a modern worldview that is compatible with the rival truth-claims of Christian doctrine and the best contemporary scientific understanding of physical reality.

Polkinghorne also acknowledges the need for a more contemporary philosophy of nature by the way he alters the classical concept of the human soul and personhood in the light of his own scientific background:

> Whatever the human soul may be, it is surely what expresses and carries the continuity of living personhood. . . . The atoms that make up our bodies are continuously being replaced in the course of wear and tear, eating and drinking. We have very few atoms in our bodies today that were there even two years ago. What does appear to be the carrier of continuity is the immensely complicated "information-bearing pattern" in which that matter is organized. This pattern is not static; it is modified as we acquire new experiences, insights and memories, in accordance with the dynamics of our living history. It is this information-bearing pattern that is the soul.[7]

Earlier in the book Polkinghorne says that he is presupposing here a philosophical understanding of physical reality known as "dual aspect monism."[8] Yet Polkinghorne does not go on to explain in detail what he means by dual-aspect monism.

Dual-aspect monism clearly implies that one and the same "stuff" or basic physical reality can simultaneously have both mental and material properties. An "information-bearing pattern" for the organization of material components, for example, would be an instance of dual-aspect monism. But then what is meant by

7. Polkinghorne, *The God of Hope*, 105–6.
8. Ibid., 96–97.

"information-bearing pattern"? The term seems to have some affinity with the notion of a formal cause in Aristotelian-Thomistic metaphysics. But much depends here upon whether one interprets Aristotle's understanding of material, formal, efficient, and final causality in a relatively static or in a more dynamic way.[9] Polkinghorne himself simply concludes: "Just as relativity theory has integrated matter and energy into a single account, so one might hope for an eventual discovery . . . that would integrate the triad: matter-energy-information. That achievement would be a significant step in the search for a dual aspect monism."[10] The irony, of course, is that Whitehead's understanding of an actual entity as both immaterial self-constituting subject of experience and its "superject," a material reality that can be prehended by subsequent actual entities, is a clear instance of such dual-aspect monism within an already-existing well-organized metaphysical system.[11] So process philosophy in some modified form might well be the best candidate for a systematic synthesis of the rival truth-claims of religion and science even though Polkinghorne continues to look to the future for such a comprehensive metaphysical scheme.

A Systems-oriented Approach to Belief in Eternal Life

In what follows then I will use my own revision of Whiteheadian metaphysics as set forth in earlier chapters of this book not to "prove" Christian belief in the resurrection of Jesus and the validity of the promise of resurrection and entrance into eternal life for the faithful

---

9. Mariusz Tabaczek, "The Metaphysics of Downward Causation: Rediscovering the Formal Cause," *Zygon* 48 (2013): 394–400.
10. Polkinghorne, *The God of Hope*, 97.
11. Alfred North Whitehead, *Process and Reality: An Essay in Cosmology*, corrected edition, ed. David Ray Griffin and Donald W. Sherburne (New York: Free Press, 1978), 27–28. Hereafter: *PR*.

after the death of the body, but only to argue for the rational plausibility of these religious beliefs in the light of a nonpartisan philosophical cosmology. Accordingly, I first ask what is meant by a physical body. Is it a relatively stable and unchanging entity or is it a set of dynamically interrelated and hierarchically ordered processes that are constantly undergoing minor changes in their internal relations to one another and in their collective relation to an ever-changing physical environment? Clearly, for me it is the latter alternative. Adapting Polkinghorne's notion of an information-bearing pattern to Whitehead's category of society, one can then say that the pattern of self-constitution for each actual entity at the end of its process of concrescence and even more for the "common element of form" for societies of actual entities is an information-bearing pattern.[12] As Whitehead notes in *Process and Reality*, his understanding of a common element of form for societies has an affinity with the Aristotelian notion of substantial form. But, unlike the substantial form within Aristotelian metaphysics that is active with respect to the material elements that it organizes and unifies, the common element of form for a Whiteheadian society is purely passive, the moment-by-moment outcome of the dynamic interrelation of its constituent actual entities.

The value of this Whiteheadian understanding of information-bearing pattern as opposed to the Aristotelian-Thomistic version is that everything that happens to a human person in the course of a lifetime can in principle be recorded in the information-bearing pattern of his life as a body-soul unity (in Whiteheadian terms, as a complex structured society of actual entities stretching over a lifetime). This information-bearing pattern proper to the individual human being could likewise be progressively integrated into the

---

12. Ibid., 34.

comprehensive information-bearing pattern of the divine life as a higher-order process or system shared with creatures, what Sacred Scripture calls "the kingdom of God." If this is possible, it constitutes objective immortality for a human person within the everlasting divine life, although it is not yet resurrection or subjective immortality, namely, conscious awareness of the pattern of one's life after death as a result of full integration into the divine life. Presumably, however, at the moment of death the limitations of life in space-time are lifted; as a result, the human being sees for the first time the entire pattern of her life-history as a small part of Salvation History, the history of the God-world relationship from the Big Bang onwards. Subjective immortality as thus understood is, of course, a gift from the divine persons so as to enable a human being to participate consciously in eternal life. Hence, belief in subjective immortality is a truth-claim based on revelation rather than reason. Objective immortality for a human being within the divine consequent nature, however, can be rationally justified on the basis of Whitehead's philosophical cosmology: "He [God] saves the world as it passes into the immediacy of his own life. It is the judgment of a tenderness which loses nothing that can be saved. It is also the judgment of a wisdom which uses what in the temporal world is mere wreckage."[13]

Naturally, as a philosopher and not a theologian, Whitehead is much more ambiguous on the issue of subjective immortality for finite actual entities within the divine consequent nature. In *Process and Reality*, he simply says: "In everlastingness, immediacy is reconciled with objective immortality."[14] The immediacy of an actual entity as a subject of experience, however, is its subjective self-awareness and responsiveness. Only if this subjective self-awareness

13. Ibid., 346.
14. Ibid., 350–51.

of an actual entity can likewise be incorporated into the divine consequent nature, would the actual entity be both subjectively and objectively immortal within the divine life. Marjorie Suchocki, however, proposes a modest revision of Whitehead's scheme at this point so as to allow for subjective immortality within Whitehead's metaphysical scheme. At the end of its process of self-constitution, an actual entity presumably experiences a brief moment of "satisfaction," a subjective awareness of what it has just become.[15] Then, if God prehends the actual entity precisely in that brief moment of satisfaction, God can endow it with both subjective and objective immortality within the divine consequent nature. In this way, as Suchocki comments, an actual entity is twice-born: "first through its own self-creation, and second through God's total prehension of this self-creation. Its temporal birth is as fleeting as the concrescence that generated it; its divine birth, grounded in God's own concrescence [as the only enduring actual entity], is as everlasting as God. The occasion is therefore reborn to subjective immortality" within the divine life.[16]

Supposing the legitimacy of this modest rethinking of Whitehead's metaphysical scheme, one can then further claim that when human beings as complex societies of such subjectively immortal actual entities die and are fully incorporated by God into the divine life, they experience themselves for the first time as a finished product or completed reality. That is, upon incorporation into the divine life at the moment of death human beings will see their true self-worth both in the eyes of other human beings and, above all, in the eyes of God. This moment of personal enlightenment might well be reason for unexpected surprise and joy, or it might be reason for acute

15. Marjorie Hewitt Suchocki, *The End of Evil: Process Eschatology in Historical Context* (Albany: State University of New York Press, 1988), 85–89.
16. Ibid., 96.

embarrassment and pain. More likely, it will be a cause of both joy and pain at the same time as one sees oneself for the first time as who one really is. Furthermore, this moment of full self-understanding for human beings at the moment of death will presumably involve a decision either to accept or to reject the full truth about oneself. If one decides to accept the truth of one's role within Salvation History, even if it is here and now somewhat embarrassing or even painful, one will be in heaven. If on the contrary one decides to reject it as too humiliating, too contrary to what one has always believed about oneself, then one will end up in a hell of one's own making. Surely, the divine persons will not leave that human being alone in such an isolated existence. They will keep extending to that unhappy human being the offer of divine forgiveness and the chance for a life of happiness with themselves and all the redeemed finite creatures of this world. In this way, over time that person may well repent of this decision to live apart from others and make the decision to ask for forgiveness from the divine persons and all those whom she offended during her earthly life. When and if this happens, that person will be in heaven. As John's Gospel makes clear, to know the truth about oneself and to accept it is finally to be free to enjoy a new and better life (John 8:32).

Implicit in this argument, of course, is a prior understanding of the relation between time and eternity. As I see it, our human experience of time is always an experience of "perpetual perishing,"[17] an ongoing flow or continuous movement from the future in terms of what one sees as possible for oneself right now, into the present where one makes a decision about what to do next, and from there into the past as a fully determined event in one's life-history.[18] Eternity,

17. Whitehead, *PR*, 340.
18. Robert Cummings Neville, *Eternity and Time's Flow* (Albany: State University of New York Press, 1993), 95–105.

on the contrary, as can be imagined even here and now, will be experienced as a dynamic togetherness of past, present, and future. In eternity one sees the fullness of one's life-history as an integral part of a higher-order process that never ends, namely, the divine communitarian life or, in biblical terms, the kingdom of God. A human being who has entered into eternal life thus lives in both time and eternity simultaneously. In eternity one sees one's life-history both as a set of past moments and as a completed whole. Thus understood, one's experience of eternity is not timeless but an ongoing process of self-transcendence within the even bigger process of the divine life. Life in eternity with the divine persons, accordingly, has its own time-system or duration that is entirely different from the ongoing succession of moments in this life. "With the Lord one day is like a thousand years and a thousand years like one day" (2 Pet. 3:8). All this, of course, is fully consistent with a systems-oriented understanding of reality in which higher-order and lower-order systems harmoniously coexist and impact on one another without loss to their individual ontological integrity as a result. Time exists as itself within eternity, and eternity is shaped by what happens in time. That is, we remain what we have become through our time in this world, however long or short that may be, and yet we are simultaneously transformed by our ongoing participation in the divine communitarian life as a social reality so much bigger than ourselves as individuals.

But what is to be said about the resurrection of the body within this line of argument? The human body, after all, is not self-aware except in and through the workings of the mind. Furthermore, in contrast to the mind or soul, the body is a tangible physical reality that undergoes many changes throughout life and after death rapidly decomposes. Within a process-oriented understanding of physical reality, however, the body of a human being or of any other living organism is not a fixed material reality, but an intricate set of physical processes or systems. These processes or systems in and through the interrelated activity of their constituent actual entities generate enduring patterns of existence and activity for the body as a unified organic whole. It is these patterns of existence and activity (rather than the body as a material thing) that survive the passage of time. But if enduring patterns for the human body are progressively incorporated into what Whitehead calls the divine consequent nature (in my scheme the comprehensive structured field of activity for three divine persons and all their creatures, i.e., the Kingdom of God), then everything that ever bodily happened to a human being is preserved for all eternity in the same way that all the conscious events of that person's life are preserved within the structured field of activity proper to the divine communitarian life or the kingdom of God.

Accordingly, if a human being after the death of the body can recognize the enduring pattern of all the events of its life on earth, then that same human being is still a bodily person even after entrance into eternal life. That is, the person who has entered the kingdom of God experiences on a feeling-level and thus identifies with all the events of his life in the body over an entire lifetime. But at the same time that person transcends whatever pain or suffering accompanied those past events in and through the possession of a new "glorified body" (1 Cor. 15:42-44) that he or she possesses as part of participation in the kingdom of God. This is the new creation (Rev. 21:1-5) destined by the divine persons as the next stage in Salvation History for humankind. For the same reason, it is also a new beginning in the history of the cosmic process even apart from human beings. That is, the patterns or structures of existence and activity that were constitutive of all the animals, plants, and even inanimate things in the past history of the earth still belong to them as the equivalent of their "glorified body" within the overall structured field of activity proper to the kingdom of God. Nothing is lost; everything is saved, albeit in a transformed state within the divine life.

Related Questions about the Credibility of this Hypothesis

Yet still other questions need to be answered here: one from the perspective of the scientific community about the eventual end of the world as a result of the workings of entropy on a cosmic scale; the other from Christians in terms of traditional belief in the Last Judgment as a fitting close to Salvation History. I answer these important questions separately. With respect to the anticipated dissolution of the physical universe as a result of the workings of entropy, I argue once again that from moment to moment of the cosmic process only patterns of existence and activity, not physical entities as such, survive. These patterns are incorporated into what Whitehead calls the divine consequent nature or what I prefer to call the inner life of God as shared with finite creatures—in biblical terms, the kingdom of God. So if the visible order and complexity of the universe gradually collapses in accord with the principle of entropy and eventually is reduced to its elementary components, subatomic particles, that universe still survives as an overall corporate reality within the divine consequent nature or the kingdom of God. Within Whitehead's scheme, the past universe and all the objectified actual entities within it enjoy objective immortality in the memory of God as the sole nontemporal or enduring reality. In my own conception of the kingdom of God, the final actual entities for every animal, plant, or inanimate thing in the universe that has just come to an end still exist in their own right as immaterial subjects of experience that enjoy their own form of subjective immortality within eternity, however simple it may be by comparison with the subjective immortality of human beings within eternity as highly complex body-soul realities.

In this way, there is no tragic loss of what human beings and the other creatures of our current universe may have achieved by the way they shaped the world around them. Everything of value is preserved in different ways within the divine consequent nature for Whitehead and the kingdom of God in my scheme. In fact, the end of one universe could possibly become the starting-point for another universe based on another Big Bang or cosmic explosion of energy within both Whitehead's cosmology and my own. For Whitehead the divine consequent nature is without beginning or end. Within my cosmological scheme the structured field of activity proper to the divine persons and shared with all the creatures from one universe could also be the context for still another universe or set of universes to follow our own at its demise. Moreover, there should be no problem of overcrowding within the divine life if it is home to several universes in succession, because all that survives from any given universe are immaterial subjects of experience: the divine persons and the final set of actual entities for all the finite persons and things that ever existed in that universe. Being immaterial realities, they take up no physical space as they prehend (contemplate) the magnificent order and complexity of their universe that now exists as an intricate set of patterns woven into the fabric of the divine life. Given the rational plausibility of these reflections about the end of the world, there should be no despondency or sense of futility for contemporary human beings in thinking about the eventual collapse of our universe because of the inexorable workings of the principle of entropy. In the end, what really counts is the cosmic process itself as a triumph of divine and creaturely creativity. As such, it gives glory to God as its transcendent source of existence and activity and deep satisfaction to finite creatures insofar as they are able to appreciate what they have helped to bring about.

The other question has to do with traditional Christian belief in the Last Judgment at the end of the world and the resurrection of the body as well as the soul for eternal life either with God in heaven or apart from God in hell. Even though it runs counter to the literal description of the Last Judgment in Sacred Scripture, I myself am inclined to believe that the judgment of the individual human being at the moment of death and the Last Judgment of the entire human race at the end of the world happen at the same time for each person who has died. At the moment of death one sees one's past life as a completed reality in and through recognition of the pattern of one's life that has been woven into the complex structure of the kingdom of God. But, if the cosmic process as a whole is only part of the duration or time-span of the divine communitarian life, then every moment in the duration or time-span of an individual's life would be part of the divine "now" or present moment of the divine life. On the assumption that the human being after the death of the body is no longer constrained by the limits of space and time proper to the cosmic process but instead is incorporated into the space-time parameters or "duration" of the divine life, then one's birth, entire earthly life, death, Particular Judgment, and the Last Judgment for the whole human race are all taking place at the same "time" for that human being.

Yet isn't this too big a departure from the texts of Sacred Scripture about the Last Judgment? Everything depends upon how literally one interprets the texts in question. Here I side with Kathryn Tanner in her belief that these texts are metaphors with a religious meaning for the religious believer rather than prophecies of historical events to come. To quote Tanner, a Christian eschatology should have "no more stake in whether or how the world ends than a Christian account of creation has in whether or how the world had a beginning (say, by means of a big bang)."[19] In both cases, one is dealing with metaphors or images rather than scientifically established hypotheses. The metaphor of God's creating the world in seven days (Genesis 1 & 2) and the metaphor of God bringing the current temporal order to a close with a final judgment forever separating the saved and the damned and making all things new (Matt. 25:31-46; Rev. 21:1-8) are both intended to convey the religious truth that creation is dependent on God for its finite existence and activity whether it has a temporal beginning and end or not.[20] Thus understood, Christian eschatology should not be focused on the future of the temporal order but on one's relation to God here and now: "By grace—by virtue, that is, of a life-giving relationship with Jesus—we enjoy something like the sort of life in God that Jesus lives. We (and the whole world) are to live in God as He does, through Him . . . like Christ, the only existence we have is in and through God."[21]

In that same essay for *The End of the World and the Ends of God*, Tanner advocates a more comprehensive cosmic teleology: "Such an eschatology would be comprehensively cosmic in the sense that its preoccupations would not center on the world of the future but on the world as a whole and on an ongoing redemptive (rather than simply creative) relation to God that holds for the world of the past, present and future."[22] Noting that Sacred Scripture, above all, the epistles of Saint Paul, speak frequently of a passage from life to death as a result of a personal conversion to Jesus, his teaching, and way of life, she argues that "after death (as before death) we are taken up into the life of God as the very mortal creatures we are. It is only in God

19. Kathryn Tanner, "Eschatology without a Future?," in *The End of the World and the Ends of God*, 224.
20. Ibid., 225.
21. Ibid., 230.
22. Ibid., 225.

that we gain immortality; considered independently of this relation to God we remain mortal. We are immortal pre- and post-mortem only in virtue of our relation to an eternal God."[23] Yet, in her view, this approach to the deeper meaning of Christian eschatology does not undercut work for a better future in this world in God's name. "Action is the proper response to take with respect to a world that it is not the way it should be, because, although human action does not bring about life in God (that is God's unconditional gift to us), human action of a certain sort [here and now] is what life in God requires of us."[24] One does not depend upon success in working to change the world in order to continue to believe in God's providential care for the world in which we live. "A hope, then, to counter despair in the present comes not from the idea that God Himself is the coming future; but from the fact that despite appearances to the contrary in a world of sin, God has in fact already assumed our lives in Godself [the inner life of the immanent Trinity]."[25]

In his book *Space, Time and Incarnation*, Thomas Torrance follows a similar line of thought with respect to the relation between time and eternity. He sets in tension with one another two basic Christian beliefs about the doctrine of the Incarnation. First, "the Son of God has become man without ceasing to be the God He ever was." Second, "after the Incarnation He is at work within space and time in a way that He never was before."[26] So, even though God in His eternal self-existence "remains quite free and cannot be known in the determinate way things are known" and "creation also remains free in its utterly contingent character and is therefore to be known in its natural processes only out of itself,"[27] yet "Jesus Christ is the

23. Ibid.
24. Ibid., 234.
25. Ibid., 235.
26. Thomas F. Torrance, *Space, Time and Incarnation* (New York: Oxford University Press, 1969), 53.

place of contact and communication between God and man in a real movement within physical existence, involving interaction between God and nature, divine and human agency."[28] Hence, "the transcendent God is present and immanent within this world in such a way we encounter His transcendence in this-worldly form in Jesus Christ, and yet in such a way that we are aware of a majesty of transcendence in Him that reaches out infinitely beyond the whole created order."[29] This perspective on the doctrine of the Incarnation is logically opposed to the claim by Ted Peters and others that the economic Trinity with its emphasis on the work of the Divine Word and the Holy Spirit in Salvation History is the eschatological fulfillment of the immanent Trinity: "God becomes fully God-in-relationship when the work of salvation—when the economic Trinity—is complete."[30] It may well be true that the world "becomes fully itself only by transcending itself, by transcending its current state of otherness over against God."[31] But this self-transcendence of the world will be accomplished by its integration into the immanent Trinity, the higher-order process of the divine life from all eternity, not by claiming that the immanent Trinity "is consummated eschatologically" through integration into the time-bound lower-order process of the economic Trinity.[32]

In a later book *Space, Time and Resurrection*, Torrance describes the risen Jesus or cosmic Christ as the Lord of space and time.[33] Here too, he keeps time and eternity, the humanity and divinity of Jesus in dynamic interrelationship:

27. Ibid., 59.
28. Ibid., 78.
29. Ibid., 79.
30. Ted Peters, *God as Trinity: Relationality and Temporality in Divine Life* (Louisville: Westminster John Knox, 1993), 181.
31. Ibid.
32. Ibid.
33. Thomas F. Torrance, *Space, Time and Resurrection* (Grand Rapids: Eerdmans, 1976), 159–93.

However difficult it may be for us, the message of the resurrection is inseparably bound up with the objective structures of the space and time of the created cosmos, but the fundamental reality inherent in it all, which the resurrection itself unveiled, is that in Jesus Christ God himself has come in person into our world and manifested himself in the body, in the wholeness and undiminished integrity of human being, yet in such a way as to redeem and transform what he has assumed through the birth, life, passion and resurrection of Jesus.[34]

Otherwise, Jesus' claim in the Fourth Gospel—"I am the way and the truth and the life. No one comes to the Father except through me" (John 14:6)—is incredible, a statement that could only be made by an extremely arrogant human being completely out of touch with reality. One can always object, of course, that we have no assurance that Jesus himself actually spoke these words. Perhaps it was the writer of John's Gospel putting words into Jesus' mouth as verbal confirmation of his own religious belief about Jesus. Yet even here one would have to concede that this otherwise extraordinary belief of the sacred writer in the divinity of Jesus came from his experience of the risen Jesus as both divine and human at the same time.

Torrance then makes an important comparison between Christian belief in the divinity of the risen Jesus and the established beliefs of natural science about the laws of nature. They "overlap with one another within the structures of space and time which are the bearers of rational order within the created universe, and therefore are intelligibly interconnected."[35] But they also inevitably diverge from one another within that same area of overlap and interconnection, since theology inquires into the transcendent source and ground, and natural science into the contingent nature and pattern, of all created order. Hence, two different methodologies and two different rationally ordered thought-systems can end up producing a level

34. Ibid., 179.
35. Ibid., 180.

234

of intelligibility for a concrete empirical event or a theoretical hypothesis about that event that would be impossible for either of them acting separately. This possibility is fully in accord with my own systems-oriented understanding of reality wherein a higher-order system and lower-order system can be in dynamic interrelation, with each having significant influence on the mode of operation of the other and yet without either system fully incorporating the other into its own ongoing self-identity in what is natural versus what is deemed supernatural.

Scriptural Accounts of the Resurrection and its Aftermath

One final question or objection must be dealt with before bringing this chapter on resurrection and eternal life to a close. If Jesus in his human nature entered into eternal life immediately after dying on the cross, what is one to say about the empty tomb and the appearances of Jesus to the holy women and the Apostles on Easter Sunday in the resurrection accounts of the four Gospel writers? This is not an easy question to answer since it involves both an explicit reference to historical evidence and an implicit appeal for faith in a new way of life inspired by the life and preaching of Jesus in the Gospel narratives. Yet both sources of information should be involved in whatever answer one ultimately employs. I would argue, for example, that the best historical evidence for the claim that Jesus died and rose again is that the message of Jesus during his earthly life continues to be a source of inspiration for those who call themselves Christians. Trusting in the historical reality of the resurrection of Jesus Christ as empirical verification of Jesus' saving message has dramatically changed the lives of many Christians over the centuries since Jesus lived and died. They have moved from a basically self-centered to an other-centered form of personal existence and activity, attaching much more value to love of God and neighbor than to protection of the self with its narrow interests and values. The alleged fact of the empty tomb on Easter Sunday morning only serves as indirect confirmation of what they already believe in terms of their own religious experience.

Moreover, no one saw the resurrection take place; no one watched as the badly disfigured corpse of Jesus suddenly became a living human being again, this time with a "heavenly" body (1 Cor. 15:36-40). As a result, there might be other possible explanations for the empty tomb that would not demand supernatural intervention but in their own way would still be in accord with the laws of nature. For example, if the human body (as I have claimed) is a hierarchically ordered set of physical systems that after death slowly but surely collapse, until only atoms and molecules that are invisible to normal sight remain, then conceivably God could arrange for that process of gradual decomposition of Jesus' body to be enormously accelerated and thus be complete by Easter Sunday morning when the stone was rolled back by an angel (Matt. 28:2). This explanation, moreover, seems to be in accord with the law of the conservation of energy. That is, the physical energy that kept Jesus alive during his lifetime was not completely destroyed but preserved as part of the total energy-pool of the cosmic process for use elsewhere. This, of course, is conjecture on my part rather than proof of what actually happened on Easter Sunday morning.

Likewise, the various Gospel narratives that describe the appearances of the risen Jesus to his followers on Easter Sunday testify not only to the reality of the resurrection but even more strikingly to the fact that Jesus no longer inhabits an earthly body subject to the limits of space and time. When he appears to the disciples in the upper room on Easter Sunday, for example, he does not first knock and ask to be admitted into their presence behind locked doors. He is suddenly there, comforts the disciples in their grief at his totally unexpected death, and then just as suddenly is no longer there (John 19:19-29). When Mary Magdalene realizes that the stranger standing behind her at the empty tomb is not the gardener but Jesus himself in his risen body, she rushes to embrace him (John 20:11-18). But he gently tells her that this expression of love for him is no longer appropriate since he has "not yet ascended to the Father." Jesus seems thereby to imply that what she sees and tries to embrace is only a temporary and partial manifestation of his new life in full union with the Father and the Holy Spirit within the divine communitarian life. After the Ascension he would instead be present to his followers interiorly (i.e., in their minds and hearts through the power of the Holy Spirit), not exteriorly through some sort of unexpected physical appearance. Finally, at the Parousia or the coming of the risen Jesus on the clouds of heaven in great power and glory at the end of the world (Mark 13:26-27), it will be the divinity of Jesus more than his humanity that will be somehow revealed not only to the followers of Jesus but also to all the peoples of the world.

In brief, then, accounts of Jesus' resurrection and of his post-resurrection appearances to his followers are a blend of reasonably reliable historical testimony and overt religious belief in a reality that transcends the natural order and thereby testifies to the reality of a higher-order pattern of existence and activity beyond what is naturally possible. This accords very nicely with my own systems-oriented understanding of reality wherein a higher-order and a lower-order process can be dynamically linked in producing one composite reality without loss to the ontological integrity of either level of existence and activity in its own mode of operation. What I am proposing here, of course, is only a theory, not a factual statement, about the nature of reality. But I am encouraged in putting forth this hypothesis by what I take to be a similar line of thought in *Space, Time and Resurrection* by Thomas Torrance. I end this chapter by summarizing what I believe to be his understanding of the relation between the natural and supernatural in human life and then indicate how his proposed cosmology and my own allow for both the transcendence of God to creation and the immanence of God in creation to be simultaneously fulfilled.

In the final chapter of *Space, Time and Resurrection* titled "The Lord of Space and Time," Torrance sums up his own understanding of the interconnected workings of the natural and the supernatural in the event of the resurrection of Jesus as follows:

> In fulfillment of his eternal design God has acted in the resurrection of Jesus from the dead in such a way that, far from setting aside or infringing or interfering with the spatio-temporal order of the universe which he created (and which we try to formulate in what we call "laws of nature"), he accepts and affirms its reality, but he introduces into the situation a transcendently new factor which brings about an utterly astonishing transformation of it which is quite inexplicable in terms of anything we are able to conceive merely within the intelligible structures of the world, or in accordance with our scientific formulations of them.[36]

What he seems to imply here and elsewhere in his book is that one and the same empirical event can allow for two quite different explanations. First, the resurrection of Jesus is a one-time, nonrepeatable event in the natural order that has definite empirical consequences for Jesus' followers but that in itself cannot be explained in terms of the known laws of nature at present. Second, for a Christian who believes in the divinity of Jesus, his resurrection on Easter Sunday is historically connected both with the doctrine of the Incarnation and with belief in the Second Coming of Jesus, the Parousia at the end of the current temporal order. The three

36. Ibid., 190.

mysteries of faith combine to give a rational explanation of the deeper meaning and value of Jesus' life, death, and resurrection, and ultimate vindication as the Lord of space and time.[37] That is, if the Son of God is born into this world as a human being, he will in due time die either by natural causes or violently at the hands of his enemies; but afterwards he will just as inevitably rise from the dead and live a new life as a result of the singular self-giving way of life which he both taught to others and personally practiced his entire life. "Whoever wishes to save his life will lose it, and whoever loses his life for my sake and that of the Gospel will save it" (Mark 8:35).

There is then no contradiction involved in studying the alleged event of the resurrection of Jesus in terms of two interrelated thought-systems: from a naturalistic perspective as the historical starting-point of Christianity, one of the major world religions, and from a supernatural perspective as one of the three key doctrinal beliefs of institutional Christianity. The Christian interprets the resurrection of Jesus, so to speak, from within the Christian belief-system, and the professional historian interprets it from outside that belief-system as a major factor in the empirical origin and historical growth of institutional Christianity. Moreover, from the perspective of natural science, in line with proper scientific method one should suspend judgment whether or not it really happened as described, given current understanding of the laws of nature, and how it might have come about through supernatural rather than natural causal forces. In this way, the autonomy of the natural and supernatural orders is respected even as one concedes that for the Christian believer there is a higher-order layer of meaning and value if one can find a way to synthesize the truth-claims of the natural and the supernatural levels of existence and activity within nature in

37. Ibid., 154–55.

one comprehensive explanatory scheme or philosophical/theological cosmology.

Torrance seems to be making much the same point in his claim that the risen Lord meets us only on the actual ground of the historical Jesus:

> The whole life of Jesus from his birth to his resurrection and beyond is an indivisible continuum, in which the historical Jesus is consistently and indissolubly one with the life of the risen Jesus, so that now after the resurrection the historical Jesus confronts us only as suffused with the light of the risen Lord. . . . [T]he life of the risen Jesus takes up the life of the historical Jesus into itself as its permanent material content so that the risen Lord meets us only on the actual ground of the historical Jesus, in his birth, life and passion.[38]

The Gospel narratives, in other words, are both reasonably reliable historical accounts of the public ministry of Jesus in Judea and Galilee before his unexpected arrest, trial, and execution at the hands of his enemies, and at the same time faith-documents, theological interpretations of the meaning and value of Jesus' message and way of life. Accordingly, while historico-critical analysis of the Gospel texts is quite important in understanding how these documents relate to one another and to various outside sources, both oral and written (e.g., the so-called "Q" document), it "has only a limited validity, beyond which it can only lead to the destruction of meaning."[39] That is, it would artificially separate empirical and theoretical components in the New Testament text and inevitably impose the interpreter's own subjective bias on the proper interpretation of that text. Here too, objective reason and subjective belief in divine revelation should work in tandem with one another, rather than be seen in competition

38. Ibid., 169.
39. Ibid.

with one another, within the mind of the spiritually minded reader of the sacred text.

Thus with reference to the Gospel narratives dealing with the bodily resurrection of Jesus on Easter Sunday and his intermittent appearances to his followers during a period of forty days until his ascension into heaven, one should be particularly careful to respect the different methods of inquiry and truth-claims of legitimate historical scholarship and authoritative religious belief. They are not in open contradiction with one another, but their full compatibility is likewise not apparent. For example, an open-minded reading of these same texts reveals minor inconsistencies in the factual account of what really happened on Easter Sunday and afterwards. Each of the Gospels has a slightly different story-line, attesting to the different oral traditions about the risen Jesus at work in the early Christian communities. So a professional historian would necessarily have to suspend judgment on the precise details of what happened on Easter Sunday. Yet the same professional historian could readily join with Christian theologians in noting how the followers of Jesus were profoundly changed in their understanding of Jesus and his message as a result of what they experienced on Easter Sunday. These followers of Jesus lost their antecedent "fear of the Jews" (John 20:19) and at the risk of their own lives openly proclaimed the Good News of salvation in Jesus Christ through the power of the Spirit to anyone who would listen to them. As a result, they converted a great number of people to a Christ-like way of life everywhere in the Mediterranean world and beyond it, "baptizing them in the name of the Father, and of the Son, and of the Holy Spirit, teaching them to observe all that I have commanded you" (Matt. 28:20). For the professional historian, why this happened remains unclear. For the Christian theologian, it is quite clear: "And behold, I am with you always, until the end of the age" (Matt. 28:20). Belief in divine revelation thus adds a new level of meaning and value to the bare historical account of what happened on Easter Sunday and in the years that followed up to the present day.

Postscript

Robert John Russell in a recently published book uses his broad knowledge of theoretical physics and Christian systematic theology to outline a way in which natural science can illuminate the traditional beliefs of Christianity, and the way in which these religious beliefs when suitably revised in the light of contemporary natural science can help to resolve longstanding metaphysical issues in the natural sciences.[40] With this project, I am completely in accord since it nicely correlates with the basic project of this book. But I have reservations about Russell's strong reliance on the theology of Wolfhart Pannenberg to set forth his own understanding of the philosophical relation between time and eternity in connection with the doctrine of the Trinity and the role of Jesus within salvation history. As I indicated in chapter 6 on the Trinity, Pannenberg's endorsement of "Rahner's Rule" (the identity between the so-called immanent and economic Trinity in Salvation History) is ambiguous. On the one hand, he seems to reaffirm the traditional understanding of the transcendence of God as Creator to the world of creation; but, on the other hand, he also says that, once creation came into being as a result of a free decision by the divine persons, the Lordship of the Father must include the Father's Lordship over creation as well as the Lordship of the Father within the immanent Trinity from all eternity. Russell in his understanding of the Lordship of the Father seems to follow the lead of Ted Peters in claiming that "[t]he existence of God

40. Robert John Russell, *Time in Eternity: Pannenberg, Physics, and Eschatology in Creative Mutual Interaction* (Notre Dame: University of Notre Dame Press, 2012).

as Trinity depends upon the future of God's coming kingdom [in this world]; and the coming of the Kingdom depends upon the person of Jesus—in the form of the anticipation of its future and as revealing the love of God."[41] Based upon my proposal of a systems-oriented approach to panentheism from a Trinitarian perspective in this book, I beg to differ. In what follows, I simply lay out my own position without trying to defend it with further argument.

First of all, since I share with Whitehead the conviction that actual entities, momentary self-constituting subjects of experience, are the ultimate constituents of all open-ended systems in this world, I claim that *pace* Pannenberg and Russell there is no ontological priority of the future over the past and the present in Salvation History (the historical process proper to the human race in its ongoing relation to God). All three time dimensions (past, present, and future) are involved in the self-constitution of every actual entity in all the various subsystems within the overall system proper to Salvation History. If there is any ontological priority among the three time-dimensions, it should belong to the present as the moment of decision in which a potentiality available in the projected future of the actual entity is actualized and, a moment later, is added to the determinate reality of the past history of the actual entity. Within the process proper to Salvation History, accordingly, there is no strictly predetermined goal of the process but only a directionality and, to borrow a term from the life-sciences, an "attractor" which draws the evolution of the system to itself without predetermining the outcome.[42]

Secondly, *pace* Russell, I do not believe that Jesus of Nazareth by his life, preaching, death, and resurrection inaugurated a New

41. Peters, *God as Trinity*, 135.
42. Joseph A. Bracken, *Does God Roll Dice? Divine Providence for a World in the Making* (Collegeville, MN: Liturgical, 2012), 32–36.

Creation within the cosmic process. Rather, Jesus by his life, death, and resurrection revealed "the plan of the mystery hidden from ages past in God who created all things" (Col. 1:26). The New Creation, in other words, has been going on since the Big Bang and will continue until the end of the cosmic process at some future date. It consists in the progressive incorporation of everything that happens within the cosmic process into the divine communitarian life along the lines indicated above in this chapter. What Jesus did for us human beings was to reveal how to live in this world so as to share more fully in the New Creation after death: "I am the way and the truth and the life. No one comes to the Father except through me" (John 14:6). Non-Christian but religiously oriented human beings will likewise be saved through Christ in ways that we do not at present understand. Finally, nonhuman creation in terms of all the actual entities at work in this world will be saved through Christ in ways that are proper to their own pattern of existence and activity as indicated earlier in this chapter. Perhaps the best description of how the New Creation presumably works to redeem all the entities of this world is provided by Whitehead in his description of how the consequent nature of God works at every moment of the cosmic process:

> The revolts of destructive evil, purely self-regarding, are dismissed into their triviality of merely individual facts; and yet the good they did achieve in individual joy, in individual sorrow, in the introduction of needed contrast, is yet saved by its relation to the completed whole. The image—and it is but an image—the image under which this operative growth of God's nature is best conceived, is that of a tender care that nothing be lost.[43]

Thirdly, as a final inference from my systems-oriented understanding of the God-world relationship, I claim that time is fulfilled in eternity; eternity is not fulfilled in time. The lower-order set of subsystems

---

43. Whitehead, *PR*, 346.

proper to the world of creation is progressively being incorporated into the higher-order system of the divine community. As Pannenberg says in his *Systematic Theology* as noted above, the Lordship of God the Father within the immanent Trinity is extended to the Father's Lordship over the world of creation both here and now in a hidden way and later at the end of the cosmic process in full visibility. The movement of incorporation of creation into the divine communitarian life is, to use a spatial metaphor, upwards, not downwards. A lower-order system is incorporated into a higher-order system, not vice versa. At the same time, of course, as indicated earlier in this chapter, the higher-order system of the divine communitarian life is enriched (though not essentially reconstituted) by its incorporation of the lower-order system into itself. In other words, the divine persons are enriched in their relations both to one another and to all their creatures through incorporation of Salvation History into their own "history" as a divine community. Yet we human beings have no way of knowing whether the three divine persons have brought into existence other forms of intelligent life within our universe[44] or, given an infinity of existence for the three divine persons, whether they have brought into being universes that existed before our own, that currently exist at the same time as our own, or that will exist after the end of our universe. It is, accordingly, presumptuous to believe that our own Salvation History has made a decisive impact on the communitarian life of the three divine persons. It is much safer simply to believe that we are part of a reality much bigger than ourselves and our world, namely, the ongoing "history" of God.

---

44. Thomas F. O'Meara, *Vast Universe: Extraterrestrials and Christian Revelation* (Collegeville, MN: Liturgical, 2012), 1–17.

Conclusion

In the Introduction to this book, I noted how Wentzel van Huyssteen has tried to bridge the current gap between scientifically oriented and religiously inspired worldviews in the postmodern Western world by proposing a new kind of interdisciplinary rational reflection, namely, what he calls "transversal rationality."[1] This new type of rationality is not theory-based or purely cognitive but likewise a performative praxis: "the practice of responsible judgment, that is at the heart of a postfoundationalist notion of rationality, and that enables us to reach fragile and provisional forms of coherence in our interpersonal and interdisciplinary conversations."[2] My counterargument was that, while transversal rationality is a valuable tool for sustaining interdisciplinary conversation between scientists and philosopher/theologians, it may not be enough to create a new commonly accepted worldview for use in the religion-and-science dialogue. Only a common language, use of the same foundational concepts both in the sciences and in philosophy and theology, has a chance to bring about over time a common overarching worldview. Aquinas succeeded in persuading the philosophers and theologians

---

1. J. Wentzel van Huyssteen, *Alone in the World? Human Uniqueness in Science and Theology* (Grand Rapids: Eerdmans, 2006), 23.
2. Ibid.

of his day to use in their own disciplines the metaphysical language of Aristotle who was both scientist and philosopher. But, given the changes of perspective in the natural and social sciences since the beginning of the modern era, it is certainly debatable whether the philosophy of Aristotle and the theology of Aquinas are well suited for the current religion-and-science dialogue. A new common language based on a new worldview is needed in our age to keep the dialogue going.

Now in this brief Conclusion, I compare and contrast the work of another distinguished theologian/philosopher of science, the late Gordon Kaufman, with my own project in this book. I find myself largely in agreement with Kaufman on key methodological issues but disagreeing with him on the way he applied this methodology to a contemporary understanding of Christian theology. In particular, I am wary of his attempt to find common ground with scientists via a strictly naturalistic approach to Christian theology that nevertheless lays heavy emphasis on the absolute transcendence of God to this world as Ultimate Reality or Divine Mystery. For, rather than finding common ground with scientists on various controversial issues, he seems thereby to have yielded the higher ground to them and then appealed to God as Divine Mystery to relativize what might otherwise be seen as absolute claims to truth and objectivity on the part of some scientists. The basic point of my book, however, has been to claim (a) that philosophers and theologians could possibly share much more common ground with natural and social scientists if they would exchange the language and worldview of classical metaphysics for the language and worldview of a systems-oriented approach to reality, and (b) that scientists for their part could benefit from accepting, at least in principle, the possibility of a trans-empirical or supernatural dimension to physical reality over and above their empirically grounded understanding of the laws of nature. In contrast to Kaufman, then, I have consciously tried to "naturalize" the supernatural order and "supernaturalize" the natural order of things by describing both the natural and the supernatural dimensions of reality in terms of a common process- or systems-oriented approach to reality.

Review and Critique of Kaufman's Approach

Accordingly, in what follows I will first make clear where in my judgment Kaufman is "on the mark" in his methodological assumptions and then where in my view he is "off the mark" in his efforts to set forth a naturalistic understanding of the God-world-self relation that equivalently eliminates any reference to the possible workings of the supernatural in human life. In the opening chapter of *In Face of Mystery*, Kaufman asserts that contemporary theologians "must develop their conceptions of God, the world and the human in dialectical interrelationship with one another, instead of trying to derive any of these from the other(s) in linear fashion."[3] I completely agree. This is why I proposed at the beginning of this book that a new worldview employing the language of integrated processes or systems may be needed to exhibit the logical interdependence of key terms for both scientists and theologians who profess to be Christians. This is not simply a word game, a change of terminology simply for form's sake. Thinking in terms of processes or systems carries with it the further metaphysical implication that physical reality is intrinsically social. That is, physical reality is based on relationships between specifically corporate realities made up of interacting parts or members (living organisms, communities, or environments) rather than on contingent relationships between individual entities as

---

3. Gordon Kaufman, *In Face of Mystery: A Constructive Theology* (Cambridge, MA: Harvard University Press, 1993), 14.

fundamentally separate realities (Aristotelian "substances"). Precisely for this reason I welcome Kaufman's evaluation of the Christian doctrine of the Trinity as pivotal for the dialectical interrelationship of the concepts of God, self, and the world within a Christian worldview: "The trinitarian idea breaks decisively with the substantialistic assumptions of our philosophical traditions—that reality consists fundamentally of *substances* ("thing-like" somethings), and that it is with the concept of 'substance,' therefore, that we designate most precisely that which is truly real."[4] Instead, the notion of *perichoresis*, mutual indwelling of the divine persons in one another's existence and activity, should be the model for understanding the physical world and all the individual entities that inhabit it.

But in his elaboration of what he means by a Trinitarian God, Kaufman ends up affirming a philosophical monism that stands in sharp contrast to the notion of panentheism as developed by myself and others in chapters 3 and 4 of this book. That is, all of us affirmed in different ways that the notion of panentheism mediates between the rival concepts of ontological dualism (an irreducible opposition between matter and spirit) and ontological monism (either the derivation of matter from antecedently existing spirit or the derivation of spirit from antecedently existing matter). Instead, the basic presupposition of panentheism is that all of finite reality exists within God as its ontological source and ultimate goal, but still remains distinct from God in its current finite existence and activity. Kaufman's understanding of the doctrine of the Trinity, however, is unmistakably monistic in its philosophical implications:

> In this interpretation of Christian faith, the symbol "God" is intended to designate (a) the ultimate reality (mystery) with which we humans

4. Ibid., 412.

have to do, a reality regarded as the creativity which is at work in and through all things (first motif); that which (b) is thus present in and with all realities of our world . . . as that which enables them to be real, their very "reality" so to speak (third motif); and which (c) is at work, therefore, within the evolutionary-historical trajectory which has produced our humanness and is moving us toward a more profound humaneness, a trajectory manifest in and paradigmatically identified by the Christ-event (second motif).[5]

The "persons" of the Trinity are thus ultimately identical with "motifs" or "intentions" of a monistic cosmic process that includes an evolutionary-historical trajectory aimed at the achievement of humaneness among human beings as active participants in the cosmic process.

At the same time, I understand and appreciate what Kaufman has in mind with his description of God as *serendipitous creativity* since "it enables us to connect important theological concerns with central features of modern/postmodern thinking about the cosmos, the evolution of life, and the emergence and biohistorical development of human life and culture on planet Earth."[6] It avoids, to be sure, thinking of God as a personal being or agent as in traditional Christian theology. But, as Karl Peters perceptively notes, "this creativity is not an additional cause operative in the universe, beyond those causes that are discoverable by empirical and scientific inquiry. Rather *serendipitous creativity* is a unifying symbol for all creative physical, chemical, biological, and historical causal processes. . . . It includes the human creativity that constructs the story of this scientifically grounded epic of creation, this 'big history' of our universe including ourselves."[7] Hence, even though the term "creativity" is not much used in reports on scientific research and

5. Ibid., 423.
6. Gordon Kaufman, *In the Beginning . . . Creativity* (Minneapolis: Fortress Press, 2004), 76.
7. Karl E. Peters, "A Christian Naturalism: Developing the Thinking of Gordon Kaufman," *Zygon* 48 (2013): 581.

technological development, it applies equally to a generic understanding of God, self, and the world. Moreover, insofar as creativity is serendipitous rather than destructive in its workings, creativity even as a symbol remains mysterious and unpredictable, pointing to something beyond human comprehension.[8] Why is there something rather than nothing? God, understood as serendipitous creativity, seems to be the only answer.

Yet I remain dissatisfied with this understanding of God as serendipitous creativity not only on theological grounds, that is, its radical departure from the traditional Christian understanding of God as Trinity or at least as transcendent personal agent and Creator of heaven and earth. My deeper dissatisfaction with the notion of God as serendipitous creativity is rather metaphysically grounded since in my view creativity is an activity, not an entity in its own right. As such, it passes from potentiality to actuality only in and through its instantiation in entities, whether the entity be God or some finite entity. Whitehead makes basically the same claim in the opening pages of *Process and Reality*, even though he uses the word "accident" rather than "instantiation" to point to the necessary actualization of creativity as a unifying activity in entities.[9] Creativity, when understood as an activity rather than an entity, thus has the same basic meaning as Be-ing in classical metaphysics when understood as a verb, rather than a noun. That is, it empowers beings to act in line with their nature or substantial form. Similarly, creativity empowers God and all finite entities to exist and consistently to act in accord with one another.

I still agree, of course, with Kaufman and Karl Peters that it is very difficult to establish a strictly philosophical understanding of

8. Ibid.
9. Alfred North Whitehead, *Process and Reality: An Essay in Cosmology*, corrected edition, ed. David Ray Griffin and Donald W. Sherburne (New York: Free Press, 1978), 7. Hereafter: *PR*.

God. As Whitehead noted in *Science and the Modern World*, since the time of Aristotle the notion of God in Western philosophy has been grounded much more in ethical and religious presuppositions than in purely rational argument.[10] To regain a strictly philosophical understanding of God, he himself describes God simply as "the Principle of Concretion."[11] By that he means that from a strictly philosophical perspective God sets limits to the possibilities for the self-actualization of each actual entity in its process of self-constitution. Creativity, in other words, is by nature boundless in terms of the possibilities for existence and activity that it offers to individual actual entities for their self-realization. Hence, over and above creativity, there must be a transcendent personal agent at work to limit these possibilities so that the actual entity in the end will have some significance and value for the cosmic process of which it is here and now a momentary part.[12] Admittedly, for Kaufman and Peters, part of the mystery of serendipitous creativity is the very fact that it is consistently serendipitous and not destructive, a positive rather than a negative factor in the cosmic process. But, in line with Whitehead's thinking in *Science and the Modern World*, I would say that there is indeed mystery within the workings of creativity, but the mystery attaches to the existence of God as the Principle of Concretion for the cosmic process, not to creativity whose sole task it is to keep providing possibilities for the self-realization of actual entities, whether or not these possibilities are consistent with the overall order and purposive directionality of the cosmic process. Creativity as the principle of process within an evolutionary worldview thus empowers the independent decision of the actual

10. Alfred North Whitehead, *Science and the Modern World* (New York: Free Press, 1967), 173–74.
11. Ibid., 174.
12. Ibid., 178.

entity; it does not overpower it in line with its own alleged goals and values.

One more feature of Kaufman's revisionary systematic theology needs attention before I end this discussion of our differing views on the proper approach to the religion-and-science dialogue from a Christian perspective. I completely agree with Kaufman that from a Christian perspective the triad of God-self-world must be expanded to include Christ as a necessary fourth component. Belief in the role of Christ as a transcendent reality directly impacts upon the Christian understanding of self and the world as well as on the Christian understanding of God. But Kaufman and I differ in how we understand that role of Christ in the cosmic process. Kaufman proposes a "wider view" of Christology than what is customary in traditional Christian belief: "'Christ' is understood to refer to and name major features of the whole complex of events and relationships surrounding, including, and following upon the ministry and death of Jesus. On this view it is the appearance of a new communal ethos in history, rather than a metaphysically unique individual, that is the matter of central importance."[13] By "new communal ethos" Kaufman has in mind "an inclusive egalitarian community that welcomes all sorts and conditions of women and men, no matter what their racial, religious, or ethnic background."[14] He thus distinguishes sharply between the historical Jesus of the Gospel narratives and the cosmic Christ in the Pauline epistles to the Colossians and the Ephesians (Col. 1:15-20; Eph. 1:3-23). The cosmic Christ is no longer "a single supernatural individual" but a powerful symbol of what human beings are destined to become in pursuit of greater humanness and humaneness.

---

13. Kaufman, *In Face of Mystery*, 396.
14. Ibid., 396–97.

While I would agree with Kaufman that there is a significant difference between the historical Jesus and the cosmic Christ, I would argue that the historical Jesus and the cosmic Christ refer to one and the same individual entity who is both human and divine at the same time. Here I appeal to the process-oriented understanding of the doctrine of the Incarnation that I elaborated in chapter 5 of this book. That is, two processes are at work here. The one process is characteristic of the person of Christ as the Divine Word or Eternal Son of the Father. The other process is characteristic of Jesus of Nazareth as a member of the human race at a given time and place in human history. As I see it, the process proper to the human Jesus is incorporated into the process proper to Christ as the Divine Word or Eternal Son of the Father within the divine life. But it retains its own ontological identity, its distinct form of existence and activity, as a lower-order process within the higher-order process of the divine life. During the earthly life of Jesus of Nazareth, the process proper to the Divine Word was active, but its impact upon Jesus was constrained by the limits of the lower-order process proper to Jesus as a human being. Accordingly, whatever the Divine Word did in conjunction with the humanity of Jesus had a finite empirically verifiable effect. Even when Jesus allegedly performed a miracle, the result was always something finite and within the natural order of things. A blind person began to see clearly again. A leper was cured of his leprosy. The only indication that the supernatural agency of the Divine Word was at work in this miraculous event was that it was so unusual, so unlike the normal course of events in human life. Calling such an unusual event a miracle would be due to one's antecedent belief in the existence and activity of the supernatural order of things in the workings of the natural order. All that the senses empirically confirm is that it was an unexpected event beyond human comprehension at the present time.

After the bodily resurrection of Jesus, however, the roles of the divine and the human processes in the person of the risen Christ are reversed. At this point, the process proper to the humanity of Jesus continues to exist but in clear subordination to the workings of the process of the divine life proper to Jesus as the eternal Son of the Father become incarnate in this world for our salvation (John 1:14). Jesus was thus no longer bound by the conditions of space and time in his appearances to the apostles and to the holy women. He appeared and disappeared without prior notice. Moreover, they did not always recognize him when he appeared (e.g., his appearance first to Mary Magdalene and then to the two disciples on the way to Emmaus). Yet upon closer inspection he was evidently the same person that they knew and cared for during his earthly life. Thus Kaufman's notion of the cosmic Christ as an "inclusive egalitarian community"[15] does not refer to Christ as an individual entity (the Risen Lord) but to what Christians following St. Paul have traditionally called the Mystical Body of Christ (1 Cor. 12:12-27). Christians as the Body of Christ certainly need the life-giving connection to the risen Christ as their Head, but even here Christ is an individual person, not a symbol for the network of Christians throughout the world.[16] The real symbolic value of the image of Christ as the Head of the Mystical Body is, in my view, that it points to the possibility that the higher-order process of the divine life in and through the person of Jesus can be active in the lower-order process of human life and thereby "redeem" it, lift it to a higher-order form of existence and activity than would be possible by human effort alone.

15. Ibid.
16. Ibid., 397.

Overview of the Contents of This Book

With these brief comments on how Kaufman and I try to align Christian systematic theology better with current scientific understanding of the world in which we live, I have highlighted many of the leading ideas of Part Two of this book without having to summarize the details of each chapter in linear fashion. But for the sake of completeness, I offer in the next few paragraphs a quick overview of the contents of the entire book. In the Introduction, I made reference to Wentzel van Huyssteen's interdisciplinary approach to topics in religion and science via the concept of transversal rationality before setting forth my own proposal of a new common language for analysis of controversial issues in the religion-and-science debate. Accordingly, in chapters 1 and 2 I proposed that theologians and scientists cease talking about individual entities (Aristotelian substances) in relation to one another and instead start talking about systems of such individual entities in dynamic interrelation. Within these systems the individual entities come and go, but the patterns of their interrelation remains to condition (though not totally control) the interplay of new individual entities that take their place within the system. The focus of attention is then no longer on entities but on the enduring patterns of their dynamic interrelation. Moreover, as I see it, such a systems-oriented approach to physical reality is easier to explain if one uses a somewhat revised understanding of the category of "society" in the metaphysics of Alfred North Whitehead. That is, while Whitehead himself proposes that a society is a genetically linked set of actual entities (momentary self-constituting subjects of experience) with a common element of form or defining characteristic, I suggest instead that a society is an enduring field of activity that has been structured by successive sets of actual entities with this common element of form or defining characteristic. As an objective reality that endures over time, a structured field of activity together with its ever-changing constituent actual entities can be considered a process that has from moment to moment the objective reality of a system. To commonsense experience, it appears to be a stable individual entity, but closer examination reveals that it is a system with a consistent mode of operation. Yet, since its components are self-constituting subjects of experience (actual entities) whose common element of form itself slowly evolves over time in response to an ever-changing environment, the system is invariably open-ended, not closed or completely fixed in its ongoing mode of operation.

In chapters 3 and 4, I used this systems-oriented approach to Whiteheadian societies to analyze various theories about the notion of panentheism as a suitable middle-ground position between monism (either matter alone or spirit alone as the basic "stuff" of physical reality) and dualism (matter and spirit in dialectical opposition as the "stuff" of the universe). For panentheism by definition claims that all finite things exist within God but retain their own ontological identity, albeit in dependence on God as the vital source of their existence and activity. Yet, whereas all the other versions of panentheism reviewed in chapter 4 presuppose that God is an infinite or all-encompassing individual entity that somehow includes within itself all finite individual entities, I instead argue that the Trinitarian God is a complex system composed of subsystems, each subsystem corresponding to one of the divine persons. In this way, the three divine persons together co-constitute the higher-order system of a divine community. The divine community, however, like all Whiteheadian societies, is the enduring structured field of activity for the interaction of its constituent parts or members, in this case the divine persons. Within this divine energy-field the current cosmic process originated and continues to exist to this day.

As the *imago Dei or* finite counterpart to the corporate reality of God, the cosmic process is a complex system of subordinate systems. These subsystems in turn have still more subsystems, the ultimate components of which are momentary self-constituting subjects of experience, Whiteheadian actual entities, as "the final real things of which this world is made up."[17]

The God-world relationship as a whole is then an all-comprehensive or super-system in which the divine system, the communitarian life of the divine persons, serves as both the ontological source and ultimate goal of the cosmic process as itself composed of hierarchically ordered subsystems. The superiority of this systems-oriented approach to the notion of panentheism is that systems can be hierarchically ordered without the subsystems losing their ontological identity as subsystems with their own mode of operation within a still larger system. This is not so readily accomplished if one is dealing with individual entities rather than systems. In an Aristotelian-Thomistic setting, lower-order entities cannot be incorporated into higher-order entities without losing the actuality of their own substantial form, at least while they are components of the higher-order entity.

In Part Two of the book I indicated in chapters 5 and 6 how this systems-oriented approach to reality addresses longstanding controversial issues within Christian systematic theology as to the proper understanding of the doctrines of the Incarnation and the Trinity. To say that Jesus has both a divine and a human nature is to claim that Jesus is a full participant in two systems, one divine and one human, with the human system integrated into the divine system but still retaining its own ontological integrity as a finite system of existence and activity. Likewise, to say that God is three persons and

17. Whitehead, *PR*, 18.

yet only one God is to claim that God is a Whiteheadian structured society, a society of interrelated subsocieties or subsystems.[18] In chapter 7 I proposed that the Church is an unfinished historical process rather than a corporate entity with a fixed institutional structure through the centuries. In chapter 8, I explored the role of miracles within the natural order of things in this world, above all, with reference to the recurrent problem of natural and moral evil within a panentheistic understanding of the God-world relationship. Finally, in chapter 9 I offered arguments for the rational plausibility of life after death for human beings and in some measure also for the nonhuman creatures of this world, given that the cosmic process is a set of systems that originated in and continue to participate in the overarching system of the divine life.

In brief, then, what I have set forth in this book is a hypothesis about the nature of the God-world relationship that is grounded in three philosophical presuppositions that in turn have significant consequences for theological reflection on basic Christian beliefs (as indicated in points 4 and 5 below):

1. A commonly accepted philosophical worldview is indispensable for fruitful dialogue between theology and science. Consciously or unconsciously, both theology and science presuppose an underlying philosophical worldview. If the two worldviews are in conflict with one another, then theologians and scientists will invariably clash over more particular issues. But if they share the same worldview or at least have two very similar worldviews, then theologians and scientists are much more likely to agree on these more particular issues.

2. The best philosophy for this ongoing dialogue between theology and science should be grounded in the conviction that reality is socially organized into integrated processes or systems with individual entities as their constitutive parts or members. Unlike

18. Ibid., 99.

classical metaphysics, therefore, whose starting-point is the ontological priority of the individual entity to the community or environment in which it finds itself, this more socially oriented approach to reality presupposes the ontological priority of the community or environment to its constituent parts or members here and now. Relationality is operative in both worldviews. But in classical metaphysics it is primarily the relation of individual entities to one another; in this metaphysical system it is primarily the relation of integrated systems to one another.

3. Finally, the ultimate constituent parts or members of these integrated systems are mini-organisms, momentary self-constituting subjects of experience with internal rather than external relations to one another. The systems themselves are not organisms, subjects of experience, but rather the objective byproduct or result of the interaction of these mini-organisms with one another from moment to moment. As momentary self-constituting subjects of experience, the organisms come and go; the systems with their relatively fixed patterns or modes of operation remain. The systems, to be sure, also evolve in terms of their patterns or modes of operation but only in virtue of ongoing interaction with other lower-order or higher-order systems. So from top to bottom, reality is hierarchically ordered into integrated systems.

4. From a theological perspective, this systems-oriented approach to reality nicely correlates with a Trinitarian understanding of God as a specifically social reality, namely, as a community of divine persons whose communitarian life is both the starting-point and endpoint of the cosmic process. For, if God is a corporate or systems-oriented reality, then creation as the finite collective image of God should also be socially organized, composed of a vast network of dynamically interrelated systems.

5. Likewise, other key Christian beliefs can be rethought and represented within the context of a systems-oriented approach to reality: for example, the doctrine of the Incarnation, the nature of the Church, the role of miracles as signs of Divine Providence in a world process marked by trial and error, and finally the possibility of eternal life, the New Creation, for all God's creatures.

Index

ᵓSIA information can be obtained
www.ICGtesting.com
nted in the USA
HW081913110820
ᵕ982BV00008B/315